THE ENGLAND
OF DICKENS

BY

WALTER DEXTER

AUTHOR OF

"THE LONDON OF DICKENS," "THE KENT OF DICKENS"

I am both a town traveller and a country traveller, and am always on the road. Figuratively speaking, I travel for the great house of Human Interest Brothers, and have rather a large collection in the fancy goods way.
The Uncommercial Traveller.

PHILADELPHIA

J. B. LIPPINCOTT COMPANY

Printed in Great Britain

PREFACE

The England of Dickens is a country of actuality as well as of romance; and Dickens knew his England fairly thoroughly.

The impressionable part of his knowledge was gained in the days before the railway was heard in the land; when the proverbial "Slow-coach" was still the only means of locomotion, hence it was not until his later books that the shriek of the locomotive engine resounded in his pages. Certain it is that he cast a halo around the coaching days; no other Dickens came after to do the like by the horse of iron and steel.

Dickens's knowledge of England was obtained in many ways; by the exercise of his early profession of reporter, when he travelled into Suffolk and into Devonshire to report election speeches; by his holiday jaunts with Hablot K. Browne (Phiz) in 1838, first into Yorkshire and then through the Midlands to Wales, Liverpool and Manchester; by a trip to the West in 1842 with his friend and biographer, John Forster, and his artist friends, Daniel Maclise and Clarkson Stanfield, just after his return from seeing all the glories that the New World had to show him; by his own family holidays at Broadstairs, where he was a constant visitor over a period of years, at Dover, at Folkestone, and at the Isle of Wight; by his "Splendid Strolling" play-acting with Mark Lemon, Douglas Jerrold and others in aid of Shakespeare's House, Leigh Hunt, and the Guild of Literature and Art, when the larger cities such as Manchester, Liverpool, Sheffield and Birmingham were visited; by his Readings, first in aid of the local Working Men's Institutions—the forerunners of our Public Libraries—at Folkestone, Chatham, Coventry, and elsewhere; and by the three great Reading Tours, for his own benefit, when all the principal towns were visited, from Carlisle and Berwick in the North, to Plymouth and Dover in the South.

▼

The letters he wrote to his family and friends during these excursions are as full of quaint observations of life and character as are his novels, and it has been our object in this book to place them in a permanent position in the towns to which they refer, thus enabling the reader to see at a glance how Dickens's visits to various places were reflected—often almost immediately—in his writings.

A certain amount of repetition of fact and quotation has been rendered unavoidable by the desire of the author to make each section devoted to a place, as complete as possible.

If the reader in glancing at the table of contents should wonder at the absence of a chapter on London, or should consider that scant courtesy has been afforded to the Dickens county of Kent, we would remind him that the present volume is already of somewhat ample proportions, and that the subjects of *The London of Dickens* and *The Kent of Dickens* have already been dealt with by the present writer in separate volumes bearing these titles.

We offer no apology for this, the third and final volume of the English Topography of Dickens. The growing desire for knowledge of all things relating to his life and work is its all-sufficient justification.

It seems but an inadequate means of thanking my old and valued friend, Mr. B. W. Matz, to put on record here how much this book owes to the immense amount of useful knowledge he has collected during his twenty years editorship of *The Dickensian;* but I do so most gratefully. To Kitton's *The Dickens Country*, acknowledgments are also recorded, and likewise to the Librarians of the towns visited by Dickens for their verification of the dates, and other interesting details, which, in many cases, would have been unobtainable but for their kind assistance, and finally to Messrs. Macmillan & Co., Ltd., for permission to quote freely from *The Letters of Charles Dickens*.

WALTER DEXTER.

Highbury,
7th February, 1925.

CONTENTS

vii

Contents

CHAPTER EIGHT

On the Track of Little Nell

CHAPTER NINE

The Dotheboys Route to Yorkshire and the North

CHAPTER TEN

A Lazy Tour for Idle Dickensians

Contents

CHAPTER ELEVEN

The Hard Times Country

CHAPTER TWELVE

A Pickwick Pilgrimage to the Copperfield Country

INDEX TO PLACES

LIST OF ILLUSTRATIONS

THE ENGLAND OF DICKENS

CHAPTER ONE

ALONG THE OLD RED ROYAL DOVER ROAD

I

"THE Old Red Royal Dover Road" was Dickens's description in a letter to a friend concerning the red jacketed postilions he turned out on it when Longfellow paid him a visit at Gad's Hill in 1868, and it is only fitting that this our first pilgrimage through the England of Dickens should be over the road with which he was so familiar and that had such a fascination for him.

Even when a small boy at Chatham, he used to delight in being taken by his father for a walk to the top of Gad's Hill to see the house there which in the hey-day of his fame he purchased, and where he died in 1870, and in his first great story he made Mr. Pickwick and his friends journey by coach along the first half of the Dover Road to see Rochester; and following that came little David Copperfield on his long and weary tramp to his aunt's at Dover.

Mr. Dorrit also made the journey, but in quite the "grand manner," his magnificent equipage being "waylaid at Dartford, pillaged at Gravesend, rifled at Rochester, fleeced at Sittingbourne, and sacked at Canterbury." Then, too, in the later books, *Great Expectations* and *Edwin Drood*, the scene is often set about the Dover Road, and Dickens himself often tramped it, so altogether we have a " glorious host " to bear us company along the seventy odd miles.

It is from northward beyond the General Post Office, that we should properly commence this Pickwickian-Copperfield Pilgrimage; for here, in that portion of what is now the Goswell Road that lies between Aldersgate and a little beyond Old Street, was the original Goswell Street. Here Mrs.

Bardell let her second floor front to Mr. Pickwick, who on the morning of the 13th May, 1827, "threw open his chamber window and looked out upon the world beneath." Having surveyed Goswell Street to the right, to the left, and over the way, and being sure that he was not content "to gaze on Goswell Street for ever, without one effort to penetrate to the hidden countries which on every side surround it." Mr. Pickwick descended, "his portmanteau in his hand, his telescope in his greatcoat pocket, and his note-book in his waistcoat" and walked to "the coach stand in St. Martin's le Grand." From here it was "Only a bob's vorth" to the Golden Cross at Charing Cross, then situated where the Nelson Monument now stands; here he met his three fellow Pickwickians, and joined by Mr. Alfred Jingle, they started by the Commodore Coach to Rochester. And so begun the topography of Dickens; and Rochester became the centre of what is now known as the Kentish Dickensland.

By way of Whitehall and Westminster Bridge went the Commodore Coach, but the Dover Road proper is reached via London Bridge and the Borough, both of which have many unforgettable memories with Dickens's life and works: for the immortal Sam Weller made his first bow to a vast appreciative public in the yard of the White Hart Inn in the Borough; and a little lower down stood the Marshalsea, famous as the birthplace of Little Dorrit; near by still stands St. George's Church, where she was married to Arthur Clennam. Over the way is Lant Street, where Dickens lodged as a boy while his father was in the Marshalsea: and here, too, he made Bob Sawyer lodge with Mrs. Raddle, and give his famous party.

There is no account of the Dover Road given in *Pickwick*. The party were too engrossed with Mr. Jingle's stories to give much attention to the road they were traversing: so we have to turn to *David Copperfield*, *A Tale of Two Cities*, and several of *The Uncommercial Traveller* papers to make up for the deficiency.

The roads from London Bridge and Westminster Bridge both join at the St. George's Circus, where once stood the obelisk, now removed to outside Bethlehem Hospital near by. This was the scene of David Copperfield's bad start, for at the Obelisk, Blackfriars Road, he was robbed of his box and his half-guinea:

I ran after him as fast as I could. . . . I narrowly escaped being run over, twenty times at least, in half a mile.

. . . At length, confused by fright and heat, and doubting whether half London might not by this time be turning out for my apprehension, I left the young man to go where he would with my box and money; and, panting and crying but never stopping, faced about for Greenwich, which I had understood was on the Dover Road. . . .

That night he slept at Blackheath beneath a haystack, within sight of his old school, Salem House, and the next day tramped the road to Rochester.

Elsewhere the writer has given a full account of the Dickens interest in the Borough, Blackheath, Greenwich, and the whole course of the Dover Road,* and we have now only space to recall its chief associations.

On Shooter's Hill we conjure up the picture of the Dover mail "lumbering up" and of Mr. Jarvis Lorry on a journey between the "two cities": and we see Pip, come into his expectations, riding to town listening to the conversation of the two convicts; and so we go:

Over the road where the old Romans used to march, over the road where the old Canterbury pilgrims used to go, over the road where the travelling trains of the old imperious priests and princes used to jingle on horseback between the Continent and this Island through the mud and water, over the road where Shakespeare hummed to himself, "Blow, blow, thou winter wind," as he sat in the saddle at the gate of the inn-yard noticing the carriers; all among the cherry orchards, apple orchards, cornfields and hop-gardens; . . . by Canterbury to Dover.

Dickens's earlier recollections of a coach journey on the Dover Road appear in the paper entitled "Dullborough Town," in which he recalls leaving Chatham for London at the age of eleven.

As I left Dullborough in the days when there were no railroads in the land, I left it in a stage coach . . . melodiously called Timpson's Blue-eyed Maid . . . Timpsons was a moderate sized coach office (in fact, a little coach office) with an oval transparency in the window, which looked beautiful by night, representing one of Timpson's coaches in the act of passing a milestone on the London road with great velocity.

* *The London of Dickens* and *The Kent of Dickens*. Published by Cecil Palmer, London.

In the concluding part of *The Seven Poor Travellers* we get another personal touch, and a true one, for Dickens often tramped the Dover Road between Rochester and London.

> As for me, I was going to walk by Cobham Woods, as far upon my way to London as I fancied. . . . Christmas begirt me, far and near, until I had come to Blackheath, and had walked down the long vista of gnarled old trees in Greenwich Park and was being steam-rattled through the mists now closing in once more, towards the lights of London.

II

Gravesend used to be a popular holiday resort in Dickens's day. In *Bleak House* we are told how, in the long vacation, " all the young clerks are madly in love, and . . . pine for bliss with the beloved object, at Margate, Ramsgate or Gravesend," and in "The Tuggses at Ramsgate" Mr. Joseph Tuggs suggested Gravesend as the place for the family holiday, but "the idea was unanimously scouted. Gravesend was *low*."

The next village on the road is Chalk, about a mile from Gravesend. It was here that Dickens spent his honeymoon in 1836. The house where the newly-married couple stayed is now marked with a couple of memorial tablets.

It is interesting to note that both Walter Gay in *Dombey and Son* and Tommy Traddles in *David Copperfield*, spent their honeymoons in Kent.

Almost midway between Gravesend and Rochester, standing a little way back on the right, is the house that is familiarly and affectionately known to the innumerable band of Dickens devotees the world over as Gad's Hill, its full and correct name being Gad's Hill Place. This was Dickens's home from 1857 until his death in 1870.

But years before it became his home—indeed from his very earliest years when a small boy at Chatham—he conceived a great attachment to the house. He used to like to be taken out to see it by his father, and it was a cherished ambition of his life to be in a position to buy the house and live there.

He has confirmed this in his paper, "Travelling Abroad," in *The Uncommercial Traveller*, in which as he is journeying along the road to Dover there crosses it a vision of himself:

> So smooth was the old high road, and so fresh were the horses, and so fast went I, that it was midway between

Gravesend and Rochester, and the widening river was bearing the ships, white-sailed or black-smoked, out to sea, when I noticed by the wayside a very queer small boy.

"Holloa!" said I, to the very queer small boy, "where do you live?"

"At Chatham," says he.

"What do you do there?" says I.

"I go to school," says he.

I took him up in a moment, and we went on. Presently, the very queer small boy says, "This is Gadshill we are coming to, where Falstaff went out to rob those travellers, and ran away."

"You know something about Falstaff, eh?" said I.

"All about him," said the very queer small boy. "I am old (I am nine), and I read all sorts of books. But *do* let us stop at the top of the hill, and look at the house there, if you please!"

"You admire that house?" said I.

"Bless you, sir," said the very queer small boy, "when I was not more than half as old as nine, it used to be a treat for me to be brought to look at it. And now I am nine, I come by myself to look at it. And ever since I can recollect, my father, seeing me so fond of it, has often said to me, ' If you were to be very persevering, and were to work hard, you might some day come to live in it.' Though that's impossible!" said the very queer small boy, drawing a low breath, and now staring at the house out of window with all his might.

I was rather amazed to be told this by the very queer small boy; for that house happens to be *my* house, and I have reason to believe that what he said was true.

Here is an account of the situation of the house, written by Dickens in July, 1858, in a letter to his French friend, de Cerjat:

At this present moment I am on my little Kentish freehold looking on as pretty a view out of my study window as you will find in a long day's English ride. My little place is a grave red brick house (time of George the First, I suppose) which I have added to and stuck bits upon in all manner of ways, so that it is as pleasantly irregular, and as violently opposed to all architectural ideas, as the most hopeful man could possibly desire. It is on the summit of

B

Gad's Hill.   The robbery was committed before the door, on the man with the treasure, and Falstaff ran away from the identical spot of ground now covered by the room in which I write.   A little rustic alehouse, called the Sir John Falstaff, is over the way—has been over the way, ever since, in honour of the event.   Cobham Woods and Park are behind the house; the distant Thames in front; the Medway, with Rochester, and its old castle and cathedral on one side.   The whole stupendous property is on the old Dover Road, so when you come, come by the North Kent Railway (not the South Eastern) to Strood or Higham, and I'll drive over to fetch you.

The grounds, which still contain the tiny gravestone of Dickens's pet birds, including the "wilderness" on the opposite side of the main road, and reached by a tunnel: and part of the interior of the house—the library and the dining-room, are usually shown to visitors on Wednesday afternoons.

III

There is no town in Great Britain—perhaps not in all the world—that has so fascinated a writer throughout his whole life as Rochester fascinated Dickens.   Although not his actual birthplace it was, as Forster says, "the birthplace of his fancy"; and his thoughts always turned to it in his writings.

Dickens was only four years of age when the family came from Portsmouth to live in the adjacent town of Chatham— and here the family resided for seven years, and Dickens has left more than one record of the mental pictures he made during that time of the city and its people.

In the preface to the cheap edition of *Nicholas Nickleby* in 1848 we find him speaking of being " a not very robust child, sitting in bye-places, near Rochester Castle, with a head full of Partridge, Strap, Tom Pipes and Sancho Panza" and when the time came for the father to fill a post in London, deep was his grief at parting with the city he had learnt to love so well.

Forster has left us an impression of this based on an actual conversation with Dickens:

"It was the birth-place of his fancy; and he hardly knew what store he had set by its busy varieties of change and scene, until he saw the falling cloud that was to hide its pictures from him for ever.   The gay bright regiments

GADS HILL PLACE

ROCHESTER CASTLE FROM THE BRIDGE

always going and coming, the continual paradings and firings, the successions of sham sieges and sham defences, the plays got up by his cousin in the hospital, the navy-pay yacht in which he had sailed to Sheerness with his father, and the ships floating out in the Medway, with their far visions of sea—he was to lose them all. He was never to watch the boys at their games any more, or see them sham over again the sham sieges and defences. He was to be taken away to London inside the stage-coach Commodore; and Kentish woods and fields, Cobham Park and Hall, Rochester Cathedral and Castle, and all the wonderful romance together, including a red-cheeked baby he had been wildly in love with, were to vanish like a dream."

Rochester figures under its own name in *The Pickwick Papers*, *David Copperfield* and *Christmas Stories*. As "Dullborough Town," "Mudfog," and "Great Winglebury," it appears in *Sketches by Boz*. In *Great Expectations* it is "The Market Town" and referred to as "Up town" and "Our town," and in *Edwin Drood*, "Cloisterham"; and although Dickens often wrote of Rochester under a fictitious name, he made no concealment otherwise, that he was referring to the city he loved so dearly.

It is in *The Pickwick Papers* that Rochester first appears under its real name; and it is this book that commenced the romance centred in the city. "Mr. Pickwick and his three companions had resolved to make Rochester their first halting place."

With notebook and telescope Mr. Pickwick descended on the city, and a fund of genuine good humour, perennial in its freshness, was the result; and pilgrimages are made to Rochester, not so much to see its historic castle and ancient cathedral, as to see the places associated with the "Immortal Pickwick."

It was not until 1854 that Rochester again figured to any large extent in the stories he wrote. This time, the house known as Watts's Charity for Six Poor Travellers, was the subject of one of the Christmas numbers, which he entitled *The Seven Poor Travellers*, Dickens himself making the seventh traveller.

In 1860, *Great Expectations* appeared, and the "Market Town" of that book was, of course, Rochester, near to which he had lately come to reside.

Ten years later came *Edwin Drood*, and his fancy again turned to the cathedral city as the setting for the story; and he called the city Cloisterham.

An ancient city, Cloisterham, and no meet dwelling-place for anyone with hankerings after the noisy world. . . . A drowsy city, Cloisterham, whose inhabitants seem to suppose, with an inconsistency more strange than rare, that all its changes lie behind it, and that there are no more to come. . . . So silent are the streets of Cloisterham (though prone to echo on the smallest provocation), that of a summer-day the sun-blinds of its shops scarce dare to flap in the south wind; . . . the streets of Cloisterham city are little more than one narrow street by which you get into it and get out of it; the rest being mostly disappointing yards with pumps in them and no thoroughfare—exception made of the Cathedral-close, and a paved Quaker settlement . . . up in a shady corner.

In a word, a city of another and a bygone time is Cloisterham, with its hoarse cathedral-bell and its hoarse rooks hovering about the Cathedral tower.

His last description of Rochester and its Cathedral is as beautiful as any he ever penned:

A brilliant morning shines on the old city. Its antiquities and ruins are surpassingly beautiful. Changes of glorious light from moving boughs, songs of birds, scents from gardens, woods and fields . . . penetrate into the Cathedral, subdue its earthly odour, and preach the Resurrection and the Life. The cold stone tombs of centuries ago grow warm; and flecks of brightness dart into the sternest marble corners of the building, fluttering there like wings.

He was writing this in the Chalet at Gad's Hill on the afternoon of the June day that was to be his last on earth; a very few more words and *The Mystery of Edwin Drood* was laid aside for ever, to prove a mystery that is perhaps unsolvable. A few days before he had been seen in Rochester, "peeping about" the nooks and corners he loved so much, and it was thought that this last number would contain other word-pictures of the city; but no notes remained.

IV

For a ramble round Rochester and Chatham, we cannot do better than follow in the tracks of Richard Doubledick and the Pickwickians and enter by the bridge across the Medway. It is not, however, the same bridge as that over which Doubledick "limped" or Mr. Pickwick leaned his portly frame "contemplating nature, and waiting for breakfast," and surveyed

> The ruined wall, broken in many places, and in some, overhanging the narrow beach below in rude and heavy masses. . . . Behind it rose the ancient castle, its towers roofless, and its massive walls crumbling away, but telling us proudly of its own might and strength, as when, seven hundred years ago, it rang with the clash of arms, or resounded with the noise of feasting and revelry.

It is a rather ugly utilitarian sort of affair; but we can nevertheless get a glimpse of the Castle and Cathedral from between the ironwork, and echo the cry of Mr. Augustus Snodgrass.

> "Magnificent ruin" said Mr. Augustus Snodgrass with all the poetic fervour that distinguished him. . . .
> "What a sight for an antiquarian" were the very words which fell from Mr. Pickwick's mouth, as he applied his telescope to his eye.
> "Ah! Fine place" said the stranger, "glorious pile, frowning walls—tottering arches . . . old cathedral too."

We now enter the "long straggling High Street," which Dickens as a boy used to think "was at least as wide as Regent Street, London," but which on revisiting in manhood, he found to be "little better than a lane."

The Crown Hotel at the foot of the bridge may have been the Crozier of *Edwin Drood*. It was formerly "Wright's"—the "next house" referred to by Mr. Jingle, when he cautioned Mr. Pickwick and his friends on no account to stay there. "Dear—very dear—half-a-crown in the bill if you look at the waiter—charge you more if you dine at a friend's than they would if you dined in the coffee room—rum fellows—very."

It was at the Bull almost next door that they had alighted, and Jingle's encomium "Good house—nice beds" is an excellent advertisement which the proprietor does not fail to use.

Although the Bull figures in *Great Expectations* as the Blue Boar and in *The Seven Poor Travellers*, its principal claim to remembrance rests with *The Pickwick Papers*, and the Ballroom upstairs is intact as it was when Dickens peopled it with the "dockyard people of upper rank" who didn't know "dockyard people of lower rank" who in turn didn't know "small gentry" and so on.

The "elevated den" in which "the musicians were securely confined" is still to be seen.

The stairs leading up to the Ballroom, are, as described in "The Great Winglebury Duel,"

> A great wide rambling staircase, three stairs and a landing —four stairs and another landing—one step and another landing—half a dozen stairs and another landing—and so on.

and we recall that they figure in Phiz's drawing of Jingle in Mr. Winkle's dress clothes with the P.C. button, defying Dr. Slammer, which as we all know, resulted in the famous duel at Fort Pitt the next day, when the innocent Mr. Winkle was discovered to be "the wrong man" at the eleventh hour.

Mr. Winkle's bedroom was inside Mr. Tupman's, and we find these two rooms in Nos. 13 and 19. Room No. 17 is Mr. Pickwick's room, the same as Dickens himself is said to have occupied more than once.

Opposite the Bull is the Town Hall, " a grave red-brick building," an edifice which Dickens informs us in "Dull-borough Town" had appeared to him in his boyhood's days, "so glorious a structure that I had set it up in my mind as the model on which the Genie of the Lamp built the Palace for Aladdin."

"A queer place" thought Pip when he went there to be bound apprentice to Joe, "with higher pews in it than in a church . . . and with some shining black portraits on the walls, which my unartistic eye regarded as a composition of hardbake and sticking-plaister."

Almost opposite, the Cathedral can be seen and we reach it by passing " an old stone gatehouse crossing the close with an arched thoroughfare passing beneath it." This is known as Jasper's Gate House from its connection with Dickens's last story, *Edwin Drood:* passing through the archway we find the house of the Verger Tope on the left.

Rochester Cathedral has many associations with Dickens, particularly with *Edwin Drood*, in which book the city is thinly disguised as Cloisterham. Said Mr. Sapsea in show-ing the principal sights of his city:

> This is our Cathedral, sir. The best judges are pleased to admire it, and the best among our townsmen own to being a little vain of it. . . . Mr. Datchery admired the

Cathedral and Mr. Sapsea pointed it out as if he himself had invented and built it.

Previous to the advent of the " old buffer " Dick Datchery, Mr. Grewgious had visited the Cathedral, and " Crossing the Close, paused at the great western folding door of the Cathedral, which stood open on the fine and bright, though short-lived, afternoon, for the airing of the place. ' Dear me,' said Mr. Grewgious, peeping in, 'it's like looking down the throat of Old Time.' "

Dickens tells us in *The Seven Poor Travellers* that he " had been wandering about the neighbouring Cathedral and had seen the tomb of Richard Watts, with the effigy of worthy Master Richard starting out of it like a ship's figurehead."

Below this effigy of Watts is a tablet of brass to connect the memory of Dickens " with the scenes in which his earliest and his latest years were passed and with the associations of Rochester Cathedral and its neighbourhood which extended over all his life."

Returning to the Cathedral Close we see the little burial ground where Dickens expressed a desire to be buried, but it was found to be full and the greater claim of Westminster Abbey prevailed.

The famous Sapsea vault with its inscription was in this burial ground and plays an important part in the story of *Edwin Drood*.

The Cathedral Close is also often referred to in *Edwin Drood*, Sir Luke Fildes's picture, " Under the Trees," depicts a part of it; for here the breaking off of the engagement between Edwin and Rosa, was first suggested: and here, after they had taken a walk by the river, they decided to say good-bye to each other.

Beyond the west door of the Cathedral we can easily reach Minor Canon Row to which reference is made in *The Seven Poor Travellers*:

A wonderfully quaint row of red-brick tenements inhabited by the Minor-Canons. They had odd little porches over the doors, like sounding-boards over old pulpits; and I thought I should like to see one of the Minor-Canons come out upon his top step, and favour us with a little Christmas discourse about the poor scholars of Rochester.

This was the Minor Canon Corner of *Edwin Drood*, where

the Rev. Canon Crisparkle lived with his Ma, the "China Shepherdess."

Minor Canon Corner was a quiet place in the shadow of the Cathedral, which the cawing of the rooks, the echoing footsteps of rare passers, the sound of the Cathedral bell, or the roll of the Cathedral organ seemed to render more quiet than absolute silence.

On Boley Hill is situated the one-time residence of Richard Watts, called Satis House. It is said that Dickens transferred the name of this house to Restoration House (see page 15) when giving a home to Miss Havisham in *Great Expectations*.

Returning to the High Street, and turning to the right, we see the quaintly gabled Watts's Charity, better known as the House of the Seven Poor Travellers after the Christmas story of that name.

Strictly speaking, there were only six Poor Travellers; but, being a traveller myself, though an idle one, and being withal as poor as I hope to be, I brought the number up to seven. This word of explanation is due at once, for what says the inscription over the quaint old door?

RICHARD WATTS, ESQUIRE
by his will dated 22nd August, 1579
founded this Charity,
for Six Poor Travellers
Who, not being Rogues or Proctors
May receive gratis for one Night,
Lodging, Entertainment
and Fourpence each.

It was in the ancient little city of Rochester, in Kent, of all the good days in the year upon a Christmas Eve, that I stood reading this inscription over the quaint old door in question. . . . I stepped backward into the road to survey my inheritance. I found it to be a clean, white house, of a staid and venerable air, with the quaint old door already three times mentioned (an arched door), choice little long low lattice-windows, and a roof of three gables.

Dickens then proceeds to give us an interesting pen picture of the High Street and the Castle.

The silent High-street of Rochester is full of gables, with old beams and timbers carved into strange faces. It is oddly garnished with a queer old clock that projects over the pavement out of a grave red-brick building, as if Time carried on business there, and hung out his sign. Sooth to say, he did an active stroke of work in Rochester, in the old days of the Romans, and the Saxons, and the Normans; and down to the times of King John, when the rugged castle—I will not undertake to say how many hundreds of years old then—was abandoned to the centuries of weather which have so defaced the dark apertures in its walls, that the ruin looks as if the rooks and daws had pecked its eyes out.

Having seen over the house, Dickens hit upon the idea of entertaining the Six Poor Travellers that evening, and himself making a seventh.

With this in view he returned to the Bull Hotel, and from his bedroom "could smell a delicious savour of Turkey and Roast Beef rising to the window." Here he "made a glorious jorum" of Wassail, in a brown pitcher.

On the stroke of nine he set out for Watts's Charity, carrying his "brown beauty" (the pitcher of Wassail) in his arms, the supper following in procession:

"As we passed along the High Street, comet-like, we left a long tail of fragrance behind us which caused the public to stop, sniffing in wonder."

A little further along the High Street on the same side as Watts's Charity is a venerable brick edifice, now a museum, known as Eastgate House, which figured in *Edwin Drood* as the Nuns' House, the Seminary for Young Ladies, kept by Miss Twinkleton, at which Rosa was a pupil:

> In the midst of Cloisterham stands the Nuns' House: a venerable brick edifice, whose present appellation is doubtless derived from the legend of its conventual uses. On the trim gate enclosing its old courtyard is a resplendent brass plate flashing forth the legend: "Seminary for Young Ladies. Miss Twinkleton." The house-front is so old and worn, and the brass plate is so shining and staring, that the general result has reminded imaginative strangers of a battered old beau with a large modern eye-glass stuck in his blind eye.

The house is marked with a tablet bearing the City Arms and an inscription connecting it with Dickens.

"Over against the Nuns' House" was, we are told, the residence of Mr. Sapsea, auctioneer, "the purest jackass in

Cloisterham"; and there, opposite us, is a quaint collection
of gabled houses.

Mr. Sapsea's premises are in the High-street, over against
the Nuns' House. They are of about the period of the
Nuns' House, irregularly modernised here and there, as
steadily deteriorating generations found, more and more,
that they preferred air and light to Fever and the Plague.
Over the doorway is a wooden effigy, about half life-size,
representing Mr. Sapsea's father, in a curly wig and toga,
in the act of selling.

At one time a carved wooden figure of an auctioneer,
such as Dickens describes, actually did grace the doorway.

The first turning on the right after passing Watts's Charity,
is the Maidstone Road.

When Jasper made his first tour of inspection with
Durdles, he returned in this direction from the Cathedral
crypt.

They have but to cross what was once the vineyard,
belonging to what was once the Monastery, to come into
the narrow back lane wherein stands the crazy wooden
house of two low stories currently known as the Travellers' Twopenny:—a house all warped and distorted,
like the morals of the travellers, with scant remains of a
lattice-work porch over the door, and also of a rustic fence
before its stamped-out garden.

The Vineyard referred to is now a public garden, called
the Vines, and there is a pleasant walk across it into Minor
Canon Row and the Cathedral.

On the evening of his disappearance Edwin wandered in
this direction and met the old opium woman, who warned
him that Edwin was a "threatened name."

Opposite the Vines is an ancient house of striking picturesqueness, known as Restoration House; but to Dickens's
readers it is the house of Miss Havisham, that figures so
largely in *Great Expectations*.

Miss Havisham was "an immensely rich and grim lady,"
who, we are told, lived "in a large and dismal house barri-
caded against robbers and who led a life of seclusion." Pip
thus made his first acquaintance with it!

Within a quarter of an hour we came to Miss Havisham's
house, which was of old brick, and dismal, and had a
great many iron bars to it. Some of the windows had

been walled up; of those that remained, all the lower were rustily barred. There was a court-yard in front, and that was barred; so, we had to wait, after ringing the bell, until some one should come to open it.

A walk in this direction was a great favourite with Dickens. "He would turn out of Rochester High Street" says Forster, "through the Vines (where some old buildings, from one of which called Restoration House he took Satis House for *Great Expectations*), had a curious attraction for him."

It is on record that the day before his death he took this walk and was noticed resting near the spot, and so attentively engaged in observing the house, that it was thought likely he would introduce it into the story. The chapter he wrote on his return—the last—had reference to the spot.

At the commencement of Star Hill, is the Conservative Club, formerly the Theatre Royal, where Jingle acted and which Dickens often visited when a boy.

We now arrive at about the spot where Rochester ends and Chatham begins; we will not attempt to define it, preferring to remain in the happy ignorance of Richard Doubledick (*The Seven Poor Travellers*), who said:

"If anybody . . . knows to a nicety where Rochester ends and Chatham begins, it is more than I do."

v

At the top of Star Hill we follow New Road, which branches off to the left. To the right are the recreation grounds, rented from the military authorities by the Corporation of Chatham. Across the recreation grounds to the right is Fort Pitt, and beyond it a meadow, the scene of the memorable duel that was to have been between Mr. Winkle and Dr. Slammer.

Leaving Fort Pitt and turning to the left we reach Ordnance Terrace. Here at No. 11 (then No. 2) Charles Dickens lived as a boy, from 1817, for about three years. The house bears a tablet to the effect that Charles Dickens lived there from 1817 to 1821.

Dickens's first school, not reckoning the primary lessons he received at his mother's knee, was near the railway station, not far from Ordnance Terrace. Behind the school was the playing field of many pleasant memories, but also, like many other things, it has gone.

Here Dickens received his earliest impressions which in due time were transferred to his earliest *Sketches by Boz*.

Leaving the station by way of Railway Street, we reach High Street, Chatham, once again. Crossing the road, and continuing straight on down Military Road, we find on our right a street oddly called The Brook. A short way down this street, on the right-hand, is a lodging-house, No. 18, St. Mary's Place, bearing a tablet announcing that Charles Dickens lived there from 1821 to 1823. The factory next door was at one time a chapel presided over by a Baptist minister, whose son, William Giles, kept a school, to which young Charles was forthwith sent.

It was in this Chatham house that he made acquaintance with the books that had so great an influence on his later life, as he told us in *David Copperfield* :

> My father had left a small collection of books in a little room upstairs to which I had access (for it adjoined my own), and which nobody else in our house ever troubled . . . a glorious host, to keep me company. They kept alive my fancy, and my hope of something beyond that place and time. . . . When I think of it, the picture always rises in my mind, of a summer evening, the boys at play in the churchyard, and I sitting on my bed, reading as if for life. Every barn in the neighbourhood, every stone in the church, and every foot of the churchyard, had some association of its own, in my mind, connected with these books, and stood for some locality made famous in them. I have seen Tom Pipes go climbing up the church-steeple; I have watched Strap, with the knapsack on his back, stopping to rest himself upon the wicket-gate; and I *know* that Commodore Trunnion held that club with Mr. Pickle, in the parlour of our little village alehouse.

When Dickens was eleven, the family left Chatham for London.

Chatham Lines are not far from The Brook, and we soon reach the scene of the "grand review" which Mr. Pickwick visited, where he lost his hat, and found an acquaintance in the jovial Mr. Wardle and family.

Forster tells us that one of the favourite walks of Dickens, when he came to live at Gad's Hill, was "by Rochester and the Medway, to the Chatham Lines. He would . . . pass round by Fort Pitt, and coming back by Frindsbury would bring himself by some cross fields again into the high-road."

In the High Street of Chatham is the Mitre Inn, which has a personal association with the boyhood of Dickens. In the days when the Dickens family lived in Chatham the landlord of the Mitre was John Tribe and the two families were on visiting terms, and young Charles and his sister Fanny used to sing duets at parties held there.

In *The Holly Tree Inn* there is a distinct reference to the Mitre:

> There was an Inn in the cathedral town where I went to school. . . . It was the Inn where friends used to put up, and where we used to go to see parents, and to have salmon and fowls, and be tipped. It had an ecclesiastical sign—the Mitre—and a bar that seemed to be the next best thing to a bishopric, it was so snug.

Nearly opposite the Mitre stood the Mechanics' Institute, in aid of the funds of which Dickens gave several readings from his works.

David Copperfield reached Rochester at the end of the second day of his tramp to Dover, and

> Toiling into Chatham,—which, in that night's aspect, is a mere dream of chalk, and drawbridges, and mastless ships in a muddy river, roofed like Noah's arks,—crept at last, upon a sort of grass-grown battery overhanging a lane, where a sentry was walking to and fro. Here I lay down, near a cannon; and, happy in the society of the sentry's footsteps, . . . slept soundly until morning.

It was at Chatham that he decided to sell his jacket. " It was a likely place to sell a jacket in; for the dealers in second-hand clothes were numerous, and were, generally speaking, on the look-out for customers at their shop-doors." He found one that "looked promising, at the corner of a dirty lane, ending in an enclosure full of stinging-nettles." Here he encountered the ugly old man who, with his "eyes and limbs," "lungs and liver," "oh goroo goroo," bid him "go fer fourpence"!

VI

When at length David got free of the old clothes-dealer at Chatham, he was "faint and weary" and "limped seven miles" upon the road.

My bed at night was under another haystack. . . .
When I took the road again next morning, I found that it
lay through a succession of hop grounds and orchards.
. . . I thought it extremely beautiful, and made up my
mind to sleep among the hops that night, imagining some
cheerful companionship in the long perspective of poles,
with the graceful leaves twining round them.

This must have brought him to about Newington, thirty-
seven miles from London. It was on the Tuesday morning
that he fell in with the tramping tinker, probably near Sittingbourne. That night he slept among the hops again, and in
the heat of the following day passed through " the sunny
street of Canterbury, dozing as it were in the hot light;
and with the sight of its old houses and gateways, and the
stately, grey cathedral, with the rooks sailing round the
towers."

When at length he reached his aunt's and it was decided
to send him to school, it was to Canterbury he went, to the
house of Mr. Wickfield, his aunt's lawyer, the original of
which is said to be at No. 71 St. Dunstan's Street, near to
the West Gate. It is described as follows:

A very old house bulging out over the road; a house
with long, low lattice-windows bulging out still farther,
and beams with carved heads on the ends bulging out too,
so that I fancied the whole house was leaning forward,
trying to see who was passing on the narrow pavement
below.

Dr. Strong's school, to which David was sent by his aunt,
is said to have had its prototype in the King's School. It
was "a grave building in a courtyard with a learned air about
it that seemed very well suited to the stray rooks and jack-
daws who came down from the Cathedral Towers to walk
with a clerkly bearing on the grass plot."

Uriah Heep's "'umble dwelling" is said to have been
situated in North Lane, but the house is now demolished.

The "County Inn" at which Mr. Dick put up was
probably the Fountain Hotel, at which Dickens stayed on
his reading tour in 1861.

Another Canterbury inn, also figuring in *David Copperfield*,
was no doubt the Sun Inn, close to the Cathedral:

It was a little inn where Mr. Micawber put up, and he
occupied a little room in it, partitioned off from the commercial room, and strongly flavoured with tobacco smoke.

I think it was over the kitchen, because a warm, greasy smell appeared to come up through the chinks in the floor, and there was a flabby perspiration on the walls. I know it was near the bar, on account of the smell of spirits and jingling of glasses.

This visit was on the occasion of Mr. Micawber's prospecting in the Medway coal trade.

We saw, I think, the greater part of the Medway . . . being so near here. Mr. Micawber was of the opinion that it would be rash not to come on and see the Cathedral. Firstly, on account of its being so well worth seeing, and our never having seen it; and secondly, on account of the great probability of something turning up in a Cathedral city.

It was at the Sun Inn that David, his aunt, Mr. Dick and Traddles stopped when they went down to Canterbury to assist Mr. Micawber in the unmasking of Uriah Heep.

On 4th November, 1861, Dickens gave a reading at Canterbury and wrote to his daughter Maimie the same evening, calling it "Windy night," from the Fountain Hotel :

An excellent house to-night, and an audience positively perfect. The greatest part of it stalls and an intelligent and delightful response in them, like the touch of a beautiful instrument. *Copperfield* wound up in a real burst of feeling and delight.

VII

And now, we, like David Copperfield, come upon " the bare, wide downs near Dover."

In reaching " the place so long desired " he felt that he had reached the " first great aim " of his journey. Even then he was not certain his aunt actually did live at Dover; his enquiries of Peggotty had been rather vague and he was told that " Miss Betsy lived near Dover, but whether at Dover itself, at Hythe, Sandgate, or Folkestone, she could not say." However, finding out that all these places were close together, he had set out for Dover, and had arrived there at last, on the sixth day of his flight.

He tells us how he enquired about his aunt among the boatmen first, and received various answers, mostly " jocose " and all " disrespectful." At length, worn out, he describes himself as " deliberating " whilst " sitting on the step of an empty shop at a street corner, near the market-place."

This shop is claimed to be that of a firm of bakers, Messrs. Igglesden & Greaves, who have fixed a tablet to their new premises, on the site of the old shop, to record the fictional incident.

Through the help of a good-natured fly-driver he became acquainted with his aunt's maid, and followed her until he came to

> A very neat little cottage with cheerful bow-windows: in front of it, a small square gravelled court or garden, full of flowers carefully tended, and smelling deliciously.

Here, he discovered his aunt—busy with her donkey scaring, and Phiz's excellent drawing of the meeting will at once be called to mind, no less than Dickens's description of the memorable scene.

There is no cottage at Dover that can be said to have been the original of that of Miss Trotwood. It is thought probable that Dickens simply transferred the locale from Broadstairs, where the original of David's aunt is said to have been a reality—see page 34. Dickens wrote a portion of the book at Broadstairs, and although Dover was known to him, yet, so far as we can trace, he had not stayed there for any length of time prior to writing the story.

Dickens took up his residence in Dover for three months in 1852, living at No. 10 Camden Crescent: he was engaged on *Bleak House* at the time. His opinion of the place, expressed in a letter written at the time, was that it was not quite a place to his taste, being too prone to itinerant music, and "infinitely too genteel." "But" he added:

> The sea is very fine, and the walks are quite remarkable. There are two ways of going to Folkestone, both lovely and striking in the highest degree; and there are heights and downs, and country roads, and I don't know what, everywhere.

The town undoubtedly attracted Dickens, for we find him writing from the Ship Hotel there in April and May 1856, speaking of his walks to Deal and back, and " over the downs towards Canterbury in a gale of wind." Three years later *A Tale of Two Cities* was written, and with it an account of Dover, as viewed by Mr. Jarvis Lorry in a walk after breakfast.

The Royal George Hotel, where Mr. Lorry always stayed, was undoubtedly the Ship where Dickens himself used to put up at. Later he stayed at the Lord Warden, and was on very friendly terms with the proprietor, Mr. Birmingham, and his wife. One letter from the Lord Warden Hotel—to Wilkie Collins—dated 24th May, 1861, is worth quoting:

> Of course I am dull and penitent here, but it is very beautiful. I can work well, and I walked, by the cliffs, to Folkestone and back to-day, when it was so exquisitely beautiful that, though I was alone, I could not keep silence on the subject. In the fourteen miles I doubt if I met twelve people.

On the 5th November, 1861, he gave a reading at Dover and described the audience as that with the greatest sense of humour.

> The effect of the readings at . . . Dover really seems to have outdone the best usual impression; . . . they wouldn't go but sat applauding like mad . . . the audience with the greatest sense of humour certainly is at Dover. The people in the stalls set the example of laughing, in the most curiously unreserved way; and they laughed with such really cordial enjoyment when Squeers read the boys' letters, that the contagion extended to me. For one couldn't hear them without laughing too.

．   ．   ．   ．   ．

For fuller particulars of *The Kent of Dickens*, the reader is referred to a volume of that title by the present writer, published by the same publisher as this book, *price 6/- nett*.

CHAPTER TWO

THE BIRTHPLACE PILGRIMAGE

I

THE road that leads to Portsmouth, the birthplace of Dickens, is somewhat overshadowed by the road that had a far greater fascination for him, with which we have dealt in our first chapter. Chatham and Rochester, which he knew when the first real rememberings of life dawned upon him, meant far more to him than any part of Portsmouth, and there is only one connection between his native place and any of his books, and that is in *Nicholas Nickleby*.

Nicholas, freed from the Yorkshire school, and befriending poor Smike, paid but a fleeting visit to London, and then went off, on foot, to seek fortune elsewhere.

Newman Noggs insisted on accompanying them on the first part of their journey, and enquired, "Which way?" "To Kingston, first," replied Nicholas; but he would give no further indication of his destination, because, as he said, he hardly knew himself. However, his plans had been a little more definitely fixed in his mind, as after Newman had left them, Nicholas informed Smike that they were bound for Portsmouth, hoping, as Portsmouth was a seaport town, to get some employment there on board ship.

Kingston was passed by Betty Higden in her flight from the terror of the workhouse, and in *Oliver Twist*, when dealing with the Chertsey burglary, we read that Blathers and Duff set off for Kingston on hearing that two men and a boy were in the cage there, apprehended under suspicious circumstances, only to find that they had no connection whatever with the burglary.

The description of the first day's journey of Nicholas and Smike is unfortunately lacking in topographic details, and might appertain to any walk along the highway on a summer's day; but it is worth repeating here:

A broad, fine, honest sun lighted up the green pastures and dimpled water with the semblance of summer, while it left the travellers all the invigorating freshness of that early time of year. The ground seemed elastic under their feet; the sheep-bells were music to their ears; and exhilarated by exercise, and stimulated by hope, they pushed onward with the strength of lions.

The day wore on, and all these bright colours subsided, and assumed a quieter tint, like young hopes softened down by time, or youthful features by degrees resolving into the calm and serenity of age. But they were scarcely less beautiful in their slow decline, than they had been in their prime; for nature gives to every time and season some beauties of its own; and from morning to night, as from the cradle to the grave, is but a succession of changes so gentle and easy, that we can scarcely mark their progress.

There is no mention of the town of Guildford, with its projecting " moon faced clock " in the High Street, to remind Dickens of his beloved Rochester. Guildford, however, was the place from which Mr. Vincent Crummles and his company had proceeded to Portsmouth, having fulfilled an engagement there " with the greatest applause "; and in a later chapter, Mr. Lillyvick explains his escape from the jealousies of the Kenwigs family, and tells Nicholas:

" Henrietta Petowker (it was settled between us) should come down here to her friends, the Crummleses, under pretence of this engagement, and I should go down to Guildford the day before, and join her on the coach there; which I did, and we came down from Guildford yesterday together."

It was somewhere in the neighbourhood of Guildford that David Copperfield spent a day of great bliss with Dora, when " it was all Dora " to him. "The sun shone Dora and the birds sang Dora." Such was his ecstasy that he hardly knew where they went, but thought it was " near Guildford." " It was a green spot on a hill, carpeted with soft turf. There were shady trees, and heather, and, as far as the eye could see, a rich landscape." Here it was that he met that mortal foe " Red Whisker."

II

In Guildford we are reminded that it is only twelve miles to Dorking by a road turning off to the left of the main road;

at Dorking the redoubtable Mrs. Weller kept the Marquis of Granby public house, to which on a certain occasion Mr. Samuel Weller, in his best clothes, journeyed " on the top of the Arundel Coach."

The Marquis of Granby in Mrs. Weller's time was quite a model of a road-side public-house of the better class—just large enough to be convenient, and small enough to be snug. On the opposite side of the road was a large sign-board on a high post, representing the head and shoulders of a gentleman with an apoplectic countenance, in a red coat with deep blue facings, and a touch of the same blue over his three-cornered hat, for a sky. Over that again were a pair of flags; beneath the last button of his coat were a couple of cannon; and the whole formed an expressive and undoubted likeness of the Marquis of Granby of glorious memory.

The bar window displayed a choice collection of geranium plants, and a well-dusted row of spirit phials. The open shutters bore a variety of golden inscriptions, eulogistic of good beds and neat wines; and the choice group of countrymen and hostlers lounging about the stable-door and horse-trough, afforded presumptive proof of the excellent quality of the ale and spirits which were sold within. Sam Weller paused, when he dismounted from the coach, to note all these little indications of a thriving business, with the eye of an experienced traveller; and having done so, stepped in at once, highly satisfied with everything he had observed.

On the occasion of Sam's visit to the Marquis after the death of his mother-in-law, we read:

It was just seven o'clock when Samuel Weller, alighting from the box of a stage-coach which passed through Dorking, stood within a few hundred yards of the Marquis of Granby. It was a cold, dull evening; the little street looked dreary and dismal; and the mahogany countenance of the noble and gallant Marquis seemed to wear a more sad and melancholy expression than it was wont to do, as it swung to and fro, creaking mournfully in the wind. The blinds were pulled down, and the shutters partly closed; of the knot of loungers that usually collected about the door, not one was to be seen; the place was silent and desolate.

What a pity it is that Dickens did not know Dorking better; or that he did not locate the " Markis Gran," as the elder

Weller once wrote it, in a place with which he was familiar, and call it by its proper name. There is no Marquis of Granby at Dorking; the nearest approach to it at the present time is the King's Arms; although, the White Horse also claims that distinction.

The writer of an article in *All the Year Round* for September 18th, 1869, stated that the King's Head (now the Post Office) a great coaching house on the Brighton Road in the old days, was "the famed house, where the fatal widow beguiled old Weller." This statement must have come under Dickens's notice, yet we can hardly believe the "road-side public house" of Mrs. Weller to have had its origin in so important a coaching house as the King's Head.

III

Godalming, not quite half-way, was chosen by Nicholas, who had borrowed a map for the purpose, as the resting-place for the first night. "To Godalming they came at last," we read, and here "they bargained for two humble beds, and slept soundly."

The second day found Nicholas and Smike crossing Hindhead, and of this portion of the road, Dickens gives an excellent pen picture:

It was a harder day's journey than yesterday's, for there were long and weary hills to climb; and in journeys, as in life, it is a great deal easier to go down hill.

They walked upon the rim of the Devil's Punch Bowl; and Smike listened with greedy interest as Nicholas read the inscription upon the stone which, reared upon that wild spot, tells of a murder committed there by night. The grass on which they stood, had once been dyed with gore; and the blood of the murdered man had run down, drop by drop, into the hollow which gives the place its name. "The Devil's Bowl," thought Nicholas, as he looked into the void, "never held fitter liquor than that!"

The stone by the roadside tells the story to which Dickens refers, of the unknown sailor who was brutally murdered at this spot and whose body was flung into the valley below.

Onward they kept, with steady purpose, and entered at length upon a wide and spacious tract of downs, with every variety of little hill and plain to change their verdant surface. Here, there shot up, almost perpendicularly, into the sky, a height so steep, as to be hardly accessible to any but the sheep and goats that fed upon its sides, and there, stood a mound of green, sloping and tapering off so delicately, and merging so gently into the level ground, that you could scarce define its limits. Hills swelling above each other; and undulations, shapely and uncouth, smooth and rugged, graceful and grotesque, thrown negligently side by side, bounded the view in each direction; while frequently, with unexpected noise, there uprose from the ground, a flight of crows, who, cawing and wheeling round the nearest hills, as if uncertain of their course, suddenly poised themselves upon the wing and skimmed down the long vista of some opening valley, with the speed of light itself.

By degrees, the prospect receded more and more on either hand, as they had been shut out from rich and extensive scenery, so they emerged once again upon the open country.

This is a very truthful picture of the road from the top of Hindhead, over Butser Hill and across the Oxenbourne Downs, to Petersfield beyond which, at a roadside inn, the travellers halted. "Thus, twilight had already closed in, when they turned off the path to the door of a road-side inn, yet twelve miles short of Portsmouth."

The Coach and Horses is the inn that is there to-day, but this was not in existence in those days. Mr. C. G. Harper in "The Portsmouth Road," points out that the gamekeeper's cottage near by, was formerly known as the Bottom Inn, and must have been the one Dickens had in mind, as there was no other inn for miles about.

Here Nicholas made the acquaintance of Vincent Crummles and his two boys. The next day, in the "vehicle of unknown design," drawn by the "strange four legged animal . . . which he called a pony," Mr. Crummles conveyed Nicholas and Smike to Portsmouth.

IV

Dickens was born at that part of Portsmouth which is called Landport, on the 7th February, 1812. The address at that time was 1, Mile End Terrace, Portsea; but it is now known as 393, Commercial Road, Portsmouth, and the house has been the property of the Corporation since 1903 and is open to the public as a museum.

It is a small house of four rooms and two attics. The front bedroom is believed to be the room in which Dickens

DICKENS'S BIRTHPLACE

[Photo by T. W. Tyrrell

THE HARD, PORTSMOUTH

[Photo by Walter Dexter

was born. The family left this house for another in Hawke Street, when Dickens was about two years of age.

Dolby, in his book, " Charles Dickens as I Knew Him," tells an amusing story connected with Dickens's reading in Portsmouth in May, 1866, where his first provincial tour with Dolby as his manager, ended.

"In the hope that the sea breezes might have the effect of relieving Mr. Dickens of the cold from which he was still suffering, we decided to visit Southsea before the Portsmouth Reading. And here two amusing incidents occurred.

"On the morning after our arrival we set out for a walk, and turning the corner of a street suddenly found ourselves in Landport Terrace. The name of the street catching Mr. Dickens's eye, he suddenly exclaimed, 'By Jove! here is the place where I was born'; and, acting on his suggestion, we walked up and down the terrace for some time, speculating as to which of the houses had the right to call itself his cradle. Beyond a recollection that there was a small front garden to the house he had no idea of the place—for he was only two years old when his father was removed to London from Portsmouth. As the houses were nearly all alike, and each had a small front garden, we were not much helped in our quest by Mr. Dickens's recollections, and great was the laughter at his humorous conjectures. He must have lived in one house because " it looked so like his father"; another one must have been his home because it looked like the birthplace of a man who had deserted it; a third was very like the cradle of a puny, weak youngster such as he had been; and so on, through the row. According to his own account, Southsea had not contributed much to his physical strength, neither indeed had Chatham; for, he used to say, he always was a puny, weak youngster, and never used to join in games with the same zest that other boys seemed to have. He never was remarkable, according to his own account, during his younger days, for anything but violent spasmodic attacks, which used to utterly prostrate him, and for indomitable energy in reading: cricket, 'chevy,' top, marbles, 'peg in the ring,' 'tor,' 'three holes,' or any of the thousand and one boys' games, had no charm for him, save such as lay in watching others play. But as none of the houses in Landport Terrace could cry out and say, as he recounted these facts, 'That boy was born here!' the mystery remained unsolved, and we passed on.

"The other incident occurred in the course of the same walk. It is well-known what interest Mr. Dickens took in all matters connected with prison life; and Mr. Wills having mentioned that he was intimately acquainted with the governor of a military prison somewhere in Gosport (the name of which, also the name of the governor, he had forgotten), a search was made, in the hope of refreshing Wills's memory. After walking some distance through clouds of dust, driven by a cold easterly wind (by no means unusual in England in the month of May), and meeting no one on the road, either of a civil, naval, or military character, able to give any information about the prison, it was suggested that the institution existed only in Wills's imagination; a suspicion which broadened into a fact when inquiries were made of the landlord of a most comfortable-looking hostelry on the roadside.

"Returning to Southsea by another road, we suddenly found ourselves in a sort of elongated ' square,' that should be called ' oblong,' open at each end, such as is to be met with in Dutch towns; the houses on each side resembled a scene ' set ' for the comic business of a pantomime; they were of red brick, with clean windows and white window frames, while green jalousie blinds of the most dazzling description added a little to the ' tone of the place.' Here the temptation to Mr. Dickens to indulge his predilections for imitating the frolics of a Clown—of the Grimaldi, Flexmore, and Tom Matthews type—presented itself. The street being entirely free from people, Mr. Dickens mounted three steps leading to one of the houses, which had an enormous brass plate on its green door; and having given three raps on the doorpost, was proceeding to lie down on the upper step, clown fashion, when the door suddenly opened and a stout woman appeared, to the intense amusement of the ' pantaloon ' (myself) and Wills, who immediately beat a retreat in the style known in pantomime as a 'rally', followed by Mr. Dickens with an imaginary policeman after him. The wind, which was very high at the time, added to the frolic, driving Mr. Dickens's hat before it, in the direction of the river, causing us to forget the situation and eagerly chase the hat to catch it ere the frolicsome blast drove it into the water. Then, and then only, we turned to take a parting look at the scene of action, when, to our dismay, we saw every doorstep and doorway occupied by the amused tenants of the houses. There was another stampede, which was stopped by an open drain, from which emanated an odour of anything but a pleasant character, suddenly making the party pale as ghosts, and necessitating the administration, medicinally, of course, of a strong dose of brandy-and-water at the nearest hotel."

Two readings were given on this occasion, at the St. George's Hall, Portsea, on 24th and 25th May, these being the final ones in Portsmouth. The only other occasion on which Dickens gave Readings in his native town was on the 11th November, 1858, when he read both in the afternoon and evening, also at the St. George's Hall. We are indebted to Mr. James Hutt, the Chief Librarian of Portsmouth, for this information, and it may be taken as final as regards Dickens's readings in Portsmouth, other dates having been discarded only after thorough search.

Dickens possessed no special regard for his birthplace, as the story of Dolby would go to show, and his only official visits to his native town were on the above-mentioned occasions of his readings in 1858 and 1866.

According to Forster, Dickens and he made a journey to Portsmouth in 1838, for local colour for the Crummles scenes.

"I perfectly recollect" says Forster, "that, on our being at Portsmouth together while he was writing *Nickleby* he recognised the exact shape of the military parade seen by him as an infant, on the same spot, a quarter of a century before."

When Nicholas Nickleby and Smike arrived at Portsmouth with Mr. Vincent Crummles, we read that:

They arrived at the drawbridge at Portsmouth, when Mr. Crummles pulled up.

"We'll get down here," said the manager, "and the boys will take him round to the stable, and call at my lodgings with the luggage. You had better let yours be taken there, for the present."

Thanking Mr. Vincent Crummles for his obliging offer, Nicholas jumped out, and, giving Smike his arm, accompanied the manager up High Street on their way to the theatre; feeling nervous and uncomfortable enough at the prospect of an immediate introduction to a scene so new to him.

They passed a great many bills, pasted against the walls and displayed in windows, wherein the names of Mr. Vincent Crummles, Mrs. Vincent Crummles, Master Crummles, Master P. Crummles, and Miss Crummles, were printed in very large letters, and everything else in very small ones; and, turning at length into an entry, in which was a strong smell of orange-peel and lamp-oil, with an under-current of saw-dust, groped their way through a dark passage, and, descending a step or two, threaded a little maze of canvas screens and paint-pots, and emerged upon the stage of the Portsmouth Theatre.

The old Portsmouth Theatre was in the High Street, where the Cambridge Barracks now stand.

After some trouble Nicholas found suitable lodgings in The Hard, over a tobacconist's:

> There is no lack of comfortable furnished apartments in Portsmouth, . . . eventually . . . they stumbled upon two small rooms up three pair of stairs, or rather two pair and a ladder, at a tobacconist's shop, on the Common Hard; a dirty street leading down to the dockyard. These Nicholas engaged, only too happy to have escaped any request for payment of a week's rent before-hand.

It was in a street quite close, Hawke Street, that the Dickens family lived at No. 16, after young Charles's birth, and before removing to Chatham.

The lodgings occupied by other members of the theatrical company were closer to the Theatre.

St. Thomas's Street is parallel with High Street, and here the Crummles's lived.

> Mr. Crummles lived in Saint Thomas's Street, at the house of one Bulph, a pilot, who sported a boat-green door, with window-frames of the same colour, and had the little finger of a drowned man on his parlour mantel-shelf, with other maritime and natural curiosities. He displayed also a brass knocker, a brass plate, and a brass bell-handle, all very bright and shining; and had a mast, with a vane on the top of it, in his back yard.

Miss Snevellicci had lodgings in Lombard Street, which runs at right angles to St. Thomas's Street.

> At the stipulated hour next morning, Nicholas repaired to the lodgings of Miss Snevellicci, which were in a place called Lombard Street, at the house of a tailor. A strong smell of ironing pervaded the little passage; and the tailor's daughter, who opened the door, appeared in that flutter of spirits which is so often attendant upon the periodical getting up of a family's linen.

The only other references to Portsmouth in Dickens's works are brief ; a mere passing mention in *The Uncommercial Traveller*, and a record in *Great Expectations* of the fact that the returned convict Magwich landed in Portsmouth under the name of Provis.

In October, 1860, Dickens was in Portsmouth, to see his son Sydney, dubbed "The Admiral," safely in his new quarters on board the "Britannia." He had just passed as a Naval Cadet, and was, so Dickens described him, "all eyes and gold lace."

Writing at the time Dickens said:

> Every maritime person in the town knew him. He seemed to know every boy on board the "Britannia," and was a tremendous favourite evidently. It was very characteristic of him that they good naturedly helped him, he being so small, into his hammock at night. But he couldn't rest in it on these terms, and got out again to learn the right way of getting in independently. Official report states that 'after a few spills, he succeeded perfectly, and went to sleep.'

v

Three years previously Dickens had seen another son off aboard from the neighbouring port of Southampton. This was Walter, and in a letter to Edmund Yates on the 19th July he tenderly expresses his grief at parting with his sons.

The Walter of fiction, in *Dombey and Son*, also went to sea, and the loss of the " Son and Heir " in which he sailed was first heard of in Southampton, by the report of the Barque " Defiance " at that port.

Southampton is mentioned in *Nicholas Nickleby* by Mr. Folair, who knew for certain of " fifteen and sixpence that came to Southampton one night last month to see me dance the Highland Fling."

Dickens gave two Readings at the Royal Victoria Rooms, Portland Terrace, Southampton, on the 9th and 10th November, 1858. He stayed at the Royal Hotel.

Winchester is mentioned once or twice in *Nicholas Nickleby*. In the first place, Nicholas's attention is drawn to it in connection with a press paragraph displayed in the lodgings of Miss Snevellicci at Portsmouth, which stated that that lady had sprained her ankle "by slipping on a piece of orange-peel flung by a monster in human form . . . upon the stage at Winchester; and it was to this town that Mr. Vincent Crummles and his company were to proceed after Nicholas left them.

Richard Carstone, in *Bleak House*, was educated at Winchester School.

(time, ten in the morning) and an Italian box of music on the steps—both in full blast.

However, in spite of this the charm of Broadstairs still continued to hold him.   In 1848 he spent " an idle summer " there, with only *The Haunted Man* to finish.

The following year (1849) Dickens was in the throes of *David Copperfield*: he was unsettled as to summer holidays and sought a change from Broadstairs, and a visit to the Isle of Wight was arranged: but he found the air too relaxing; his daughter Maimie was taken ill, so in the September the family returned to their old favourite Broadstairs. As soon as he was in Broadstairs, he became more settled in his mind about the book and decided to put a great part of the MS. of his own life, on which he had been busy some time previously, into Number 4 of the story; this was Chapter Eleven, which is mostly autobiographical.

The location of Betsey Trotwood at Dover was purely imaginary, as the original was Mary Strong, who lived in the house in Nuckell's Place, Broadstairs, now called Dickens House and marked with a tablet to the effect that in the house "lived the original of Betsey Trotwood in *David Copperfield* by Charles Dickens, 1849."

The gardens in front of the house facing the sea were meadow-land in those days, and Miss Strong, it is said, had as decided an antipathy to donkeys as Miss Betsey.

In July, 1850, Dickens was at last able to secure Fort House from the July for a few months, and here *David Copperfield* was completed.

The house has undergone several alterations since then, including the altogether unnecessary change of name to Bleak House—a tribute to Dickens, no doubt; but it was not the Bleak House of the story, nor was any portion of *Bleak House* planned or written there.

On an outer wall of the house is a granite tablet bearing a bronze bust of Dickens, encircled by a wreath bound with ribbons upon which are inscribed the names of some of the works. It is a pity that *Barnaby Rudge* and *The Old Curiosity Shop*, both partly written at Broadstairs, should be omitted, and *Bleak House* and other works having no association with the place included.

He took a fond farewell of Broadstairs in a paper in *Household Words* for 2nd August, 1851, entitled "Our Watering Place":

Half awake and half asleep, this idle morning in our sunny window on the edge of a chalk-cliff in the old-

FORT HOUSE, BROADSTAIRS

CHICHESTER HOUSE, BRIGHTON

[*Photos by Walter Dexter*

fashioned watering-place to which we are a faithful resorter, we feel a lazy inclination to sketch its picture.

His last visit was some eight years later; he was far from well at the time, as he wrote to Forster, "I have an instinctive feeling that nothing but the sea will restore me." His friend, Wilkie Collins, and his brother, were at Broadstairs at the time, and to them he wrote, "Nothing but sea air and sea water will set me right. I want to come to Broadstairs next Wednesday by the mid-day train and stay till Monday." Accordingly, Broadstairs welcomed him once again, and again he stayed at the Albion Hotel, from which place he wrote a very characteristic letter to his two daughters.

II

Herne Bay was also known to Dickens, but of all the Kentish seaside towns, Broadstairs had the preference.

In a letter to Douglas Jerrold, written on a cold, wet day in June, 1843, he dismisses the proposal of a visit there, rather curtly:

Herne Bay. Hum. I suppose it's no worse than any other place in this weather, but it is watery rather—isn't it? In my mind's eye, I have the sea in a perpetual state of smallpox; and the chalk running downhill like town milk.

Later, however, his opinion of the place undoubtedly improved, as in 1851 he wrote to Charles Knight from Broadstairs holding out an " expedition to Herne Bay, Canterbury, where not?" as an inducement to him to spend a few days there.

The larger watering-places of Thanet, Ramsgate and Margate had little charm for Dickens; he preferred the quietude offered him by Broadstairs, the situation of which, midway between the two towns, enabled him to visit either during an afternoon walk.

In *Bleak House* reference is made to the popularity of the Thanet towns for seaside holidays:

It is the hottest long vacation known for many years. All the young clerks are madly in love, and, according to their various degrees, pine for bliss with the beloved object at Margate, Ramsgate or Gravesend.

The journey from London to the Thanet towns was usually made by water from London Bridge, and this was the way Dickens most often came; and he gives descriptions of the

incidents of such journeys in " The Tuggses at Ramsgate,"
" The River " and " The Steam Excursion "; all in
Sketches by Boz.

In 1842 Dickens wrote to Forster from Broadstairs:

> Strange as it may appear to you the sea is running so
> high that we have no choice but to return by land. No
> steamer can come out of Ramsgate, and the Margate boat
> lay out all night on Wednesday with all her passengers on
> board. You may be sure of us therefore on Saturday at
> 5, for I have determined to leave here to-morrow, as we
> could not otherwise manage it in time; and have engaged
> an omnibus to bring the whole caravan by the overland
> route. . . . We cannot open a window, or a door; legs
> are of no use on the terrace; and the Margate boats can
> only take people aboard at Herne Bay!

Margate comes in for a fair amount of mention in the
Sketches by Boz, although no one special story is devoted to it,
as was the case with Ramsgate. Mrs. Tuggs simply sneered
at Margate when it was suggested for the family holiday:
"Margate? . . . Worse and worse—nobody there but
tradespeople" she said.

Ramsgate was visited by Dickens during his first visit to
Broadstairs in 1837. Thus he wrote to Forster:

> I have walked upon the sands at low-water from this
> place to Ramsgate, and sat upon the same at high-ditto till
> I have been flayed with the cold.

But we cannot find he ever paid more than fleeting visits
to the town. In 1845 he wrote to Forster:

> I went to a circus at Ramsgate on Saturday night,
> where Mazeppa was played in three long acts without an
> H in it; as if for a wager.

There are, however, sundry references to Ramsgate in the
novels—more particularly in the *Sketches by Boz*, and from
the knowledge displayed of Ramsgate and Pegwell Bay in
' The Tuggses at Ramsgate," published in 1836: it is
probable that Dickens had visited the town prior to his stay
in Broadstairs in 1837.

This story gives an amusing account of the holiday spent
at Ramsgate by the Tuggs family to celebrate their inheritance of twenty thousand pounds. Where shall they go;
Gravesend was low, Margate too full of tradespeople,
" Ramsgate? . . . To be sure, how stupid they must have

been not to have thought of that before! Ramsgate was just the place of all others" and then follows an interesting and amusing account of Ramsgate and what befell them there.

III

Deal has associations with *Bleak House*, where Esther Summerson says:

> I could only suggest that I should go down to Deal where Richard was then stationed. . . . We all went to London that afternoon and finding two places on the mail, secured them. At our usual bed-time Charley and I were rolling away seaward, with the Kentish letters. . . . At last we came into the narrow streets of Deal and very gloomy they were, upon a raw misty morning. The long flat beach with its little irregular houses, wooden and brick, and its litter of capstans, and great boats and sheds, and bare upright poles with tackle and blocks, and loose gravelly waste places overgrown with grass and weeds, were as dull in appearance as any place I ever saw. The sea was heaving under a thick white fog; and nothing else was moving but a few early ropemakers, who with the yarn twisted round their bodies, looked as if, tired of their present state of existence, they were spinning themselves into cordage.
>
> But when we got into a warm room in an excellent hotel . . . Deal began to look more cheerful. Our little room was like a ship's cabin, and that delighted Charley very much.

It was while walking on the beach at Deal that Esther witnessed a small boat landing from a "great Indiaman" and recognised among the officers Allan Woodcourt, returned from the East, with whom she later had an interview at the hotel.

Deal was probably the town mentioned in " Out of the Season," to which he walked from " the watering-place out of the season " (Folkestone).

> A walk of ten miles brought me to a seaside town without a cliff, which, like the town I had come from, was out of the season too. Half of the houses were shut up; half of the other half were to let; the town might have done as much business as it was doing then, if it had been at the bottom of the sea. Nobody seemed to flourish save the attorney. . . .

D

The parlor bell in the Admiral Benbow had grown so flat with being out of the season, that neither could I hear it ring when I pulled the handle for lunch, nor could the young woman in black stockings and strong shoes, who acted as waiter out of the season, until it had been tinkled three times.

Admiral Benbow's cheese was out of the season, but his home-made bread was good, and his beer was perfect.

To Dover, Dickens was also a fairly frequent visitor, and we have dealt with his visits to that town on pages 19–21.

IV

Although it was not until 1855 that Dickens spent a sea-side holiday at Folkestone, the place was well known to him before, and had often been visited during his holidays at Broadstairs.

On 13th July, 1849, we find him writing a characteristic letter from Broadstairs:

Why sir, I'm going to Folkestone on Saturday sir, not on accounts of the manifacktring of Bengal cheroots as there is there, but for the survay in 'o' the coast sir. . . . You couldn't spend your arternoon better sir. Dover, Sand-gate, Herne Bay—they're all to be wisited sir.

" There are two ways of going to Folkestone," he wrote to Mary Boyle from Dover in 1852, " both lovely and striking in the highest degree, and there are heights and downs and country roads, and I don't know what, everywhere."

In the summer of 1855 Dickens and his family took residence at No. 3 Albion Villas, Folkestone, and it was during his stay there that he decided to give a public reading from his works to assist the funds of the local institutes; this led to the idea of giving such readings for his own benefit, the first series of which was given three years later.

Thus we find him writing to Forster from Folkestone on the 16th September, 1855: " I am going to read for them here on the 5th of next month, and have answered in the last fortnight thirty applications to do the like all over England, Ireland and Scotland." And a week later:

I am going to read here next Friday week. There are (as there are everywhere) a Literary Institution and a Working Men's Institution, which have not the slightest sympathy or connection. The stalls are five shillings, and

I have made them fix the working men's admission at three pence, and I hope it may bring them together. The event comes off in a carpenter's shop, as the biggest place that can be got.

The " carpenter's shop " was a builder's saw-mills in the Dover Road, on the site now occupied by the Fire Station.

We cannot glean very much of Dickens's life at Folkestone from the published letters, as very few have reference to it.

The only references of importance to Folkestone in the works are to be found in *Reprinted Pieces*. The following extract is from " A Flight," describing the journey by train from London to Folkestone to connect with the steamer for Boulogne. The paper originally appeared in *Household Words*, 30th August, 1851.

Now fresher air, now glimpses of unenclosed Downland with flapping crows flying over it . . . now the sea, now Folkestone. . . . We are dropped slowly down to the Port, and sidle to and fro (the whole Train) before the insensible Royal George Hotel for some ten minutes. The Royal George takes no more heed of us than its namesake under water at Spithead, or under earth at Windsor, does. The Royal George dog lies winking and blinking at us, without taking the trouble to sit up ; and the Royal George's " wedding party " at the open window (who seem, I must say, rather tired of bliss) don't bestow a solitary glance upon us. . . . The first gentleman in Folkestone is evidently used up, on this subject.

There is no Royal George Hotel at Folkestone. Some years later, in writing *A Tale of Two Cities*, Dickens calls the Ship Hotel at Dover the Royal George.

To *Household Words* of 29th September, 1855, Dickens contributed an article on Folkestone under the title of " Out of Town." In it he called the place Pavilionstone. This was subsequently published in *Reprinted Pieces*.

Sitting, on a bright September morning, among my books and papers at my open window on the cliff over-hanging the sea-beach, I have the sky and ocean framed before me like a beautiful picture. . . . The name of the little town, on whose shore this sea is murmuring . . . is Pavilionstone. Within a quarter of a century, it was a little fishing town, and they do say, that the time was, when it was a little smuggling town.

The article also contained an eulogy of the Pavilion Hotel.

The following year Dickens wrote another sea-side article, " Out of the Season," already referred to. Folkestone was probably the " watering-place out of the season " that he had in his mind, although no mention is made of it by name.

.   .   .   .   .

For a complete account of *The Kent of Dickens*, by the present writer, the reader is referred to a volume bearing that title, published by the same publisher as this book, *price 6/- nett*.

V

Dickens paid only one visit to Hastings on his reading tours, and except that he has left a record that he "turned away half Hastings" and that the effect of the readings there "really seems to have outdone the best usual impression," we have no further account of the place from his pen, nor do we know if he ever visited it on any other occasion.   The date of the reading was 6th November, 1861.

Eastbourne was visited in 1860.   Forster was staying there in the October and to him Dickens wrote: " It would be a great pleasure to me to come to you, an immense pleasure, and to sniff the sea I love (from the shore); but I fear I must come down one morning and go back at night."   He then goes on to tell why; that he has his new story, *Great Expectations* in hand.   "Therefore what I hoped would be a few days at Eastbourne diminish to a few hours."

VI

Dickens's personal connection with Brighton as a seaside holiday resort was from 1837 until about 1853, during which period he was a regular visitor.

So far as can be ascertained, his first visit was in October, 1837, when after finishing *The Pickwick Papers* and during the writing of *Oliver Twist*, he spent about ten days there at the Old Ship Hotel, where he had "a beautiful bay-windowed sitting-room, fronting the sea."

On the 3rd of November he wrote to Forster regretting that he had not come down to keep him company :

I have seen nothing of B.'s brother who was to have shown me the lions, and my notions of the place are consequently somewhat confined: being limited to the pavilion, the chain-pier, and the sea. The last is quite enough for me, and, unless I am joined by some male

companion (do you think I shall be?) is most probably all
I shall make acquaintance with.

In the same letter he humorously described the weather:

It is a beautiful day and we have been taking advantage
of it; but the wind until to-day has been so high, and the
weather so stormy, that Kate has been scarcely able to
peep out of doors.   On Wednesday it blew a perfect hurri-
cane, breaking windows, knocking down shutters, carrying
people off their legs, blowing the fires out, and causing
universal consternation.   The air was for some hours darkened with a shower of black hats (second hand) which are
supposed to have been blown off the heads of unwary
passengers in remote parts of the town, and have been
industriously picked up by the fishermen.

and the theatre:

Charles Kean was advertised for " Othello," "for the
benefit of Mrs. Sefton, having most kindly postponed for
this one day his departure for London."   I have not heard
whether he got to the theatre, but I am sure nobody else
did.   They do " The Honeymoon " to-night, on which
occasion I mean to patronise the drayma.

and the letter concludes thus characteristically:

I am afraid you will find this letter extremely dear at
eightpence, but if the warmest assurances of friendship and
attachment, and anxious lookings-forward to the pleasure
of your society, be worth anything, throw them into the
balance, together with a hundred good wishes and one
hearty assurance that I am, &c., &c., Charles Dickens.   No
room for the flourish—I'll finish it the next time I write
to you.

More than three years elapsed before he again visited
Brighton, when we find him writing from the Old Ship
Hotel to George Cattermole, who was at the time illustrating
The Old Curiosity Shop.

I passed your house on Wednesday, being then atop of
the Brighton Era, but there was nobody at the door, saving
a solitary poulterer, and all my warm-hearted aspirations
lodged in the goods he was delivering.   No doubt you
observed a peculiar relish in your dinner.   That was the
cause.

The next mention of Brighton is in a letter to Forster in October, 1845, when finishing *The Cricket on the Hearth*. "Visions of Brighton come upon me, and I have a great mind to go there and finish my second part."

The railway to Brighton was opened in 1841, and it is very probable that Dickens paid several flying visits to the town between 1841 and 1847, the date of his next recorded visit, when he stayed with Mrs. Dickens, his eldest boy and Miss Hogarth at 148 King's Road, next door to the Norfolk Hotel. He fetched his two little daughters down to join them during the last week of their stay. He was still at work writing *Dombey* at the time, although his letters do not allude to it, and the Brighton scenes in that novel were all written before that time. It is therefore reasonable to suppose that Brighton saw him more frequently between the years above mentioned, although there is no record of the fact.

His next visit to Brighton was in March, 1848, this time with his wife and Mrs. Macready. They stayed first at the Bedford Hotel (where he had made Mr. Dombey and Mr. Toots put up), and then at Junction House, No. 1 Junction Road, close to the Old Steine. Macready joined them on the Sundays during their stay, and to him Dickens wrote "we have migrated from the Bedford, and come here, where we are very comfortably (not to say gorgeously) accommodated."

In the November of the same year he was again at Brighton, staying at the Bedford Hotel, and his letters contain some references to the theatre.

> I have been at work all day, and am going to wander into the theatre, where (for the comic man's benefit) ' two gentlemen of Brighton ' are performing two counts in a melodrama. I was quite addle headed for the time being and think an amateur or two would revive me.

In the same letter we read: "The Duke of Cambridge is staying in this house, and they are driving me mad by having Life Guard Bands under our windows playing *our* overtures. . . ."

The next day he wrote Mark Lemon an account of his visit to the theatre:

> I went to the play last night—fifth act of Richard the Third. Richmond by a stout *lady*, with a particularly well-developed bust, who finished all the speeches with the soubrette simper. Also, at the end of the tragedy she

came forward (still being Richmond) and said, "Ladies and gentlemen, on Wednesday next the entertainments will be for *My* benefit, when I hope to meet your approbation and support." Then, having bowed herself into the stage-door, she looked out of it, and said, winningly, "Won't you come?" which was enormously applauded.

In the February of the following year (1849) Dickens and his wife were again at Brighton, this time accompanied by the Leeches, and here they met with an amazing adventure. They had taken lodgings (the address is not given) and after they had been residing there for a week both the landlord and his daughter went mad, and the lodgers were forced to seek accommodation at the Bedford Hotel.

If you could have heard the cursing and crying of the two; could have seen the physician and nurse quoited out into the passage by the madman at the hazard of their lives; could have seen Leech and me flying to the doctor's rescue; could have seen our wives pulling us back; could have seen the M.D. faint with fear; could have seen three other M.D.'s come to his aid; with an atmosphere of Mrs. Gamps, strait-waistcoats, struggling friends and servants, surrounding the whole; you would have said it was quite worthy of me, and quite in keeping with my usual proceedings.

At this time Dickens was engaged on thinking out the title for his new story, and the matter gave him much concern; in the same letter he wrote: " A sea-fog to-day, but yesterday inexpressibly delicious. My mind running, like a high sea, no names—not satisfied yet, though." And it was not until he had left Brighton for Broadstairs that he finally decided on the title of the book we now familiarly know as *David Copperfield*. It was on this visit that he wrote an invitation in rhyme to Mark Lemon, to join him; the refrain was as follows:

> Oh, my Lemon, round and fat,
> Oh, my bright, my right, my tight 'un,
> Think a little what you're at—
> Don't stay at home, but come to Brighton.

The following year, 1850, he was again at No. 148 King's Road for a short time, and probably a part of *David Copperfield* was written here, but of this we cannot say for certain. However, "The Child's Dream of a Star" was written here on this occasion. Forster quotes a letter from Brighton dated

" Who is he? Who the Devil is he? Why don't I know him? "

When Mrs. Chick proposed sea air as the only thing to literally put little Paul Dombey on his feet, she suggested Brighton and Mrs. Pipchin in almost the same breath; and so to the "infantine boarding house of a very select description " Paul was sent to be under the supervision of Mrs. Pipchin, " a marvellous, ill-favoured, ill-conditioned old lady, of a stooping figure, with a mottled face, like bad marble, a hook nose, and a hard grey eye, that looked as if it might have been hammered at on an anvil without sustaining any injury. . . . She was generally spoken of as " a great manager " of children, and the secret of her management was, to give them everything that they didn't like, and nothing that they did—which was found to sweeten their dispositions very much.".

It is rather difficult, and perhaps futile, to attempt to identify any house in Brighton, as the original of what Dickens calls " The castle of the ogress."   All we know is that it was in a " steep by-street " so probably Upper or Lower Rock Gardens was the location.

The Castle of this ogress and child-queller was in a steep by-street at Brighton; where the soil was more than usually chalky, flinty, and sterile, and the houses were more than usually brittle and thin; where the small front-gardens had the unaccountable property of producing nothing but marigolds, whatever was sown in them; and where snails were constantly discovered holding on to the street doors, and other public places they were not expected to ornament, with the tenacity of cupping-glasses.   In the winter time the air couldn't be got out of the Castle, and in the summer time it couldn't be got in. . . . It was not, naturally, a fresh-smelling house; and in the window of the front parlour, which was never opened, Mrs. Pipchin kept a collection of plants in pots, which imparted an earthy flavour of their own to the establishment.   However, choice examples of their kind, too, these plants were of a kind peculiarly adapted to the embowerment of Mrs. Pipchin.   There were half-a-dozen specimens of the cactus, writhing round bits of lath, like hairy serpents; another specimen shooting out broad claws, like a green lobster; several creeping vegetables, possessed of sticky and adhesive leaves; and one uncomfortable flower-pot hanging to the ceiling, which appeared to have boiled over,

and tickling people underneath with its long green ends,
reminded them of spiders—in which Mrs. Pipchin's
dwelling was uncommonly prolific, though perhaps it
challenged competition still more proudly, in the season,
in point of earwigs.

Mr. Dombey used to come down once a week to see his
son and it was on one of these occasions that Major Bagstock
put himself in Mr. Dombey's way and got an introduction.
" I stay at the Bedford " Mr. Dombey informed him, and in
due course the Major had " the honour of calling at the
Bedford, Sir," and was invited to dinner.   " On Saturday
Mr. Dombey came down; and Florence and Paul would go
to his hotel, and have tea. They passed the whole of Sunday
with him, and generally rode out before dinner."

It was to the Bedford Hotel, on one of the week-end visits,
that Captain Cuttle and Walter came to ask for assistance to
meet the liabilities of old Sol Gills.

"Brighton proved very beneficial" to young Paul, and the
question of his education being discussed, Mrs. Pipchin
recommended Mr. Dombey to Dr. Blimber, "my neighbour, Sir. I believe the Doctor's is an excellent establishment."

Dickens describes Dr. Blimber's establishment as "a great
hot-house, in which there was a forcing apparatus incessantly
at work."

The Doctor's was a mighty fine house, fronting the
sea. Not a joyful style of house within, but quite the
contrary.   Sad-coloured curtains, whose proportions were
spare and lean, hid themselves despondently behind the
windows. The tables and chairs were put away in rows,
like figures in a sum: fires were so rarely lighted in the
rooms of ceremony, that they felt like wells, and a visitor
represented the bucket; the dining-room seemed the
last place in the world where any eating or drinking was
likely to occur; there was no sound through all the houes
but the ticking of a great clock in the hall, which made
itself audible in the very garrets: and sometimes a dull
crying of young gentlemen at their lessons, like the mur-
murings of an assemblage of melancholy pigeons.

Dr. Blimber's is said to have had its prototype in the
school kept at Brighton during the years 1839 to 1846 by
Dr. Proctor called Chichester House, at the corner of the
terrace of that name.

Broadstairs, which he had visited for several years, thought of Bonchurch. In the June he went to Shanklin, from which he wrote to his wife on Monday the sixteenth:

> I have but a moment.   Just got back and post going out. I have taken a most delightful and beautiful house, belonging to White, at Bonchurch; cool, airy, private bathing, everything delicious.   I think it is the prettiest place I ever saw in my life, at home or abroad.   Anne may begin to dismantle Devonshire Terrace.   I have arranged for carriages, luggage, and everything.
>
> The man with the post-bag is swearing in the passage.
>
> P.S.   A waterfall in the grounds, which I have arranged with a carpenter to convert into a perpetual shower-bath.

This house was Winterbourne, and he took it for six months, and was busy with *David Copperfield* the whole time.   John Leech and his family also had a house at Bonchurch at the same time.

The beauties of this part of the Island attracted him enormously: they were so different from what he had been accustomed to at Broadstaris.   Forster declares " he began with an excess of liking " which unfortunately did not endure. This is what he said in a letter of July 28th:

> From the top of the highest downs there are views which are only to be equalled on the Genoese shore of the Mediterranean;   the variety of walks is extraordinary; things are cheap, and everybody is civil.   The waterfall acts wonderfully, and the sea-bathing is delicious.   Best of all, the place is certainly cold rather than hot, in the summer-time.   The evenings have been even chilly. White very jovial, and emulous of the inimitable in respect of gin-punch.   He had made some for our arrival.   Ha! ha! not bad for a beginner. . . . I have been, and am, trying to work this morning; but I can't make anything of it, and am going out to think.   I am invited by a distinguished friend to dine with you on the first of August, but I have pleaded distance and the being resident in a cave on the seashore;   my food, beans;   my drink, the water from the rock.

Four days later, showed that he had settled down.   " I have just begun to get into work.   We are expecting the Queen to come by very soon, in grand array, and are going to let off ever so many guns," and a further letter, dated August 6th, described himself as continuing still at work;

but also taking part in dinners at Blackgang, and picnics of " tremendous success " on Shanklin Down.

The Swinburne family lived at Bonchurch, and Forster tells us " there was a reference in one of his letters, but I have lost it, to a golden-haired lad of the Swinburnes whom his own boys used to play with, since become more widely known."

On Friday we had a grand, and what is better, a very good dinner at " parson " Fielden's, with some choice port. On Tuesday we are going on another picnic; with the materials for a fire, at my express stipulation; and a great iron pot to boil potatoes in. These things, and the eatables, go to the ground in a cart. Last night we had some very good merriment at White's, where pleasant Julian Young and his wife (who are staying about five miles off) showed some droll new games.

This, Forster informs us, roused the ambition in Dickens to give a " mighty conjuring performance for all the children in Bonchurch," for which he sent him the necessary materials and which " went off in a tumult of wild delight."

In another letter he wrote:

There has been a Doctor Lankester at Sandown, a very good merry fellow, who has made one at the picnics, and whom I went over and dined with, along with Danby (I remember your liking Danby, and don't wonder at it), Leech, and White.

A letter towards the close of August resumed yet more of his ordinary tone:

We had games and forfeits last night at White's. Davy Roberts's pretty little daughter is there for a week, with her husband, Bicknell's son. There was a dinner first to say good-bye to Danby, who goes to other clergy-man's-duty, and we were very merry. Mrs. White unchanging; White comically various in his moods.

Although he was busy with *David Copperfield* every day until 2 o'clock in the afternoon all the time he was at Bonchurch, he found plenty of time for his usual robust exercise of walking. His daily walk was to the top of the downs. " It makes a great difference in the climate to get a blow there, and come down again " he explained. He also had plenty of illustrious visitors around him. His dear friend Talfourd had just been made a Judge, and paid a visit to Bonchurch at this time.

There are only a few references to the Isle of Wight in Dickens's books. In *Nicholas Nickleby* we hear of the Vincent Crummles Company paying a week's visit to the theatre at Ryde, after Nicholas had left them; and also in the same book we read that Mr. Lillyvick and his bride, Miss Petoker, "departed for Ryde where they were to spend the next two days in profound retirement": accompanied by the Infant Phenomenon, the "travelling bridesmaid" specially chosen because the steamboat people, deceived by her size, would carry her at half price.

The Isle of Wight has always been famous for honeymoons: small wonder is it therefore that Dickens on another occasion, should take a newly married couple there. This was in *Our Mutual Friend*, when the Lammles spent their honeymoon at Shanklin—where they both found each other out as a couple of impostors! The time comes in "about a fortnight, and it comes to Mr. and Mrs. Lammle on the sands at Shanklin, in the Isle of Wight."

Mr. and Mrs. Lammle have walked for some time on the Shanklin sands, and one may see by their footprints that they have not walked arm in arm, and that they have not walked in a straight track, and that they have walked in a moody humour; for, the lady has prodded little spirting holes in the damp sand before her with her parasol, and the gentleman has trailed his stick after him. As if he were of the Mephistopheles family indeed, and had walked with a drooping tail.

CHAPTER FOUR

ROAD AND RIVER WITH OUR MUTUAL FRIEND

I

WHEN one come to reckon up the number of times the River Thames and its towns and villages form the scene of adventures of the characters in the writings of Dickens, one is surprised at the quantity of material to be dealt with.

Much of it, however, treats of the London portion of the river, and has already been covered by the present writer in " The London of Dickens." To that book the reader is referred, and with it he can recall the exploits of Pip in *Great Expectations* between Temple Stairs and Gravesend in his endeavours to get his benefactor Magwitch safely out of the country; can see in fancy the boat of Gaffer Hexam plying its nefarious trade "between Southwark Bridge which is of iron, and London Bridge which is of stone ": can follow Arthur Clennam by way of Fulham and Putney to the cottage of the Meagles family at the river-side at Twickenham: can visit Chelsea, the birthplace of Vincent Crummles, and residence of Mr. Bayham Badger and Miss Sophia Wackles: can visit Sir Barnet Skittles at Fulham and Dora at Putney: the Pocket family and Clara Barley at Hammersmith: Betty Higden at Brentford, and Estella and Mr. Tupman at Richmond.

Our present pilgrimage follows the road and the river from London to Oxford, and we cannot do better than to start it in company with Oliver Twist and Bill Sikes en route for the burglary at Chertsey, picking up Rogue Riderhood on his way to the Lock where he was Deputy Lock-keeper, and later accompanying Betty Higden in her brave flight from the terrors of pauperism.

In Chapter XXI of *Oliver Twist*, Dickens is so precise in his description of the road to be followed, that he might very well have been writing a guide book. Our only hope

They turned round to the left, a short way past the public-house; and then, taking a right-hand road, walked on for a long time: passing many large gardens and gentlemen's houses on both sides of the way, and stopping for nothing but a little beer, until they reached a town. Here against the wall of a house, Oliver saw written up in pretty large letters, "Hampton." They lingered about, in the fields, for some hours. At length, they came back into the town; and, turning into an old public-house with a defaced sign-board, ordered some dinner by the kitchen fire.

The kitchen was an old, low-roofed room; with a great beam across the middle of the ceiling, and benches, with high backs to them, by the fire; on which were seated several rough men in smock-frocks, drinking and smoking. They took no notice of Oliver; and very little of Sikes. . . .

They had some cold meat for dinner, and sat so long after it, while Mr. Sikes indulged himself with three or four pipes, that Oliver began to feel quite certain they were not going any further. Being much tired with the walk, and getting up so early, he dozed a little at first; then, quite overpowered by fatigue and the fumes of the tobacco, fell asleep.

The tale of *Oliver Twist* as first published in "Bentley's Miscelleny," contained two pieces of description which were omitted in later editions, the first from the first publication in volume form, and the second from a still later edition.

The first lines to be omitted came immediately after the reference to the "gentlemen's houses on both sides of the way," and were:

And at length, crossing a little bridge which led them into Twickenham, from which town they still walked on without stopping for anything but some beer until they reached another town, in which, against the wall, etc.

The second omission, noticeable only in the early volume editions came almost immediately afterwards:

Turning round by a public house which bore the sign of the Red Lion they kept on by the river side for a short distance and then Sikes striking off into a narrow street walked straight to an old public house with a defaced sign-board, etc.

So far as we can find, the location of this public house has not been discovered, but it is very curious that these few lines should have been the subject of so much revision on two separate occasions. Why the reference to Twickenham was entirely omitted from the first separate edition is a complete mystery, as through that town the couple must have passed. Then came the later deletion of the name of the Red Lion Inn as a guide to the lower class public house where Sikes and Oliver dined, and where the companionable carrier gave them a lift in the direction of Lower Halliford.

The Red Lion at Hampton was probably in Dickens's thoughts when he described one of the adventures of Betty Higden in her brave flight. In *Our Mutual Friend*, Book 3, Chapter VIII, we read:

> The poor creature had taken the upward course of the River Thames as her general track. . . . In the pleasant towns of Chertsey, Walton, Kingston and Staines her figure came to be quite well known for some short weeks and then again passed on. . . .
>
> In these pleasant little towns on Thames, you may hear the fall of water over the weirs or even, in still weather, the rustle of the rushes and from the bridge you may see the young river, dimpled like a young child, playfully gliding away among the trees, unpolluted by the defilements that lie in wait for it on its course, and as yet out of hearing of the deep summons of the sea.

At one town on the last stages of her wanderings she had a fainting fit, and on coming to, and fearing being taken to the workhouse, she confessed to be quite well again and hurried on:

> She looked over her shoulder before turning out of the town and had seen the sign of the White Lion hanging across the road . . . and the old grey church, and the little crowd gazing after her, but not attempting to follow her.

The sign of the Red Lion at Hampton hangs across the road in the manner described.

To Hampton Race Course on the June Meeting, we are introduced in Chapter L of *Nicholas Nickleby*, and the events there lead up to the quarrel between Sir Mulberry Hawk and Lord Francis Verisopht, which had its culmination in the duel in "one of the meadows opposite Twickenham, by the river side."

Near Hampton, Mortimer Lightwood and Eugene Wrayburn had a summer cottage:

Quickening their pace, they turned up a road upon the left hand. After walking about a quarter of a mile, they stopped before a detached house surrounded by a wall; to the top of which, Toby Crackit, scarcely pausing to take breath, climbed in a twinkling.

"The boy next," said Toby. " Hoist him up; I'll catch hold of him."

Before Oliver had time to look round, Sikes had caught him under the arms; and in three or four seconds he and Toby were lying on the grass on the other side. Sikes followed directly.

Why Pyrcroft House in Pyrcroft Street has been associated by many writers as the original of the home of the Maylies at which the famous burglary took place, is more than we can say, but there is the house, the high wall, and indeed everything to fit in with the story, although there is no record to show that Dickens ever visited it.

It is reached through Guildford Street, which turns off to the left of the town in going through it, and in this respect follows the story although it lacks being clear of the town, to make its location certain.

There is no description of Chertsey in *Oliver Twist*, and the identity of " the cottage at some distance in the country " to which Oliver went with the Maylies after his illness, cannot be determined. Here it was that Rose was taken ill and Oliver was sent with a letter to Mr. Losberne the doctor.

It must be carried to the market-town: which is not more than four miles off, by the footpath across the fields: and thence dispatched, by an express on horseback, straight to Chertsey. The people at the inn will undertake to do this; and I can trust to you to see it done, I know. . . .

Swiftly he ran across the fields, and down the little lanes . . . nor did he stop once, save now and then, for a few seconds, to recover breath, until he came, in a great heat, and covered with dust, on the little market-place of the market-town.

Here he paused, and looked about for the inn. There were a white bank, and a red brewery, and a yellow town-hall; and in one corner there was a large house, with all the wood about it painted green: before which was the sign of " The George." To this he hastened, as soon as it caught his eye.

Mr. Percy Fitzgerald says that this picture of the market-town with its George Inn and red brewery applies to Chertsey, but we venture to think the description is of quite the ordinary variety and applicable to almost any market-town. In any case, Dickens evidently did not wish it to apply to Chertsey.

IV

Dickens was not unacquainted with Windsor, for towards the end of 1841, when recovering from an illness and prior to his departure for America, he spent some little time there. Of this time Forster tells us: " He suffered more than he let anyone perceive, and was obliged again to keep his room for some days. On the second of November he reported himself as progressing and ordered to Richmond, which, after a week or so, he changed to the White Hart at Windsor, where I passed some days with him and Mrs. Dickens, and her younger sister Georgina."

There are naturally, casual references to Windsor in several of the books, but the principal connection of the town with Dickens, although of minor importance, is to be found in the early part of *Bleak House*, when Esther Summerson opens up her narrative and tell us how her very earliest years were spent there with Mrs. Rachael, until Mr. Kenge came along and she was sent to the school kept by the twin Miss Donnys at Greenleaf, Reading.

This interview took place at Windsor, where I had passed (as far as I know) my whole life. On that day week, amply provided with all necessaries, I left it, inside the stage coach for Reading.

In *Master Humphrey's Clock*, part of which was probably written at Windsor, we read:

A good many years have passed away since old John Podgers lived in the town of Windsor, where he was born, and where, in course of time, he came to be comfortably and snugly buried. You may be sure that in the time of King James the First, Windsor was a very quaint queer old town, and you may take it upon my authority that John Podgers was a very quaint queer old fellow; consequently he and Windsor fitted each other to a nicety, and seldom parted company even for half-a-day.

and the surrounding district, known undoubtedly very well to the novelist, who was a prodigious walker, is referred to

There now arose in the distance a great building full of lighted windows. Smoke was issuing from a high chimney in the rear of it, and there was the sound of a water-wheel at the side. Between her and the building lay a piece of water, in which the lighted windows were reflected, and on its nearest margin was a plantation of trees.

"I humbly thank the Power and the Glory," said Betty Higden, holding up her withered hands, "that I have come to my journey's end."

Hurley Lock, three miles before reaching Henley, is probably the Plashwater Weir Mill Lock of the story. It fits in very well with the course of events, as the river makes a big bend between Hurley and Henley, so that the distance between the two places by road is less than half that by water.

Eugene Wrayburn, in his light boat, had made a river trip to Henley to see Lizzie Hexam, and Bradley Headstone had followed him by road.

"Plashwater Weir-Mill Lock looked tranquil and pretty on an evening in the summer time. A soft air stirred the leaves of the fresh green trees, and passed like a smooth shadow over the river, and like a smoother shadow over the yielding grass. The voice of the falling water, like the voice of the sea and the wind, was an outer memory to a contemplative listener; but not particularly so to Mr. Riderhood, who sat on one of the blunt wooden levers of his lock-gates dozing. . . . The creaking lock-gates opened slowly, and the light boat passed in as soon as there was room enough, and the creaking lock-gates closed upon it, and it floated low down in the dock between the two sets of gates, until the water should rise and the second gates should open and let it out."

"Now I must follow him," said Bradley Headstone. "He takes this river road—the fool—to confuse observation." For two days disguised as a bargeman—perilously like Riderhood himself—he kept watch on the movements of the couple, with the result we all know; and then returned to Riderhood at the Lock.

Here was enacted the final scene of the tragedy when Headstone again walked from his school to the Lock House in the snow, and refused the demands Riderhood made on him. Riderhood kept the schoolmaster under strict observation, and when he departed and "turned towards London,

Riderhood caught him up and walked at his side." For three miles they so travelled and then "Bradley turned to retrace his course. Instantly Riderhood turned likewise."

Bradley re-entered the Lock-house. So did Riderhood. Bradley sat down in the window. Riderhood warmed himself at the fire. After an hour or more, Bradley abruptly got up again, and again went out, but this time turned the other way. Riderhood was close after him, caught him up in a few paces, and walked at his side. . . .

Bradley had caught him round the body. He seemed to be girdled with an iron ring. They were on the brink of the Lock, about midway between the two sets of gates.

"Let go!" said Riderhood, "or I'll get my knife out and slash you wherever I can cut you. Let go!"

Bradley was drawing to the Lock-edge. Riderhood was drawing away from it. It was a strong grapple and a fierce struggle, arm and leg. Bradley got him round, with his back to the Lock, and still worked him backward.

"Let go!" said Riderhood. "Stop! What are you trying at? You can't drown me. Ain't I told you that the man as has come through drowning can never be drowned? I can't be drowned."

"I can be!" returned Bradley, in a desperate clenched voice. "I am resolved to be. I'll hold you living, and I'll hold you dead. Come down!"

Riderhood went over into the smooth pit, backward, and Bradley Headstone upon him. When the two were found, lying under the ooze and scum behind one of the rotting gates, Riderhood's hold had relaxed, probably in falling, and his eyes were staring upward. But he was girdled still with Bradley's iron ring, and the rivets of the iron ring held tight.

Marsh Mill, about half a mile from Henley, is pointed out as the place where Lizzie worked, and near which Betty Higden died. It is, however, a little difficult to reconcile this with the account given in Chapter VI of Book 4 that "the inn where he (Wrayburn) stayed, like the village and the Mill, was not across the river, but on that side of the stream on which he walked."

The inn above referred to was doubtless the Red Lion, which is on the same side of the river as the village itself. It has the required "patch of inn lawn, sloping gently to the river" for the purpose of the landing of a boat. Bradley

Henley is also mentioned in *Little Dorrit*: the first recorded utterance of Mr. F's aunt was that "when we lived at Henley, Barnes's gander was stole by tinkers."

VI

Reading possesses some noteworthy associations with the life of Dickens. It had the honour of inviting the novelist to represent it in Parliament. This was in 1841. Although, as he wrote, "my principles and inclinations would lead me to aspire to the distinction you invite me to seek," yet he had to decline the invitation as he could not satisfy himself that entering Parliament would enable him to pursue the honourable independence without which, as he said, he could neither preserve his own respect or that of his constituents.

The first public visit of Dickens to Reading was on December 9th, 1851, with the Amateur Company of the Guild of Literature and Art in Lord Lytton's play, "Not so Bad as we Seem," at the Town Hall, and a few years later (1854), Dickens having become president of the Reading Literary and Mechanics' Institution in succession to his friend Talfourd, who was a native of Reading, read the Carol at the Institute on December 19th, in aid of the funds. Four years later Dickens was again at Reading (8th November, 1858) at the New Hall giving one of his famous readings. The Institute was in London Street and is now a Methodist Chapel.

Reading in the novels figures but once, and that in the early chapters of *Bleak House*. It was to Reading that Esther Summerson came by stage coach from Windsor, where she had hitherto been residing with Mrs. Rachael. Chapter III of the book gives us a pretty picture of the young girl sitting on the low seat of the coach with her bird-cage on the straw at her feet, looking out of the window full of sorrow at leaving the only home she had known. It was during this journey that she first met her guardian, John Jarndyce, then unknown to her, who comforted her with "A piece of the best plum-cake that can be got for money —sugar on the outside an inch thick, like fat on mutton chops," and who left the coach "a little way short of Reading."

Her destination was Greenleaf, the school of the twin Miss Donnys, and here she passed what she described as "six happy quiet years" before coming up to the fog of London and its Chancery Courts.

We left him at a milestone. I often walked past it afterwards, and never for a long time, without thinking of him, and half expecting to meet him.

· · · · ·

There is a bare mention of Oxford in *David Copperfield* and its sole association with Dickens rests with two readings which he gave at the old Town Hall, demolished in 1891–2, on November 5th and 6th, 1858, and with the reading at the same place in the October of the following year. He does not appear to have visited Oxford on his later reading tours.

CHAPTER FIVE

TO BATH WITH MR. PICKWICK

I

At the time when *Pickwick* was written, Dickens had personal recollections of the Bath Road, possibly quite as vivid as those he had of the road to Dover with which we have already dealt.

The interval of two years between his first published sketch " Mr. Minns and his Cousin," as it is now called, and the beginning of *The Pickwick Papers*, saw Dickens making rapid strides in his profession as reporter for the " Morning Chronicle."

"To the wholesome training of severe newspaper work when I was a very young man I constantly refer my first successes," he said on one occasion, and to his experiences then, we owe the graphic pictures he has given us in *The Pickwick Papers* and elsewhere, of travelling by road, and the descriptions of the old inns and other places he visited during the elections of 1835. Now was opened up to him a wide and varied range of experience, which his genial, youthful observation made quaint and humorous.

In 1845 he made a confession of these days, in a letter to Forster, in which he said:

There never was anybody connected with newspapers, who in the same space of time had so much express and post-chaise experience as I. And what gentlemen they were to serve in such things at the old " Morning Chronicle!" Great or small, it did not matter. I have had to charge for half a dozen break-downs in half a dozen times as many miles. I have had to charge for the damage of a great-coat from the drippings of a blazing wax-candle, in writing through the smallest hours of the night in a swift-flying carriage and pair. I have had to charge for all sorts of breakages fifty times in a journey without question, such being the ordinary results of the pace which we went at. I have charged for broken hats, broken luggage, broken chaises, broken harness—everything but a broken head, which is the only thing they would have grumbled to pay for.

Forster is also able to quote a letter written by Dickens to the Editor of the " Morning Chronicle," during one of his Bath road expeditions, which shows the conditions under which the work was done. It is dated a " Tuesday morning " in May 1835, from the Bush Inn, Bristol, and states, to quote Forster, who does not give the letter verbatim:

He expects to forward " the conclusion of Russell's dinner " by Cooper's Company's coach leaving the Bush at half-past six next morning; and by the first Ball's coach on Thursday morning he will forward the report of the Bath dinner, endorsing the parcel for immediate delivery, with extra rewards for the porter. Beard is to go over to Bath next morning. He is himself to come back by the mail from Marlborough; he has no doubt, if Lord John makes a speech of any ordinary dimensions, it can be done by the time Marlborough is reached; " and taking into consideration the immense importance of having the addition of saddle-horses from thence, it is beyond all doubt, worth an effort . . . I need not say," he continues, " that it will be sharp work and will require two of us; for we shall both be up the whole of the previous night, and shall have to sit up all night again to get it off in time." He adds that as soon as they have had a little sleep they will return to town as quickly as they can; but they have, if the express succeeds, to stop at sundry places along the road to pay money and notify satisfaction. And so, for himself and Beard, he is his editor's very sincerely.

Something to the same effect he said publicly twenty years later on the occasion of his presiding, in May 1865, at the second annual dinner of the Newspaper Press Fund.

I have pursued the calling of a reporter under circumstances of which many of my brethren here can form no adequate conception. I have often transcribed for the printer, from my shorthand notes, important public speeches . . . on the palm of my hand, by the light of a dark lantern, in a post-chaise and four, galloping through a wild country, and through the dead of the night, at

the then surprising rate of fifteen miles an hour. . . .
Returning home from exciting political meetings in the
country to the waiting press in London, I do verily believe
I have been upset in almost every description of vehicle
known in this country. I have been, in my time, belated
on miry by-roads, towards the small hours, forty or fifty
miles from London, in a wheelless carriage, with exhausted
horses and drunken post-boys, and have got back in time
for publication, to be received with never-forgotten
compliments.

"London is so small," says a character in *The Uncommercial Traveller*. "If you go west you come to Hounslow,"
and Hounslow is so much a part of London to-day, that one
does not know where it begins or ends.

When Martin Chuzzlewit left Mr. Pecksniff's, he was
fortunate in getting a lift as far as Hounslow, by a driver
whose " spruce appearance was sufficiently explained by his
connexion with a large stage-coaching establishment at
Hounslow, whither he was conveying his load from a farm
belonging to the concern in Wiltshire."

Hounslow Heath is unforgettably associated with Sam
Weller and his song of " Bold Turpin vunce on Hounslow
Heath. His bold mare Bess bestrode—er."

In *Great Expectations* we are told that the woman who
was murdered by Estella's mother, was " found dead in a
barn near Hounslow Heath."

This part of the road was commented on by Dickens in
The Holly Tree Inn, the Christmas number for 1855, when
he speaks of the decay of the roadside inns especially in
this part of the country.

Casting my eyes upon my Holly-Tree fire, I next
discerned among the glowing coals the pictures of a score
or more of those wonderful English posting-inns which
we are all so sorry to have lost, which were so large and so
comfortable, and which were such monuments of British
submission to rapacity and extortion. He who would
see these houses pining away, let him walk from Basingstoke, or even Windsor, to London, by way of Hounslow
and moralise on their perishing remains; the stables
crumbling to dust; unsettled labourers and wanderers
bivouacking in the outhouses; grass growing in the yards;
the rooms, where erst so many hundred beds of down
were made up, let off to Irish lodgers at eighteenpence
a week.

II

Mr. Pickwick, having decided that he would pay " Not one halfpenny " of the costs of the case which the wily Mrs. Bardell at the instigation of Dodson and Fogg had brought against him, finally answered his own question "where shall we go next," by saying, Bath.   So to Bath they accordingly did go, and " Sam was at once despatched to the White Horse Cellar, to take five places by the half-past seven o'clock coach, next morning."   And the next morning —a damp and unpropitious one we are told, found them at the White Horse Cellar, Piccadilly, with twenty minutes to spare, so they repaired to the travellers' room " the last resource of human dejection."

Here they encountered the " stern eyed man . . . with a good deal of black hair . . . and large black whiskers," Mr. Dowler, who was " going to Bath on pleasure " with his wife, of whom he was very jealous.   At the commencement of the journey we are told of a remarkable coincidence. Mr. Winkle had got inside the coach and Mr. Pickwick was preparing to follow him, when

Sam Weller came up to his master, and whispering in his ear, begged to speak to him, with an air of the deepest mystery.

"Well, Sam," said Mr. Pickwick, " what's the matter now?"

" Here's rayther a rum go, sir," replied Sam.

"What?" inquired Mr. Pickwick.

"This here, sir," rejoined Sam.   " I'm wery much afeerd, sir, that the proprieator o' this here coach is a playin' some imperence vith us."

"How is that, Sam?" said Mr. Pickwick; " arn't the names down on the way-bill?"

"The names is not only down on the vay-bill, sir," replied Sam, " but they've painted vun on 'em up on the door o' the coach."   As Sam spoke, he pointed to the part of the coach door on which the proprietor's name usually appears; and there sure enough, in gilt letters of a goodly size, was the magic name of Pickwick.

"Dear me," exclaimed Mr. Pickwick, " what a very extraordinary thing."

"Yes, but that ain't all," said Sam, " not content with writing up Pickwick, they puts Moses afore it, vich I calls adding insult to injury."

army; but what struck Tom's fancy most was a strange, grim-looking high-backed chair, carved in the most fantastic manner, with a flowered damask cushion, and the round knobs at the bottom of the legs carefully tied up in red cloth, as if it had got the gout in its toes."

For a full account of all the happenings in this room with the "queer chair" the reader is directed to Chapter XLIX of *The Pickwick Papers*.

III

Returning to the Pickwickians themselves, we learn that the party reached Bath in safety.

At seven o'clock p.m. Mr. Pickwick and his friends, and Mr. Dowler and his wife, respectively retired to their private sitting-rooms at the White Hart Hotel, opposite the Great Pump Room, Bath, where the waiters, from their costume, might be mistaken for Westminster boys, only they destroy the illusion by behaving themselves much better.

The White Hart is gone now; it does not hold a long record in Dickensian annals, as very little indeed is said about it, and Mr. Pickwick stayed there a night or two only prior to taking lodgings in the Royal Crescent; but it will always be remembered that a Mr. Pickwick kept the Hotel in the days when Dickens visited it!

This was the Moses Pickwick to whom Sam Weller referred when the Bath Coach was standing outside the White Horse Cellar in London. His grandfather, Eleazer Pickwick, was a foundling picked up at the village of Pickwick, nine miles from Bath. Eleazer Pickwick founded the coaching business carried on by his grandson Moses, with much success; this Moses Pickwick also became the proprietor of the White Hart Inn at Bath, the starting place of the coaches. The hotel was demolished in 1867, and the present Grand Pump Room Hotel stands on its site. The effigy of the White Hart which formerly adorned the entrance is now to be seen at the White Hart Inn at Widcombe, a suburb of Bath.

If, as there is reason to suppose, Dickens visited Bath in 1837, just when the Bath chapters were being written, it must have been a peculiar experience for him, the great author of *The Pickwick Papers*, the book which everybody was reading, to travel to Bath by the Pickwick Coach and to stop at mine host Pickwick's Hotel.

The morning after their arrival at the White Hart Hotel, Mr. Pickwick was visited by Angelo Cyrus Bantam, Esq., the Master of the Ceremonies:

"Welcome to Ba-ath, sir. This is indeed an acquisition. Most welcome to Ba-ath, sir. It is long—very long, Mr. Pickwick, since you drank the waters. It appears an age, Mr. Pickwick. Re-markable!"

"It is a very long time since I drank the waters, certainly," replied Mr. Pickwick; "for to the best of my knowledge I was never here before."

"Never in Ba-ath, Mr. Pickwick!" exclaimed the Grand Master, letting the hand fall in astonishment. "Never in Ba-ath! He! he! Mr. Pickwick, you are a wag. Not bad, not bad. Good, good. He! he! he! Re-markable!"

.   .   .   .   .

"Bantam," said Mr. Dowler, " Mr. Pickwick and his friends are strangers. They must put their names down. Where's the book?"

"The register of the distinguished visitors in Ba-ath will be at the Pump Room this morning at two o'clock," replied the M.C. " Will you guide our friends to that splendid building, and enable me to procure their autographs?"

Strange to say, it was to the Assembly Rooms and not to the Pump Room that the party was conducted, for we read:

At the appointed hour, Mr. Pickwick and his friends, escorted by Dowler, repaired to the Assembly Rooms, and wrote their names down in a book. An instance of condescension at which Angelo Bantam was even more overpowered than before.

Bantam's mission was not without its object, as he succeeded in getting the party to promise to attend the Assembly Rooms that evening.

"This is a ball-night," said the M.C. . . . " The ball-nights in Ba-ath are moments snatched from Paradise; rendered bewitching by music, beauty, elegance, fashion, etiquette, and—and—above all, by the absence of tradespeople . . . who have an amalgamation of themselves at the Guildhall every fortnight, which is, to say the least, remarkable."

Prior to attending the Ball at the Assembly Rooms that evening, Mr. Pickwick took a short walk through the city, and " arrived at the unanimous conclusion that Park Street was very much like the perpendicular streets a man sees in a dream, which he cannot get up for the life of him."

The Assembly Rooms where Mr. Pickwick made the acquaintance of Lord Mutanhead, the Dowager Lady Snuphanuph, Mrs. Colonel Wugsby, and Miss Bolo, are intact.

Bath being full, the company, and the sixpences for tea, poured in, in shoals.   In the ball-room, the long card-room, the octagonal card-room, the staircases, and the passages, the hum of many voices, and the sound of many feet, were perfectly bewildering. Dresses rustled, feathers waved, lights shone, and jewels sparkled.   There was the music—not of the quadrille band, for it had not yet commenced; but the music of soft tiny footsteps, with now and then a clear merry laugh—low and gentle, but very pleasant to hear in a female voice, whether in Bath or elsewhere. . . .

In the tea-room, and hovering round the card-tables, were a vast number of queer old ladies and decrepit old gentlemen, discussing all the small talk and scandal of the day, with a relish and gusto which sufficiently bespoke the intensity of the pleasure they derived from the occupation.   Mingled with these groups, were three or four matchmaking mammas, appearing to be wholly absorbed by the conversation in which they were taking part, but failing not from time to time to cast an anxious sidelong glance upon their daughters, who, remembering the maternal injunction to make the best use of their youth, had already commenced incipient flirtations in the mislaying of scarves, putting on gloves, setting down cups, and so forth; slight matters apparently, but which may be turned to surprisingly good account by expert practitioners.

Lounging near the doors, and in remote corners, were various knots of silly young men, displaying various varieties of puppyism and stupidity. . . .

And lastly, seated on some of the back benches, where they had already taken up their positions for the evening, were divers unmarried ladies past their grand climacteric, who, not dancing because there were no partners for them, and not playing cards lest they should be set down as irretrievably single, were in the favourable situation of being able to abuse everybody without reflecting on themselves.

The very room where the famous game of cards was played is to be seen: and it is to be remembered that Dickens gave readings in the large hall on February 9th, 1867 and January 29th, 1869.

The original of Mr. Bantam was Mr. Jervois, who was the M.C. of Bath at the time *The Pickwick Papers* were written. He lived at No. 21 Portland Place, although it was in Queen Square that Dickens located this eccentric creation, to whom Sam was despatched for the tickets for the Assembly Ball.

Sam Weller put on his hat in a very easy and graceful manner, and thrusting his hands in his waistcoat pockets, walked with great deliberation to Queen Square, whistling as he went along, several of the most popular airs of the day, as arranged with entirely new movements for that noble instrument the organ, either mouth or barrel. Arriving at the number in Queen Square to which he had been directed, he left off whistling, and gave a cheerful knock, which was instantaneously answered by a powdered-headed footman in gorgeous livery, and of symmetrical stature.

Eleazer Pickwick, brother of Moses, lived at No. 10 Queen Square, in 1837. It is interesting to note that at the same time an A. Snodgrass was living at No. 16 Trim Street.

It was to Queen Square that Sam came again on the occasion of his invitation by the select company of Bath Footmen, to the " friendly swarry, consisting of a boiled leg of mutton with the usual trimmings." Here he met Mr. Joseph Smauker " leaning his powdered head against a lamp-post," and with him " walked towards High Street," and turning " down a by-street," reached " a small greengrocer's shop."

Crossing the greengrocer's shop, and putting their hats on the stairs in the little passage behind it, they walked into a small parlour; and here the full splendour of the scene burst upon Mr. Weller's view.

A couple of tables were put together in the middle of the parlour, covered with three or four cloths of different ages and dates of washing, arranged to look as much like one as the circumstances of the case would allow. Upon these were laid knives and forks for six or eight people. Some of the knife handles were green, others red, and a few yellow; and as all the forks were black, the combination of colours was exceedingly striking. Plates for a corresponding number of guests were warming behind the fender; and the guests themselves were warming before it.

The identity of the " small greengrocer's shop " has not yet been established. " The Beaufort Arms " cannot be associated with it definitely, as several seem to think; but that it was a rendezvous of the Bath Footmen at the time when Dickens visited Bath, there is not much doubt; and that " swarries " such as Dickens describes were not an uncommon event, is also a fact; but how Dickens came to know them so intimately as he makes us believe, is hard to say.

Dickens improves upon the legend associated with the foundation of Bath, by introducing " The True Legend of Prince Bladud " as a separate story, discovered by Mr. Pickwick in his lodgings in the Crescent.

He discards with a few words the story of the sagacious pig that was fond of bathing in the rich moist mud, and of Bladud who followed his example and was so cured of leprosy, and founded the famous baths as a thank-offering, and proceeds to tell us the *true* legend. The unhappy love-sick Bladud, being bound for Athens, " wandered as far out of his way as Bath."

There was no city where Bath stands, then. There was no vestige of human habitation, or sign of man's resort, to bear the name; but there was the same noble country, the same broad expanse of hill and dale, the same beautiful channel stealing on, far away; the same lofty mountains which, like the troubles of life, viewed at a distance and partially obscured by the bright mist of its morning, lose their ruggedness and asperity, and seem all ease and softness. Moved by the gentle beauty of the scene, the Prince sank upon the green turf, and bathed his swollen feet in his tears.

The story further tells, how in answer to Prince Bladud's wish that his wanderings might end in Bath.

The ground opened beneath the Prince's feet; he sunk into the chasm; and instantaneously it closed upon his head for ever, save where his hot tears welled up through the earth, and where they have continued to gush forth ever since.

It is observable that, to this day, large numbers of elderly ladies and gentlemen who have been disappointed in procuring partners, and almost as many young ones who are anxious to obtain them, repair annually to Bath to drink the waters, from which they derive much strength and comfort. This is most complimentary to the virtue of Prince Bladud's tears, and strongly corroborative of the veracity of this legend.

Less than two hundred years ago, on one of the public baths in this city, there appeared an inscription in honour of its mighty founder, the renowned Prince Bladud. That inscription is now erased.

The bath referred to was the King's Bath, which is also the subject of a facetious remark of Angelo Cyrus Bantam, M.C., on his introduction to Mr. Pickwick:

" You are the gentleman residing on Clapham Green," resumed Bantam, " who lost the use of his limbs from imprudently taking cold after port wine; who could not be moved in consequence of acute suffering, and who had the water from the King's Bath bottled at one hundred and three degrees, and sent by waggon to his bed-room in town, where he bathed, sneezed, and same day recovered. Very re-markable !"

Mr. Pickwick acknowledged the compliment which the supposition implied, but had the self-denial to repudiate it, notwithstanding.

The description of the Pump Room is a remarkably detailed one, considering the few opportunities Dickens had of seeing it.

The great pump-room is a spacious saloon, ornamented with Corinthian pillars, and a music gallery, and a Tompion clock, and a statue of Nash, and a golden inscription, to which all the water-drinkers should attend, for it appeals to them in the cause of a deserving charity. There is a large bar with a marble vase, out of which the pumper gets the water; and there are a number of yellow-looking tumblers, out of which the company get it; and it is a most edifying and satisfactory sight to behold the per-severance and gravity with which they swallow it. There are baths near at hand, in which a part of the company

wash themselves; and a band plays afterwards, to congratu-
late the remainder on their having done so. There is
another pump-room, into which infirm ladies and gentlemen are wheeled, in such an astonishing variety of chairs
and chaises, that any adventurous individual who goes
in with the regular number of toes, is in imminent danger
of coming out without them; and there is a third, into
which the quiet people go, for it is less noisy than either.
There is an immensity of promenading, on crutches and
off, with sticks and without, and a great deal of conversation, and liveliness, and pleasantry.

Dickens had surely a little fun to poke at the visitors to
the Pump Room at Bath when he says:

Mr. Pickwick began to drink the waters with the utmost
assiduity. Mr. Pickwick took them systematically. He
drank a quarter of a pint before breakfast, and then walked
up a hill; and another quarter of a pint after breakfast,
and then walked down a hill; and after every fresh quarter
of a pint, Mr. Pickwick declared, in the most solemn and
emphatic terms, that he felt a great deal better; whereat
his friends were very much delighted, though they had
not been previously aware that there was anything the
matter with him.

Mr. Weller's opinion of the Bath waters was communicated
to Mr. Smauker on their way to the "swarry."

"I thought they wos particklery unpleasant," replied Sam.
"Ah," said Mr. John Smauker, "you disliked the killi-
beate taste, perhaps?"
"I don't know much about that 'ere," said Sam. "I
thought they'd a wery strong flavour o' warm flat irons."

Dickens criticises the monotony of the life of the Bath
visitor in the following terse account of their daily round.

The regular water drinkers, Mr. Pickwick among the
number, met each other in the Pump Room, took their
quarter of a pint, and walked constitutionally. At the
afternoon's promenade . . . all the great people and
all the morning water drinkers, met in grand assemblage.
After this they walked out, or drove out or were pushed
out in bath chairs . . . After this they went home. If
it were theatre night, perhaps they met at the theatre;
if it were assembly night, they met at the rooms; and if
it were neither they met the next day.

The Pickwickians stayed in Bath for about four months.
They arrived on the 16th February and left, according to
Chapter XL, the end of the first week in Trinity term.

As Mr. Pickwick contemplated a stay of at least two
months in Bath, he deemed it advisable to take private
lodgings for himself and friends for that period; and
as a favourable opportunity offered for their securing,
on moderate terms, the upper portion of a house in the
Royal Crescent, which was larger than they required,
Mr. and Mrs. Dowler offered to relieve them of a bed-room
and sitting-room. This proposition was at once accepted,
and in three days' time they were all located in their new
abode.

The number of the house is not given, but as the houses
are practically all of one pattern, and only numbers 15 and
16 were, in those days, let out in lodgings, it is not difficult
for us to make a choice.

The landlady's name was Mrs. Craddock, the name
of the landlady of the cottage at Chalk, where Dickens spent
his honeymoon a few months before the Bath chapters were
written.

Here Mr. Winkle met with that never failing mirth pro-
voking adventure with the Sedan chair, the story of which
is worth briefly recording as follows:

Mrs. Dowler was out at a party. Mr. Dowler had promised
to wait up for her return, but fell asleep, and we read:

Just as the clock struck three, there was blown into
the crescent a sedan chair with Mrs. Dowler inside,
borne by one short fat chairman, and one long thin one,
who had had much ado to keep their bodies perpendicular:
to say nothing of the chair. But on that high ground,
and in the crescent, which the wind swept round and
round as if it were going to tear the paving stones up, its
fury was tremendous. They were very glad to set the
chair down, and give a good round loud double-knock at
the street door.

They waited some time but nobody came. At last they
aroused Mr. Winkle, who descended to the front door.

Mr. Winkle, being half asleep, . . . opened the door a
little, and peeped out. The first thing he saw, was the
red glare of the link-boy's torch. Startled by the sudden
fear that the house might be on fire, he hastily threw the
door wide open. . . . At this instant there came a

G

violent gust of wind; the light was blown out; Mr. Winkle felt himself irresistibly impelled on to the steps; and the door blew to, with a loud crash.

Here was a predicament! "Mr. Winkle, catching sight of a lady's face at the window of the sedan, turned hastily round, plied the knocker with all his might and main, and called frantically upon the chairman to take the chair away again."

"The people are coming down the Crescent now. There are ladies with 'em; cover me up with something. Stand before me!" roared Mr. Winkle. But the chairmen were too much exhausted with laughing to afford him the slightest assistance. . . . Mr. Winkle gave a last hopeless knock; the ladies were only a few doors off. He threw away the extinguished candle, which, all this time, he had held above his head, and fairly bolted into the sedan-chair where Mrs. Dowler was.

At this juncture Mrs. Craddock the landlady roused Mr. Dowler, who swore vengeance against Mr. Winkle and seizing a small supper-knife, tore into the street.

But Mr. Winkle didn't wait for him. He no sooner heard the horrible threat of the valorous Dowler, than he bounced out of the sedan, quite as quickly as he had bounced in, and throwing off his slippers into the road, took to his heels and tore round the Crescent, hotly pursued by Dowler and the watchman. He kept ahead; the door was open as he came round the second time; he rushed in, slammed it in Dowler's face, mounted to his bed-room, locked the door, piled a wash-hand-stand, chest of drawers, and table against it, and packed up a few necessaries ready for flight with the first ray of morning.

Some writers assert that Dickens was in error in stating that Winkle ran round and round the Crescent hotly pursued by Mr. Dowler and the watchman, and that he had the Circus in his mind; but we do not hold that opinion. It is on record that Dickens made several alterations in the pictures submitted by Phiz; that the houses in the drawing show the houses in the Crescent. It was quite consistent with the account that Winkle ran round and round the Crescent, that Winkle should double back when he got to the end of the semi-circular sweep, and so eventually reach safety in his own door; had he been running round the Circus he could have eluded his pursuers very well by means of one of the

LANDOR'S HOUSE, BATH

[Photo by T. W. Tyrrell

THE CRESCENT, BATH

[Photo by Walter Dexter

turnings.   There is another fact to be noted; if in the Circus, Winkle could not have observed the party in the distance coming towards him, and would not at all times have been visible to his pursuers; also Dickens describes the Crescent as an exposed and unsheltered place, which description would not apply to the Circus.

Bath has a further claim to Dickensian interest in the fact that it may be said to have been the birthplace of Little Nell. No. 35 St. James's Square bears an interesting tablet; it was once the residence of Walter Savage Landor, for whom Dickens had a real great affection and regard.   In 1840 Dickens accompanied by his wife, Maclise and Forster visited Landor, and, according to Forster "it was during three happy days passed together there that the fancy which was shortly to take the form of Little Nell first occurred to its author."

To Forster, who also wrote the life of Landor, we are indebted for the information that Landor told him he had never in his life regretted anything so much as his having failed to carry out an intention he had formed respecting this house in St. James's Square, Bath; for "he had meant to purchase it, and then and there to have burnt it to the ground, to the end that no meaner association should ever desecrate the birthpace of Little Nell."

In unveiling the tablet on the 91st anniversary of Dickens's birth, Mr. Percy Fitzgerald said that "from that modest unassuming mansion the one image had set out on its travels all over the world, and was known like a living being wherever English was read."

There is a story, recorded first we believe by Mr. Percy Fitzgerald in connection with the Saracen's Head Inn in Walcot Street, a quaint and ancient structure, to the effect that Dickens as a young reporter stayed here in 1835, and was lodged in a building across the yard up a flight of steps, still to be seen.   However delightful the story may be of his patience with the candle that would persist in going out as he crossed the yard, we are unable to accept it as a fact, without further corroboration.

There was only one other character whom Dickens "sent to Bath," and that was Miss Volumnia in *Bleak House;* she "retired to Bath . . . on an annual present from Sir Leicester. . . . She has an extensive acquaintance at Bath among appalling old gentlemen . . . and is of high standing in that dreary city."

In a later chapter she is referred to as living in "that grass grown city of the ancients, Bath."

In spite of the happy spirit displayed in the Bath chapters of *The Pickwick Papers*, Dickens does not appear to have had a very high regard for the beautiful city, according to these references to it in *Bleak House*, and in a letter to Forster written on the occasion of his last visit in January 1869 when he stayed at the White Lion Hotel.

> Landor's ghost goes along the silent streets here before me. . . . The place looks to me like a cemetery which the Dead have succeeded in rising and taking. Having built streets of their old gravestones, they wander about scantily trying to 'look alive.' A dead failure.

IV

The Bath incidents of *The Pickwick Papers* end with the "shoulder of mutton swarry" which took place at the same time as the Sedan Chair adventure of Mr. Winkle. That gentleman, wishing to escape from the wrath of the valorous Dowler, resolved to quit Bath, and we can now follow him into the neighbouring town of Bristol.

Mr. Winkle we are told, "grasped his carpet-bag, and creeping stealthily down-stairs, shut the detestable street-door with as little noise as possible, and walked off."

Bending his steps towards the Royal Hotel, he found a coach on the point of starting for Bristol, and, thinking Bristol as good a place for his purpose as any other he could go to, he mounted the box, and reached his place of destination in such time as the pair of horses, who went the whole stage and back again twice a day or more, could be reasonably supposed to arrive there.

The Royal Hotel mentioned is the present York House Hotel, and called the Royal, as Queen Victoria stayed there in 1830, when Princess. Dickens stayed here on the occasion of his visit in 1867. In 1869 he stayed at the White Lion Hotel, since demolished.

Arrived at Bristol, Winkle " took up his quarters at the Bush, designing to postpone any communication by letter with Mr. Pickwick until it was probable that Mr. Dowler's wrath might have in some degree evaporated."

The Bush is gone now; until 1864 it stood near the Guild-hall on the site now occupied by Lloyd's Bank.

His quarters fixed, Mr. Winkle walked forth to view the city, which Dickens informs us "struck him as being a shade more dirty than any place he had ever seen."

Having inspected the docks and shipping, and viewed the cathedral, he inquired his way to Clifton, and being directed thither, took the route which was pointed out to him. But, as the pavements of Bristol are not the widest or cleanest upon earth, so its streets are not altogether the straightest or least intricate; Mr. Winkle being greatly puzzled by their manifold windings and twistings, looked about him for a decent shop in which he could apply afresh, for counsel and instruction.

This he found in the surgery of "Sawyer, late Nockemorf," which it has been suggested might have been situated in Park Street, quite a different sort of thoroughfare then from what it is to-day.

In the days of Mr. Pickwick the street was much steeper, the viaduct not having yet been built, and at the bottom was an old fashioned chemist's shop that is said to have answered the description of "something between a shop and a private house."

Here Mr. Winkle encountered Mr. Bob Sawyer, late of Guy's and Lant Street, making very merry with his old friend Ben Allen, and after a convivial evening, he returned to the Bush to meet the very Mr. Dowler he had so zealously sought to avoid. However, as it turned out that both had run away from each other, friendship was soon restored.

Early next morning, Sam Weller made his appearance at the Bush and by means of a trick locked the unfortunate Winkle in his room until such time as Mr. Pickwick should arrive from Bath, and we read that "at eight o'clock in the evening Mr. Pickwick himself walked into the coffee-room of the Bush tavern, and told Sam with a smile, to his very great relief, that he had done quite right."

Ascertaining from Mr. Winkle that Arabella Allen was "immured . . . somewhere near the Downs" it was decided that Sam Weller should start next morning on an expedition of discovery.

"Away he walked, up one street and down another—we were going to say, up one hill and down another, only it's all uphill at Clifton—without meeting with anything or anybody that tended to throw the faintest light on the matter in hand."

The Clifton Suspension Bridge was not erected at that time. It was not until 1863 that it was removed from Charing Cross to Bristol, else, Dickens in viewing through the eyes of Sam, the old Hungerford Bridge, might have revived the scene of his early sufferings as a poor boy in the Blacking Factory.

Sam struggled across the Downs against a good high wind, wondering whether it was always necessary to hold your hat on with both hands in that part of the country, and came to a shady by-place about which were sprinkled several little villas of quiet and secluded appearance. Outside a stable-door at the bottom of a long back lane without a thoroughfare, a groom in undress was idling about, apparently persuading himself that he was doing something with a spade and a wheelbarrow.

Sam strolled down the lane, sat upon "a good large stone just opposite the wheelbarrow" and vainly endeavoured to elicit some information from the "surly groom" who ultimately waxed very wroth and disappeared.

Sam continued to sit on the large stone, meditating upon what was best to be done, and revolving in his mind a plan for knocking at all the doors within five miles of Bristol, taking them at a hundred and fifty or two hundred a day, and endeavouring to find Miss Arabella by that expedient.

Here Sam encountered Mary the housemaid whom he had previously met at the house of Mr. Nupkins the Mayor, at Ipswich, and to whom he had indited his famous valentine. From her, Sam learnt that Arabella Allen was living in the next house, the one to which the "surly groom" was attached and after helping Mary to shake the carpets (can we not on the spot conjure up the delightful scene?) arranged to come in the evening, when he obtained the interview with Arabella from the pear tree. The result of this was that on the following evening Mr. Pickwick, in the hope of being able to intercede with the young lady, proceeded to the garden, aided by Sam and a dark lantern.

The lantern played all sorts of tricks in the hands of Mr. Pickwick, sending its beam of light in many an unwanted direction. After Mr. Pickwick, by the aid of Sam's back had the interview with Arabella over the garden wall, Mr. Winkle declared his passion; Mr. Pickwick "keeping guard in the lane vith that 'ere dark lantern, like an amiable Guy Fawkes," to quote Sam.

"While these things were going on in the open air, an elderly gentleman of scientific attainments was seated in his library, two or three houses off, writing a philosophical treatise" and "was very much surprised by observing a most brilliant light glide through the air, at a short distance above the ground, and almost instantaneously vanish." This caused him to speculate on the origin of so strange a phenomenon.

Venturing as far as the garden gate, he met the party returning down the lane, and Sam, "seeing a man's head peeping out very cautiously within half a yard of his own, gave it a gentle tap with his clenched fist, which knocked it, with a hollow sound, against the gate. Having performed this feat with great suddenness and dexterity, Mr. Weller caught Mr. Pickwick up on his back, and followed Mr. Winkle down the lane at a pace which, considering the burden he carried, was perfectly astonishing."

The result of that evening's amusing adventure was that the scientific gentleman in a masterly treatise demonstrated "that these wonderful lights were the effect of electricity; and clearly proved the same by detailing how a flash of fire danced before his eyes when he put his head out of the gate, and how he received a shock which stunned him for a quarter of an hour afterwards; which demonstration delighted all the Scientific Associations beyond measure, and caused him to be considered a light of science ever afterwards."

At a later period in the history of the Pickwickians, Mr. Pickwick and Sam Weller hastened to Bristol in respect to the love affairs of Mr. Winkle, and again put up at the Bush, where the Bagman told that rare old story of the old coaches and of the "dead letters which these ghosts of mail coaches carry in their bags."

The next morning Mr. Pickwick, Sam, Benjamin Allen, and Bob Sawyer left for that memorable trip to Birmingham, where they were to see the elder Mr. Winkle, and smooth out the love affair of Arabella Allen and Mr. Winkle.

So long as their progress was confined to the streets of Bristol, the facetious Bob kept his professional green spectacles on, and conducted himself with becoming steadiness and gravity of demeanour; merely giving utterance to divers verbal witticisms for the exclusive behoof and entertainment of Mr. Samuel Weller. But when they emerged on the open road he threw off his green spectacles and his gravity together, and performed a great variety of practical jokes, which were calculated to attract the attention of the passers-by, and to render the carriage and those it contained, objects of more than ordinary curiosity; the least conspicuous among these feats being a most vociferous imitation of a key-bugle, and the ostentatious display of a crimson silk pocket-handkerchief attached to a walking-stick, which was occasionally waved in the air with various gestures indicative of supremacy and defiance.

The Pickwick Papers is the only book in which Bristol figures to any great extent. There is a reference to the city in *Barnaby Rudge* when a few weeks after the execution at Newgate, we are told that "Mr. Haredale stood alone in the mail coach office at Bristol . . . about to re-visit London for the last time" and we are further told that "the journey was a very different one in those days from what the present generation find it; but it came to an end as the longest journey will, and he stood again in the streets of the metropolis."

Dickens's first public appearance in Bristol was in 1851, when on November 12th his company of strolling players appeared in "Not so Bad as we Seem" at the Victoria Rooms, Clifton, in aid of the Guild of Literature and Art.

On this occasion he wrote to his wife, "We are well lodged and boarded and living high up on the Downs are quite out of the filth of Bristol."

And in another letter he gave a description of the reception the play received:

We had a noble night last night. The room, which is the largest but one in England, was crammed in every part. The effect of from thirteen to fourteen hundred people, all well dressed and all seated in an unbroken chamber, except that the floor rose high towards the end of the hall, was most splendid, and we never played to a better audience.

On Tuesday January 19th, 1858, Dickens gave his first reading in Bristol, in aid of the Athenæum.

His next visit was as a professional reader, on August 2nd, in the same year, when he wrote:

In that large room at Clifton, the people were perfectly taken off their legs by *The Chimes*—started—looked at each other—started again—looked at me—and then burst into a storm of applause.

He was again at the same hall four days later.

In another letter referring to this reading he told how "a torrent of five hundred shillings bore Arthur (Smith) away, pounded him against the wall, flowed on to the seats over his body, scratched him, and damaged his best dress suit. All to his unspeakable joy."

On May 9th and 10th, 1866, Dickens gave further readings at Clifton, when according to a letter, he stayed at the Downs Hotel. On January 20th, 1869, he was again at the Victoria Rooms, and five days later, on January 25th, witnessed his last reading with, so he wrote, his sister-in-law, "by far the best Murder yet done"; while at the same time he wrote to his daughter:

At Clifton on Monday night we had a contagion of fainting; and yet the place was not hot. I should think we had from a dozen to twenty ladies taken out stiff and rigid, at various times! It became quite ridiculous.

V

We leave Bristol by the same road as the Pickwickians travelled in so boisterous a manner to Birmingham, as described on page 91, and reach Berkeley Heath in 18 miles and notice the Bell Inn, an unpretentious roadside hostelry, announcing on its signboard that "Charles Dickens and Party lunched here 1827," which of course is not a fact; it was however a party of Charles Dickens's characters who lunched there as recorded in the *Pickwick Papers* when on this very momentous journey, one of Bob Sawyer's funny stories "was only stopped by the stoppage of the chaise at the Bell at Berkeley Heath, to change horses."

"I say! We're going to dine here, aren't we?" said Bob, looking in at the window.

"Dine!" said Mr. Pickwick. "Why, we have only come nineteen miles, and have eighty-seven and a half to go."

"Just the reason why we should take something to enable us to bear up against the fatigue" remonstrated Mr. Bob Sawyer.

Mr. Pickwick was somewhat out in the distance still to be covered to Birmingham, it being only 66 and not 87½ miles as he states. In answer to Bob, Mr. Pickwick declared it was "Quite impossible to dine at half past eleven o'clock."

"So it is" rejoined Bob, "lunch is the very thing. Hallo, you sir! Lunch for three, directly, and keep the horses back for a quarter of an hour. Tell them to put everything they have cold on the table, and some bottled ale, and let us taste your very best Madeira."

Issuing these orders with monstrous importance and bustle,
Mr. Bob Sawyer at once hurried into the house to super-
intend the arrangements; in less than five minutes he
returned and declared them to be excellent.

The quality of the lunch fully justified the eulogium
which Bob had pronounced, and very great justice was
done to it, not only by that gentleman, but Mr. Ben Allen
and Mr. Pickwick also.   Under the auspices of the three,
the bottled ale and the Madeira were promptly disposed
of; and when (the horses being once more put to) they
resumed their seats, with the case-bottle full of the best
substitute for milk-punch that could be procured on so
short a notice, the key-bugle sounded, and the red flag
waved, without the slightest opposition on Mr. Pickwick's
part.

It is a pity that so fine and ancient a city as Gloucester
should have no association with Dickens.   The Pickwickians
must have passed through it on this journey to Birmingham,
but perhaps it was the "substitute for milk-punch" with
with which the case-bottle was filled that made them oblivious
to its existence.

Gloucester, however, is a very good centre from which to
visit the remaining places of interest to the Dickens pilgrim
in the West.

The next stopping-place of the Pickwickians was Tewkesbury, ten miles from Gloucester, and here the Hop Pole
still flourishes.

At the Hop Pole at Tewkesbury, they stopped to dine :
upon which occasion there was more bottled ale, with
some more Madeira, and some port besides ; and here
the case-bottle was replenished for the fourth time.   Under
the influence of these combined stimulants, Mr. Pickwick
and Mr. Ben Allen fell fast asleep for thirty miles, while
Bob and Sam Weller sang duets in the dickey.

VI

The first reference to Cheltenham is in *Nicholas Nickleby*
when Miss Knag tells Madame Mantalini that she "had an
uncle once, who lived in Cheltenham, and had a most excellent business as a tobacconist—hem—who had such small
feet, that they were no bigger than those which are usually
joined to wooden legs."

There is also a brief mention of Cheltenham in *Little Dorrit*.

Macready the actor went to live in retirement at Cheltenham in the year 1859 ; after Dickens, who was a great friend, visited him there he wrote :

> I have rarely seen a place that so attracted my fancy. I had never seen it before. Also I believe the character of its people to have greatly changed for the better. All sorts of long visaged prophets had told me that they were dull, stolid, slow and I don't know what more that is disagreeable. I found them exactly the reverse in all respects.

His first reading at Cheltenham was on October 27th, 1859, just before Macready went there. Dickens gave two readings, one in the afternoon—the other in the evening, both at the Music Hall, Royal Old Wells. The old actor was naturally anxious to hear Dickens read, but it was not for more than two years that he had the opportunity. In October, 1861, we find Dickens writing him :

> This is a short note. But the moment I know for certain what is designed for me at Cheltenham, I write to you in order that you may know it from me and not by chance from anyone else.
>
> I am to read there on the evening of Friday, the 3rd of January, and on the morning of Saturday, the 4th ; as I have nothing to do on Thursday, the 2nd, but come from Leamington, I shall come to you, please God, for a quiet dinner that day.

These, and all subsequent readings in Cheltenham, were in the Assembly Rooms, since demolished. The effect this reading had on the famous actor was marvellous. " I swear to Heaven," he said to Dickens " that as a piece of passion and playfulness, indescribably mixed up together it does amaze me as profoundly as it moves me. But as a piece of art, and you know I . . . have seen the best art in a great time, it is incomprehensible to me."

On Friday evening and Saturday afternoon, March 23rd and 24th, 1866, Dickens again read at Cheltenham. In a letter written shortly before he said : "I am going to read at Cheltenham (on my own account) on the 23rd and 24th of this month, staying with Macready of course."

The following year he read also on the Friday evening and Saturday afternoon, April 5th and 6th.

Macready lived at No. 6 Wellington Square, and although Dickens visited his old friend there, probably on the Saturday evenings, it is doubtful if he actually stayed with Macready, as he states. He was always averse to staying with friends on these reading tours, although the readings being actually over on the Saturday afternoon, he may possibly have spent the night and Sunday with Macready. However, in a letter written to Mrs. Fitzgerald on the 7th March, 1867, he explained his decision in this respect, thus :

I never promise myself while thus engaged to make a visit. And even in the case of my old friend Mr. Macready at Cheltenham, a little while ago, I acted on the Spartan principles which at this present writing are making me very uncomfortable.

Dickens's farewell reading in Cheltenham was on Friday, January 22nd, 1869, when he gave the Sikes and Nancy scene specially for Macready. To Forster he wrote : "Macready is of opinion that the Murder is two Macbeths. He declares that he heard every word of the reading, but I doubt it. Alas! he is sadly infirm."

VII

Ross, the gateway to the beautiful Wye Valley, has a very interesting connection with Dickens. In the hall of the Royal Hotel is a tablet reading as follows :

AT THIS HOTEL
IN SEPTEMBER 1867
CHARLES DICKENS
MET HIS FRIEND AND BIOGRAPHER
JOHN FORSTER AND HERE
DECIDED UPON HIS CELEBRATED
AMERICAN TOUR
1867–8

George Dolby, Dickens's manager for the reading tours, was a native of Ross, and an interesting duel of wits took place at the Royal Hotel. Dolby had lately returned from America and had reported very favourably on the prospects of great success to be derived from a reading tour in the United States.

Forster—whose advice was much cherished by Dickens—was opposed to the idea. He was spending a few weeks at Ross, so Dickens drew up a list of pros and cons, or as he called it " The case in a nutshell," and it was posted to him

Then Dolby went home to Ross : let us tell the story in Dolby's own language :

I decided to return to my house at Ross, in which town by an odd coincidence, Mr. Forster was staying for the benefit of his health. So arrangements were made for a meeting to take place between us in ten days after my arrival there.

Up to this time, I had only met Mr. Forster at the social gatherings at "Gad's" and at the office ; and, before the interview at his hotel at Ross, had not met him in a business capacity. Being perfectly aware of the intimate relations existing between Mr. Dickens and Mr. Forster, I regarded this interview with considerable anxiety, as, in my opinion, much depended on the view Mr. Forster should take of the matter. This anxiety was not allayed by the discovery that he had in the most unreasonable manner, and without any knowledge of the subject that I could see, made up his mind that the enterprise was *not* to be; and a red rag could not have made a mad bull more ferocious than the discussion of the clauses in the moderate and business-like "case in a nutshell" made the biographer of the novelist. He had made up *his* mind, and there was an end of the matter. He urged that ever since the Staplehurst accident Mr. Dickens had been in a bad state of health, and that a sea-voyage was the very worst thing in the world for him. . . .

The unreasonableness of these arguments, and the manner in which they were laid down, produced such an unpleasant effect on my mind that I felt relieved when Mr. Forster suggested that there "was no reason why the interview should be prolonged" as he had "fully made up *his* mind that Dickens should *never go to America again.*"

It was with a sense of relief that I heard the hotel waiter announce that luncheon was served, and with a much greater sense of satisfaction that I declined an invitation to partake of that meal, and so ended a most disagreeable colloquy.

As for Forster, his parting assurance was : "I shall write to Dickens by to-night's post, and tell him how fully I am opposed to the idea, and that he must give it up."

Leaving the oracle to his reflections and his lunch, I proceeded at once to the telegraph station, and sent the following telegram to Mr. Dickens : "I can make nothing of Forster; he is utterly unreasonable and impracticable. Come down here and stay at my house, and we will tackle him together."

Mr. Forster had kept his word and had sent his manifesto to Mr. Dickens, who on receipt of it telegraphed to me that he would come to Ross by the afternoon train, as suggested; but would stay with Forster at the Hotel for fear of wounding his feelings.

I met Mr. Dickens on the arrival of the train, and conducted him to the hotel, leaving him in the care of his friend, Forster, who displayed a considerable amount of chagrin at the action I had taken.

Next morning I learned from Mr. Dickens that Mr. Forster had conducted himself in the same unreasonable manner as before, leaving the matter where it was on the previous day. . . .

When we returned to Mr. Forster he remarked at once, "I see it's of no use for me to say anything further on the subject, for by your faces it is plain you have made up your minds." Being assured that such was the case, he resignedly ordered lunch, and nothing more was said about the matter on that occasion. Later in the day Mr. Dickens returned to London, and then a sudden change came over Mr. Forster's spirit. These good qualities which had endeared him to Mr. Dickens's heart began to manifest themselves, leaving an impression in my mind that the churlishness displayed at our first interview was the outcome of his love and affection for Mr. Dickens and of an anxious desire for his welfare. The objections to the American tour were heard no more; but when Mr. Forster was leaving Ross, he gave me at the railway station a parting injunction to take care of Mr. Dickens, which would have been really comic, but for the earnestness with which it was delivered.

This incident is referred to as follows by Forster in his *Life of Dickens*:

So momentous in my judgment were the consequences of the American journey to him that it seemed right to preface thus much of the inducements and temptations that led to it. My own part in the discussion was that of steady dissuasion throughout: though this might perhaps have been less persistent if I could have reconciled myself to the belief, which I never at any time did, that Public Readings were a worthy employment for a man of his genius. But it had by this time become clear to me that nothing could stay the enterprise. The result of Mr Dolby's visit to America—drawn up by Dickens himself in a paper possessing still the interest of having given to the Readings when he crossed the Atlantic much of the form they then assumed—reached me when I was staying at Ross; and upon it was founded my last argument against the scheme. This he received in London on the 28th of September, on which day he thus wrote to his eldest daughter:

"As I telegraphed after I saw you, I am off to Ross to consult with Mr. Forster and Dolby together. You shall hear, either on Monday, or by Monday's post from London, how I decide finally."

The result he wrote to her three days later:

"You will have had my telegram that I go to America. After a long discussion with Forster, and consideration of what is to be said on both sides, I have decided to go through with it. We have telegraphed 'Yes' to Boston."

Dolby lived at Ashfield Lodge, Ross, and also at Wilton House, at both of which places he entertained Dickens on more than one occasion. Of the visit paid to Dolby in January, 1869, Dolby tells us: "He had heard so much of the beauties of the scenery in and around Ross, and expressed a wish to be taken for a walk along the prettiest road in the neighbourhood. I chose the one which is supposed by old travellers to be the 'prettiest in England' viz., from Ross to Monmouth, about eleven miles."

VIII

Writing to his sub-editor, W. H. Wills, in April, 1854, who was then spending a holiday in Malvern, Dickens said: "I know all the walks for many and many miles round about Malvern, and delightful walks they are."

This knowledge came from a stay at Knutsford Lodge, Malvern, in 1851, when Dickens took lodgings there for his wife and little daughter, Dora Annie, who were both ailing, and the air of Malvern had been recommended to him. Dickens divided his time between London and Malvern, and on March 15th wrote to Forster:

It is a most beautiful place. O Heaven, to meet the Cold Waterers (as I did this morning when I went out for a shower-bath) dashing down the hills, with severe expressions on their countenances, like men doing matches and not exactly winning! Then, a young lady in a grey polka going *up* the hills, regardless of legs; and meeting a young gentleman (a bad case I should say) with a light black silk cap on under his hat, and the pimples of I don't know how many douches under that. Likewise an old man

CHAPTER SIX

INTO THE WEST

I

THIS journey to the west—farther west than we have gone on the Bath road dealt with in the last chapter—takes us into Cornwall and as far as Land's End.

For the first ten miles, until Hounslow is reached, our road is the same as the Bath road; but at Hounslow we bear to the left along the main road to Exeter, through Bagshot and Basingstoke.

At Andover, sixty-three miles from London, two roads branch off to Exeter, both joining again at Honiton, one via Amesbury and Stonehenge, the other via Salisbury. Both these interest us in exploring the Dickens Land of the West, as in the pages of *Martin Chuzzlewit* we are often taken to the home of Mr. Pecksniff which was situated at a distance of about ten miles from "the fair old town of Salisbury."

There are many accounts of the coach ride between Mr. Pecksniff's and London, as the characters in the book are constantly moving between Wiltshire and the Metropolis.

First, Pecksniff and his daughters perform the journey by "the heavy coach," Pecksniff sleeping for the "first three stages" and then being joined by Jonas and his father, who after the visit to old Martin at the Green Dragon, had done some business at a place on the road back to London. This may have been Andover or Basingstoke, and near Andover it is that Martin probably stopped to breakfast on the morning of his departure from Mr. Pecksniff's house.

He was ten good miles from the village made illustrious by being the abiding-place of Mr. Pecksniff, when he stopped to breakfast at a little road-side ale-house; and resting upon a high-backed settle before the fire, pulled off his coat, and hung it before the cheerful blaze to dry. It was a very different place from the last tavern in which he had regaled; boasting no greater extent of accommodation than the brick-floored kitchen yielded.

Here Martin had the good luck to fall in with the driver of "a kind of light van drawn by four horses," who for the silk handkerchief Martin wore, agreed to take him as far as he went—"Hounslow, ten miles this side of London."

After Jonas had buried his father, we find him accompanying Pecksniff on this road, "seated on the outside of the coach at the back," and enquiring as to the dowries that might be given with his daughters.

Mr. Pecksniff unburdened himself at this, and Jonas became taciturn for a time, being "steadily engaged in subjecting some given amount to the operation of every known rule in figures," then became jocose and slapped his companion on the back, saying, "Let's have something." Pecksniff consenting,

Jonas got down from the coach-top with great alacrity, cut a cumbersome kind of caper in the road. After which, he went into the public-house, and there ordered spirituous drink to such an extent, that Mr. Pecksniff had some doubts of his perfect sanity, until Jonas set them quite at rest by saying, when the coach could wait no longer:

"I've been standing treat for a whole week and more, and letting you have all the delicacies of the season. You shall pay for this, Pecksniff." It was not a joke either, as Mr. Pecksniff at first supposed; for he went off to the coach without further ceremony, and left his respected victim to settle the bill.

Pecksniff, being a man of much endurance and having a great regard for Jonas "came out from the tavern with a smiling face, and even went as far as to repeat the performance, on a less expensive scale, at the next alehouse."

None of these landmarks of the road are mentioned by name, because Dickens was not very familiar with the Salisbury road. Indeed the names of the places en route are entirely absent. There is only one inn that is mentioned by name, the Bald Faced Stag, but there is no such inn on the road. Its name figures in connection with Tom Pinch's jovial ride to London, Chapter XXXVI, when Dickens describes the road and the ride, with many a "Yoho," and talks of "scampering on through light and darkness, all the same, as if the light of London, fifty miles away, were quite enough to travel by and some to spare."

As the sunlight died away, and evening fell upon the wood, he entered it. Moving here and there a bramble or a drooping bough which stretched across his path, he slowly disappeared. At intervals a narrow opening showed him passing on, or the sharp cracking of some tender branch denoted where he went; then he was seen or heard no more.

Never more beheld by mortal eye or heard by mortal ear; one man excepted. That man, parting the leaves and branches on the other side, near where the path emerged again, came leaping out soon afterwards.

This is a chapter that grips us, and makes the woods round Salisbury live in our minds for ever more.

"Leaving the body of the murdered man in one thick solitary spot . . . among the last year's leaves of oak and beach, just as it had fallen headlong down," Jonas walked on for ten miles; and then stopped at an ale-house for a coach, which he knew would pass through, on its way to London, before long; and which he also knew was not the coach he had travelled down by, for it came from another place. And "when the coach came up, which it soon did, he got a place outside, and was carried briskly onward towards home" where Nemesis overtook him at the hands of Nadgett.

II

The "little Wiltshire village, within an easy journey of the fair old town of Salisbury" where Mr. Pecksniff was guide, philosopher and friend to budding architects, is not named by Dickens but it is usually referred to as being the village of Amesbury, eight miles north from Salisbury; although there are others who claim this distinction for Alderbury which is only three miles south-east from Salisbury, and actually possesses a Dragon Inn—a Green one it is true, nevertheless. However, the fact is that the village and the inn formed a composite picture such as Dickens often drew when he was not on very familiar ground.

A little over ten miles beyond Andover and seven miles before reaching Salisbury, just after passing Lobcombe Corner, where the roads from Andover and Stockbridge join, is the Pheasant Inn, better known as Winterslow Hut. It is on record that Dickens "explored" this association with Hazlitt in 1848—five years after writing *Martin Chuzzlewit*. had visited the district before writing the book, as we point out on page 114, and may have walked the "couple of miles or so" into Winterslow, where the Lion's Head may have attracted his fancy and in course of time and travel, become the Blue Dragon that was kept by Mrs. Lupin.

Winterslow fits in with the details given by Dickens even better than Amesbury, as the village where Pecksniff resided.

It is "a couple of miles or so" away from the main London road as required by Chapter XX, and eight miles from Salisbury, against the ten miles called for in Chapter XXXI, but in this respect Amesbury is eight miles too.

The toll gate of which Dickens speaks in connection with Tom Pinch and his love for the tollman's children, we can well imagine was at this corner.

The tollman—a crusty customer, always smoking solitary pipes in a Windsor chair, inside, set artfully between two little windows that looked up and down the road, so that when he saw anything coming up, he might hug himself on having toll to take, and when he saw it going down, might hug himself on having taken it.

The finger-post at the end of the lane leading to the village is often mentioned, for here the coach always stopped and the gig was sometimes in waiting. On the occasion of Mrs. Lupin meeting the coach there with Tom Pinch's box, and handing it over to him with "a basket, with a long bottle sticking out of it" for his refreshment on the way, having said good-bye to the kindly landlady, Tom strains his eyes and thinks to himself, "And that's the last of the old finger-post where I have so often stood to see this very coach go by, and where I have parted with so many companions! I used to compare this coach with some great monster that appeared at certain times to bear my friends away into the world. And now it's bearing me away, to seek my fortune, Heaven knows where and how!"

It made Tom melancholy to picture himself walking up the lane and back to Pecksniff's as of old.

The toll-house and the finger-post all fit in so well with the various parties going between the Pecksniffs and London or Salisbury, that it is far easier to visualise it at Winterslow than it is from Amesbury.

As we have said, Mr. Pecksniff's village was one of Dickens's composite pictures, and we cannot for one moment believe he had Amesbury in his mind, more than any other place.

A careful reading of the account of the ride of Tom Pinch to London after being the victim of a duty which Mr.

to know why, and who, if required, would have stood stock still in a china-shop, with a complete dinner-service at each hoof.

We too, if it is market-day or not, can enjoy to the full the quaint narrow streets of Salisbury, and the old market-place with its picturesque butter cross, with quite as much interest as Tom Pinch, who "When he had exhausted the market-place, and watched the farmers safe into the market dinner, wandered round the town and regaled himself with the shop windows; previously taking a long stare at the bank, and wondering in what direction underground the caverns might be, where they kept the money."

The tavern at which Tom Pinch was to meet Martin is not named; there are so many of the smaller type of inn in Salisbury that it is idle to conjecture which of them was the actual place where Tom Pinch sat "in the sanded parlour of the tavern where he had left the horse" and had "his little table drawn out close before the fire and fell to work upon a well-cooked steak and smoking hot potatoes, with a strong appreciation of their excellence, and a very keen sense of enjoyment." But the Haunch of Venison in the market-place is a typical example of such an inn.

There is no further description of the inn until Chapter XXXI when Tom, after his dismissal from Mr. Pecksniff, made for Salisbury and plodded the ten miles through the wet and eventually "came into the welcome precincts of the city."

He went to the inn where he had waited for Martin and . . . ordered a bed. He had no heart for tea or supper . . . but sat by himself before an empty table in the public room. . . . It was a great relief when the chambermaid came in, and said the bed was ready. It was a low four-poster shelving downward in the centre like a trough, and the room was crowded with impracticable tables and exploded chests of drawers, full of damp linen. A graphic representation in oil of a remarkably fat ox hung over the fireplace, and the portrait of some former landlord (who might have been the ox's brother, he was so like him) stared roundly in, at the foot of the bed. A variety of queer smells were partially quenched in the prevailing scent of very old lavender; and the window had not been opened for such a long space of time that it pleaded immemorial usage, and wouldn't come open now.

The other inn at Salisbury is perhaps more easily identified. Here John Westlock, who had had the satisfaction of seeing his "father's executors cash up" redeemed his promise to Tom Pinch to "come down to Salisbury on purpose" to give him a dinner in honour of the event. His invitation included Martin, and was for dinner, as Tom said, "not at the house where you and I were either, but at the very first hotel in the town."

This could only have been the White Hart Hotel, which to-day is a capital example of an English hotel.

We can also well imagine it was to the White Hart that the wounded Tigg and Jonas came on the night of their disastrous ride from London, and knocked the people up there to send out messengers to see to the overturned carriage and the half dead Bailey Junior. It was also quite probable that Pecksniff and Tigg dined here a few days later, on that fateful evening that was to be Tigg's last. Pecksniff had fallen into the trap and had "agreed to become the last partner and proprietor in the Anglo-Bengalee, and made an appointment to dine with Mr. Montague at Salisbury, on the next day but one, and there to complete the negotiations."

A spirited account of the walk of Martin and Tom from Amesbury to Salisbury, ending at this inn, is given in Chapter XII. "A rare strong, hearty, healthy walk—four statute miles an hour—preferable to that rumbling, tumbling, jolting, shaking, scraping, creaking, villainous old gig? Why, the two things will not admit of comparison. It is an insult to the walk, to set them side by side."

The journey ended in a snowstorm "And lo! the towers of the Old Cathedral rise before them, even now! and bye and bye they come into the sheltered streets, made strangely silent by their white carpet; and so to the Inn for which they are bound."

A famous Inn! the hall a very grove of dead game, and dangling joints of mutton; and in one corner an illustrious larder, with glass doors, developing cold fowls and noble joints, and tarts wherein the raspberry jam coyly withdrew itself, as such a precious creature should, behind a lattice work of pastry. And behold, on the first floor, at the court-end of the house, in a room with all the window-curtains drawn, a fire piled half-way up the chimney, plates warming before it, wax candles gleaming everywhere and a table spread for three, with silver and glass enough for thirty—John Westlock!

IV

From Salisbury it is eight miles to Amesbury, from which Salisbury Plain and Stonehenge are best visited, and the journey continued to Exeter by way of Wincanton and Honiton.

Dickens's thoughts had apparently been on Salisbury Plain whilst in America the year previous to writing *Martin Chuzzlewit*, for in a letter to Forster at that time, he compared the Wild West very unfavourably with it.

> The widely-famed Far West is not to be compared with even the tamest portions of Scotland or Wales. You stand upon the prairie, and see the unbroken horizon all round you. You are on a great plain, which is like a sea without water. I am exceedingly fond of wild and lonely scenery, and believe that I have the faculty of being as much impressed by it as any man living. But the prairie fell, by far, short of my preconceived idea. I felt no such emotions as I do in crossing Salisbury Plain. The excessive flatness of the scene makes it dreary, but tame. Grandeur is certainly not its characteristic. . . . It was fine. It was worth the ride. . . . But to say (as the fashion is here) that the sight is a landmark in one's existence, and awakens a new set of sensations, is sheer gammon. I would say to every man who can't see a prairie—go to Salisbury Plain, Marlborough Downs, or any of the broad, high, open lands near the sea. Many of them are fully as impressive; and Salisbury Plain is decidedly more so.

No doubt his knowledge of the district was obtained in the newspaper reporting days, when he travelled this way by coach to report the speeches of Lord John Russell on his election campaign in the West. We have no direct record of a visit until 1848—five years after *Martin Chuzzlewit*, when Forster tells us that "One of its earlier months had been signalised by an adventure in which Leech, Lemon, and myself took part with him, when, obtaining horses from Salisbury, we passed the whole of a March day in riding over every part of the Plain; visiting Stonehenge, and exploring Hazlitt's 'hut' at Winterslow, birthplace of some of his finest essays."

In the opening chapter of *The Uncommercial Traveller* Dickens refers to himself as "quite a Druid, in the midst of a light Stonehenge of samples."

And in *The Holy Tree* he refers to "a good Inn down

in Wiltshire" where he put up once. It was, we read, "on the skirts of Salisbury Plain, and the midnight wind that rattled my lattice window came moaning at me from Stonehenge."

There is a more marked reference to Stonehenge, in the same story, where Dickens tells us:

> There was a hanger-on at that establishment . . . with long white hair, and flinty blue eyes always looking afar off; who claimed to have been a shepherd, and who seemed to be ever watching for the reappearance, on the verge of the horizon, of some ghostly flock of sheep that had been mutton for many ages. He was a man with a weird belief in him that no one could count the stones of Stonehenge twice, and make the same number of them; likewise, that any one who counted them three times nine times, and then stood in the centre and said "I dare!" would behold a tremendous apparition, and be stricken dead.

The George at Amesbury is usually referred to as being the Blue Dragon of *Martin Chuzzlewit*, but the objection to it is that it can hardly be considered as "a village ale-house"; whereas such a title might be applied to the Lion's Head at Winterslow or the Green Dragon at Alderbury, but on the other hand, neither would hardly have been able to accomodate old Martin and Mary, to say nothing of the other members of the Chuzzlewit family who "formally invested it." These remarks only serve to emphasise the fact that a composite picture was drawn by Dickens.

The sign of the Blue Dragon is said to be applicable to the sign of the Green Dragon at Alderbury as it was many years ago. Dickens refers to it as:

> A certain Dragon who swung and creaked complainingly before the village ale-house door. A faded and an ancient dragon he was; and many a wintry storm of rain, snow, sleet and hail, had changed his colour from a gaudy blue to a faint lack-lustre shade of grey. But there he hung; rearing in a state of monstrous imbecility, on his hind legs; waxing, with every month that passed, so much more dim and shapeless that as you gazed at him on one side of the signboard it seemed as if he must be gradually melting through it, and coming out upon the other.

At a later date it will be remembered, the sign was changed to The Jolly Tapley, consequent upon the redoubtable Mark Tapley marrying the kindly, buxom Mrs. Lupin.

If the George at Amesbury is the Blue Dragon, then possibly the King's Arms is the original of the Half Moon and Seven Stars, where Montague Tigg announced he was to be found "at any time, and open to any reasonable proposition" in regard to the common enemy, old Martin Chuzzlewit. Anthony Chuzzlewit and his son Jonas were also "economically quartered at the Half Moon and Seven Stars, which was an obscure ale-house."

Snowden Ward, in "The Real Dickens Land," went so far as to locate a house on the left hand side of the Wilsford Road, entering Amesbury, just before the cross road, as the original of the house of Pecksniff.

"In one sense, and only one, he may be said to have been a Land Surveyor on a pretty large scale, as an extensive prospect lay stretched out before the windows of his house."

This may have been the late Mr. Ward's only reason for the identification: we have been unable to find any other support for it.

V

Sherborne, ten miles south from Wincanton on the main Salisbury–Exeter Road, was the place of Macready's retirement in 1851, and there is no doubt that Dickens paid him more than one visit there.

However, it is on record that on December 21st, 1854, Dickens gave one of his earliest public readings there, for the benefit of the funds of the local Literary Institution, which, as he wrote to Mrs. Watson at the time, "is one of the remaining pleasures of Macready's life."

To Macready himself he had written previously a characteristically humorous letter:

> In that vast hall in the busy town of Sherborne, in which our industrious English novelist is expected to read next month—though he is strongly of opinion that he is deficient in power, and too old—I wonder what accommodation there is for reading, because our illustrious countryman likes to stand at a desk breast high, with plenty of room about him, a sloping top, and a ledge to keep his book from tumbling off. If such a thing should not be there, however on his arrival, I suppose even a Sherborne carpenter could knock it up out of a deal board.

The reading took place in the Literary Society's rooms later known as the Macready Institute but now an auction room. This adjoins Sherborne House, where Macready resided.

There is another Dorsetshire village about eight miles from Dorchester that Dickens must have heard of long before Macready made Sherborne the place of his retirement. It is a village six or seven miles from the nearest railway station. In *The Old Curiosity Shop* we read that Dick Swiveller was "the nephew of Rebecca Swiveller, Spinster, deceased, of Cheselbourne in Dorsetshire"; it was this lady who left him an annuity of £150, which enabled him to marry the Marchioness and live in comfort in a cottage in Hampstead.

Taunton is mentioned more than once by Dickens in his novels. In *Nicholas Nickleby* we are told by Mrs. Nickleby that when she was a girl at school she "always went at least twice every year to the Hawkinses at Taunton Vale" and in *Bleak House*, Conversation Vholes often referred to the privilege he had in supporting "an aged father in the Vale of Taunton—his native place" and he further added on one occasion that he admired that county very much.

In "The Story of Richard Doubledick" the mother of Captain Taunton lived at Frome, in Somersetshire, where she was visited by Doubledick.

VI

Exeter must be given premier honours of all Devon and Cornish towns in matters of association with Dickens. Before his days of authorship commenced Dickens came to Exeter as a reporter (1834). At the annual dinner of the Newspaper Press Fund in 1865 he narrated his experiences during this visit:

The very last time I was in Exeter I strolled into the Castle Yard, there to identify, for the amusement of a friend, the spot on which I once "took," as we used to call it, an election speech of Lord John Russell . . . in the midst of a lively fight maintained by all the vagabonds in that division of the county, and under such pelting rain that I remember two good-natured colleagues, who chanced to be at leisure, held a pocket handkerchief over my notebook, after the manner of a State canopy in an ecclesiastical procession.

In 1839 he again came to the city, this time to find a house for the settlement of his parents. This he succeeded in accomplishing, and for many years John Dickens dwelt

I

and above, a full-sized country drawing-room and three
bedrooms; in the yard behind, coal-holes, fowl-houses,
and meat safes out of number; in the kitchen a neat little
range; in the other rooms, good stoves and cupboards;
and all for twenty pounds a year, taxes included. There
is a good garden at the side well stocked with cabbages,
beans, onions, celery, and some flowers. The stock
belonging to the landlady (who lives in the adjoining
cottage), there was some question whether she was not
entitled to half the produce, but I settled the point by
paying five shillings, and becoming absolute master of
the whole.

I do assure you that I am charmed with the place
and the beauty of the country round about, though I have
not seen it under very favourable circumstances, for it
snowed when I was there this morning, and blew bitterly
from the east yesterday. It is really delightful, and when
the house is to rights and the furniture all in, I shall be
quite sorry to leave it. I have had some few things,
second-hand, but I take it seventy pounds will be the mark,
even taking this into consideration. I include in that
estimate glass and crockery, garden tools, and such like
little things. There is a spare bedroom of course. That
I have furnished too.

I am on terms of the closest intimacy with Mrs. Samuell,
the landlady, and her brother and sister-in-law, who have
a little farm hard by . . . and I really think the old
woman herself will be a great comfort to my mother. Coals
are dear just now—twenty-six shillings a ton. They
found me a boy to go two miles out and back again to
order some this morning. I was debating in my mind
whether I should give him eighteenpence or two shillings,
when his fee was announced—twopence!

The house is on the high-road to Plymouth, and,
though in the very heart of Devonshire, there is as much
long-stage and posting life as you would find in Piccadilly.
The situation is charming. Meadows in front, an orchard
running parallel to the garden hedge, richly-wooded hills
closing in the prospect behind, and, away to the left,
before a splended view of the hill on which Exeter is
situated, the cathedral towers rising up into the sky in
the most picturesque manner possible. I don't think I
ever saw so cheerful or pleasant a spot. The drawing-room
is nearly, if not quite, as large as the outer room of my old
chambers in Furnival's Inn. The paint and paper are

MILE END COTTAGE, ALPHINGTON

[*Photo by T. W. Tyrrell*

DICKENS AND HIS FRIENDS IN CORNWALL

[*Drawn by W. M. Thackeray*

new, and the place clean as the utmost excess of snowy cleanliness can be.

You would laugh if you could see me powdering away with the upholsterer, and endeavouring to bring about all sorts of impracticable reductions and wonderful arrangements. He has by him two second-hand carpets; the important ceremony of trying the same comes off at three this afternoon. I am perpetually going backwards and forwards. It is two miles from here, so I have plenty of exercise, which so occupies me and prevents me being lonely that I stopped at home to read last night, and shall to-night, although the theatre is open. Charles Kean has been the star for the last two evenings. He was stopping in this house, and went away this morning. I have got his sitting-room now, which is smaller and more comfortable than the one I had before.

Mile End Cottage still stands in Alphington on the outskirts of Exeter, but the view of which Dickens writes as being visible from the house is obscured by buildings since erected.

There is no doubt a reference to the cottage in *Nicholas Nickleby*, Mrs. Nickleby speaks of the home of her friends, the Dibabses, as "The beautiful little thatched white house, one storey high, covered all over with ivy and creeping plants, with an exquisite little porch with twining honeysuckle and all sorts of things."

This is identical with the house in Alphington as it used to be, and was undoubtedly inspired by this visit while engaged in writing the story.

He was accompanied by his wife and stayed, as he did on the occasions of his later visits, at the New London Inn. He occupied the sitting-room which had just been vacated by Charles Kean.

My quarters are excellent, and the head-waiter is *such* a waiter! By-the-bye, not the least comical thing that has occurred was the visit of the upholsterer (with some further calculations) since I began this letter. I think they took me here at the New London for the Wonderful Being I am; they were amazingly sedulous; and no doubt they looked for my being visited by the nobility and gentry of the neighbourhood. My first and only visitor came to-night, a ruddy-faced man in faded black, with extracts from a feather-bed all over him; an extraordinary and quite

"The influence of my family being local, it is their wish that Mr. Micawber should go down to Plymouth. They think it indispensable that he should be upon the spot."

So the Micawbers went to Plymouth and returned empty: "The truth is, talent is not wanted at the Custom House . . . when that branch of my family which is settled in Plymouth, became aware that Mr. Micawber was accompanied by myself, and by little Wilkins, and his sister and by the twins . . . our reception was cool."

Dickens paid two visits to Plymouth on his reading tours; the first in 1858 and the second in 1862. This was his last visit, as evidently he was not very well pleased with his reception.

You know I was very averse to going to Plymouth and would not have gone there again but for poor Arthur. But on the last night I read "Copperfield" and positively enthralled the people. It was the most overpowering effect, and . . . came behind the screen after the storm and cried in the manliest manner.

An account of the first visit is given in a letter to Miss Hogarth dated from West Hoe, Plymouth, August 5th, 1858:

Last night here was not so bright. There are quarrels of the strangest kind between the Plymouth people and the Stonehouse people. . . . We had a fair house, but not at all a great one. All the notabilities came this morning to "Little Dombey" . . . For "Mrs. Gamp" and "The Boots" to-night we have also a very promising let. But the races are on, and there are two public balls to-night, and the yacht squadron are at Cherbourg to boot. . . . The room is a very handsome one, but it is on top of a very windy and muddy hill, leading (literally) to nowhere; and it looks (except that it is new and mortary) as if the subsidence of the waters of the Deluge might have left it where it is. I have to go right through the company to get to the platform. Big doors slam and resound when anybody comes in; and all the company seem afraid of one another. Nevertheless they were a sensible audience last night, and much impressed and pleased.

And on August 7th, 1858, to his daughter Mamie: "The closing night at Plymouth was a very great scene and the morning there was exceedingly good, too."

There are many scattered references to Devonshire throughout the writings of Dickens, which show that the country visited in early manhood left its impression on the writer. *Nicholas Nickleby* is particularly rich in this respect. The Nicklebys came from "a sequestered part of the county of Devonshire" and it was in the same district that Smike breathed his last, probably quite close to the "small farm near Dawlish" which had been originally purchased by the grandfather of Nicholas; and his two children, Ralph and Nicholas went to school at Exeter. Mrs. Nickleby in her widowhood was often referring to those Devonshire days, and on one occasion speaks of "the election ball at Exeter"—a reminiscence of Dickens's reporting days, and on another refers to her friend "Miss Cropley of Exeter."

Mrs. Skewton in *Dombey and Son* had, we are informed, recently returned from a holiday in Devonshire, and in that delightful county Mr. Stryver, in *A Tale of Two Cities*, also spent his vacation, whilst Tommy Traddles in *David Copperfield* was engaged to the "Devonshire Beauty," Sophy, the curate's daughter, "Such a dear girl . . . one of ten down in Devonshire" to visit whom Traddles walked all the way from London into Devon.

Dr. Marigold the Cheap-jack, whose wife ill-treated their little girl, and was the cause of her death, tells us:

One summer evening, when, as we were coming into Exeter, out of the farther West of England, we saw a woman beating a child in a cruel manner, who screamed, "Don't beat me! O mother, mother, mother!" Then my wife stopped her ears, and ran away like a wild thing, and next day she was found in the river.

IX

Prior to writing jointly with Wilkie Collins the Christmas Number for 1860 entitled *A Message from the Sea*, the two friends made a special journey into Devonshire to obtain the local colour. They started by train from Paddington on November 1st, and reached Bideford that same evening, a twelve hours journey at that time. On arriving he wrote to Miss Hogarth:

I write (with the most impracticable iron pen on earth) to report our safe arrival here in a beastly hotel. We start to-morrow at nine on a two days' posting between this and Liskeard. . . . We had stinking fish for dinner,

Enjoining Tom to give an eye to the shop, Captain Jorgan followed Mrs. Raybrock into the little, low, backroom,—decorated with divers plants in pots, tea-trays, old china teapots, and punch-bowls,—which was at once the private sitting room of the Raybrock family and the inner cabinet of the post-office of the village of Steepways.

The Cornish village of Lanrean with its King Arthur's Arms to which Captain Jorgan went to make enquiries, does not exist outside the imagination of the author, and his attempt to coin a Cornish word, whilst very creditable as to sound, has no meaning in the ancient language.

Both Barnstaple in North Devon and Falmouth in Cornwall, are casually mentioned in this story.

X

After his return from America in 1842, Dickens spent three weeks of the autumn in Cornwall with Forster, Maclise and Clarkson Stanfield. As Forster says, "Railways helped us then not much; but where the roads were inaccessible to post-horses we walked." And Dickens adds that they "went down into Devonshire by railroad and there we hired an open carriage." The Great Western Railway was only complete as far as Bristol in those days, but they no doubt got into North Cornwall by a local line from there, as from the accounts we have the party appears to have visited Tintagel before reaching Land's End.

Dickens gave a humorous account of the trip in a letter to his American friend Professor Felton:

Blessed star of morning! Such a trip as we had into Cornwall just after Longfellow went away! We went down into Devonshire by railroad, and there we hired an open carriage from an innkeeper, patriotic in all Pickwick matters, and went on with post-horses. Sometimes we travelled all night, sometimes all day, sometimes both. . . . Heavens! If you could have seen the necks of bottles, distracting in their immense varieties of shape peeping out of the carriage-pockets! If you could have witnessed the deep devotion of the post-boys, the wild attachment of the hostlers, the maniac glee of the waiters! If you could have followed us into the earthy old churches we visited, and into the strange caverns on the gloomy sea-shore, and down into the depths of mines, and up to the tops of giddy heights where the unspeakably green water was roaring, I don't know how many hundred feet below! If you could have seen but one gleam of the bright fires by which we sat in the big rooms of the ancient inns at night, until long after the small hours had come and gone. . . . I never laughed in my life as I did on this journey. It would have done you good to hear me. I was choking, and gasping, and bursting the buckle off the back of my stock, all the way. And Stanfield got into such apoplectic entanglements that we were often obliged to beat him on the back with portmanteaus before we could recover him. Seriously, I do believe there never was such a trip. And they made such sketches, those two men, in the most romantic of our halting-places, that you would have sworn we had the Spirit of Beauty with us, as well as the Spirit of Fun.

"Tintagel was visited," says Forster, "and no part of mountain or sea consecrated by the legends of Arthur was left unexplored."

It is unfortunate that Dickens left no further record of this trip, but a letter of Maclise to Forster some years later respecting Forster's agility in gaining high places, and his steadiness when there, tells us that they clambered up the Goat Path to King Arthur's Castle at Tintagel, ascended to the cradle of the highest tower of Mount St. Michael, and rocked themselves on the Logan Stone, of which latter event, Stanfield has left an historic drawing which shows Forster perched right on the very top.

The Waterfall at St. Nighton near Tintagel was painted by both Stanfield and Maclise and exhibited at the Royal Academy in 1843. Maclise's picture contained the figure of Miss Hogarth, which Dickens purchased secretly, as he did not wish to impose upon the generosity of the artist, who when he found Dickens was the purchaser, wished to return the money.

Boase in his "Collectanea Cornubiensis" records the fact that when Dickens was at Marazion in 1842, Mr. Tippet, solicitor, and member of the Penzance Town Council, being anxious to see something of him, persuaded Mr. George Sealy, the landlord of the Marazion Hotel, to allow him to serve as one of the waiters. The dinner had nearly concluded when one of the guests in making a latin quotation placed the accent on the wrong syllable. Mr. Tippet, a fair scholar, immediately noticed the occurrence, and quite off his guard, said, "Excuse me, sir, I think that the accent by torchlight. We had had a break-down in the dark, on a stony morass some miles away; and I had the honour of leading one of the unharnessed post-horses. If any lady or gentleman, on perusal of the present lines, will take any very tall post-horse with his traces hanging about his legs, and will conduct him by the bearing-rein into the heart of a country dance of a hundred and fifty couples, that lady or gentleman will then, and only then, form an adequate idea of the extent to which that post-horse will tread on his conductor's toes. Over and above which the post-horse, finding three hundred people whirling about him, will probably rear, and also lash out with his hind legs, in a manner incompatible with dignity or self-respect on his conductor's part. With such little draw-backs on my usually impressive aspect, I appeared at this Cornish Inn, to the unutterable wonder of the Cornish Miners. It was full, and twenty times full, and nobody could be received but the post-horse,—though to get rid of that noble animal was something. While my fellow-travellers and I were discussing how to pass the night and so much of the next day as must intervene before the jovial blacksmith and the jovial wheelwright would be in a condition to go out on the morass and mend the coach, an honest man stepped forth from the crowd and proposed his unlet floor of two rooms, with supper of eggs and bacon, ale and punch. We joyfully accompanied him home to the strangest of clean houses, where we were well entertained to the satisfaction of all parties. But the novel feature of the entertainment was, that our host was a chair-maker, and that the chairs assigned to us were mere frames, altogether without bottoms of any sort; so that we passed the evening on perches. Nor was this the absurdest consequence; for when we unbent at supper, and any one of us gave way to laughter he forgot the peculiarity of his position, and instantly disappeared. I myself, doubled up into an attitude from which self-extrication was impossible, was taken out of my frame, like a clown in a comic pantomime who has tumbled into a tub, five times by the taper's light during eggs and bacon.

The above, written in 1855, must surely have been a reminiscence of the autumn holiday thirteen years before. The reference to the old Longships Lighthouse in *A Christmas Carol* is contained in the following:

The Spirit did not tarry here, but bade Scrooge hold his robe, and passing on above the moor, sped whither? Not to sea? To sea. To Scrooge's horror, looking back, he saw the last of the land, a frightful range of rocks, behind them; and his ears were deafened by the thundering of water, as it rolled and roared and raged among the dreadful caverns it had worn, and fiercely tried to undermine the earth.

Built upon a dismal reef of sunken rocks, some league or so from shore, on which the waters chafed and dashed, the wild year through, there stood a solitary lighthouse. Great heaps of seaweed clung to its base, and storm birds . . . rose and fell about it, like the waves they skimmed.

Young Walter Gay it was who used to like to hear from his uncle Sol Gills, tales of gale and shipwreck and boats "driven ashore on the coast of Cornwall" and this again must have re-called to Dickens the wild scenery he had viewed off the Cornish coast a few years previously.

In *Martin Chuzzlewit* there is a reference to "men of large stature bred in the mining districts of Cornwall," and in *Little Dorrit*, we find Mr. Panks asking Arthur Clennam if he was related to the Clennams of Cornwall, and was much disappointed to hear that he was not, for "you'd have heard of something to your advantage" he said " . . . There's a Cornish property going a-begging sir, and not a Cornish Clennam to have it for the asking."

A Cornish authority informs us that there are no Clennam's in Cornwall, and that Clennam is not a Cornish name.

K

CHAPTER SEVEN

I

On the completion of his second book, *Oliver Twist*
Dickens took two bachelor holidays with Hablot K. Browne
(Phiz). The first was in the summer of 1838 when they
journeyed into Yorkshire to investigate the matter of th
notorious schools there, and this pilgrimage is dealt with
in Chapter Nine.

The second was into North Wales, with no particula
object in view, so far as we can ascertain; but certain im
pressions were obtained on the way which served a ver
useful purpose in *The Old Curiosity Shop* written som
twelve months later, and to a lesser extent, aided by late
visits, the background to some of the incidents in *Dombe*
and Son.

Dickens's Diary commenced on January 1st of that year an
closed after a trial of only a few days with the words, "Her
ends this brief attempt at a diary, I grow sad over this checkin
off my days, and can't do it," was for some unaccountabl
reason re-opened on the occasion of this trip and from it w
can obtain some very interesting information of the way th
party travelled, and although we deal with each place visite
in its due place upon the journey, it is useful to view as
whole the journey as Dickens and Phiz took it.

On Monday, October 29th, 1838 he notes: "Started fro
Coach Office near Hungerford Street with Browne—agreeab
ride but cold." A further note tells us that the fares
Leamington were 17s. each and that the tips to coachma
guard and porter amounted to no less than 14s. The nig
was spent at Copp's Hotel, Leamington, "excellent inn
where the bill for the night amounted to no less tha
£2 19s.

On Tuesday, October 30th, they proceeded to Kenilwort
Warwick and Stratford-on-Avon, where they stayed th
night.

Monday, OCTOBER 29, 1838.

302nd day. Hare Hunting begins.

	£	s	d
Hatfield expences on Saturday —	1	12	0
Fares to Leamington 17/- each —	1	14	0
Coach to Stop - coach office —		2	6
coachmen, guard, and porter —		14	
Lunches —		6	

Started from coach office near Hungerford street with Browne — agreeable ride, but cold — Leamington, Copp's Hotel - Excellent Inn.

Tuesday, OCTOBER 30, 1838.

303rd day.

	£	s	d
Bile at Leamington —	2	19	0
Book of Kenilworth Castle, and visit —		6	
Expences at Warwick Castle —		6	6
Turnpikes —		1	6
Horses and post boy —	1	13	0

away to Kenilworth — delightful - beautiful beyond expression — mem: what a Summer resort! — three months — lie about the ruins — books - hunting — seriously turn this over for next year

FACSIMILE OF ENTRIES IN DICKENS'S DIARY

134

On Wednesday, October 31st, the journey was continued through Birmingham and Wolverhampton to Shrewsbury, where the night was spent at the Lion Hotel.

On Thursday, November 1st, in the afternoon, they took the Post-chaise to Llangollen and stayed at the Hand Hotel.

On Friday, November 2nd, they posted to Bangor and from there to Capel Curig where they spent the night.

On Saturday, November 3rd, they posted from Capel Curig to Chester and stayed there until Monday when an entry shows they paid the "bill at Chester £3 18s." and then went on to Birkenhead. There is no entry in the diary under Sunday, nor any mention of the Hotel at which they stayed at Chester.

From Birkenhead they probably went on to Liverpool, as the entry on the Tuesday states "Bill at Adelphi £4 10s. 9d." Forster tells us that he met Dickens at Liverpool at this time, so that accounts for the entry of three fares to Manchester on the following day.

On Tuesday, November 6th, appears this entry in the diary: "3 fares to Manchester 3 times." We are at a loss to explain why three separate journeys were necessary to Manchester. We should imagine the party left Liverpool on the Tuesday, as there is a note of having paid the bill at the Adelphi on that day; and it is probable they went to Manchester and then on to Cheadle.

On Wednesday, November 7th, there is an entry "Chaise to Cheadle £1 1s." but whether the journey was made on that day or the day previous is difficult to say. There is also noted on this date "Bill at Inn £4" and "Fares to London £7 13s."; so probably the return was made on the Wednesday or Thursday, and so the holiday finished.

The first part of the Great North Road as far as Barnet is common also to the Holyhead Road which runs through the Midlands and which is the subject of the present chapter; the Great North Road from Barnet covering the Dotheboys Route of *Nicholas Nickleby* is dealt with in Chapter Nine.

A portion of this journey is also associated with Little Nell's wanderings with her Grandfather; with this we deal separately in the next chapter.

II

The Great North Road was second only to the Dover Road in the affections of Dickens, and so it has left its impress in his works. First and foremost perhaps is the journey made by Nicholas Nickleby in the company of Mr. Squeers to Dotheboys Hall in Yorkshire, following quickly upon a journey of inspection made by Dickens himself in January 1838 in company with Hablot K. Browne, the artist who is better known as Phiz.

Oliver Twist made his first acquaintance with London by this road entering it via Barnet and Islington, and the same road is associated with Noah Claypole, and with Bill Sikes in his flight after the murder of Nancy. The same road, too, witnessed the arrival of John Browdie and his bride, and saw the departure of Esther Summerson, Ada and Richard, for Bleak House, near St. Albans.

So far as the first portion of the Great North Road is concerned, it passes through Islington, Holloway, Highgate and Finchley to Barnet and has many associations with both Dickens personally and with his novels. The City Road leading to Islington is indelibly associated with the Micawbers, who lived in Windsor Terrace; and at Islington itself, Tom Pinch lived with his sister Ruth, and the walk of Oliver and the Dodger, from the Angel, Islington, to Fagin's in Field Lane, is very clearly described in *Oliver Twist*.

Mr. Micawber once had lodgings at Pentonville, so did Nicodemus Dumps, Guppy and Panks. Mr. Brownlow lived here, as actually did Grimaldi and George Cruikshank.

A noteworthy picture of stage coach travelling is given in the opening of the Christmas Story for 1855, *The Holly Tree Inn*.

There was no Northern Railway at that time, and in its place there were stage-coaches; which I occasionally find myself, in common with some other people, affecting to lament now, but which everybody dreaded as a very serious penance then. I had secured the box-seat on the fastest of these.

This coach started from the Peacock at Islington.

When I got up to the Peacock,—where I found everybody drinking hot purl, in self-preservation, I then discovered that I was the only passenger. However, I took a little purl (which I found uncommonly good), and got into the coach. When I was seated, they built me up with straw to the waist, and, conscious of making a rather ridiculous appearance, I began my journey.

It was still dark when we left the Peacock . . . and we were rattling for Highgate Archway over the hardest ground I have ever heard the ring of iron shoes on. As we got into the country, everything seemed to have grown old and gray. The roads, the trees, thatched roofs of cottages and homesteads, the ricks in farmer's yards . . . little turnpike houses had blazing fires inside, and children (even turnpike people have children, and seem to like them) rubbed the frost from the little panes of glass with their chubby arms, that their bright eyes might catch a glimpse of the solitary coach going by.

At the Archway Tavern, Highgate, the road forks. To the right Archway Road leads to Barnet. This was the road by which Oliver Twist, accompanied by the Dodger, arrived in London ; this was the road to and from Bleak House which was near St. Albans. Through Highgate Archway, the one that was replaced by the present bridge, Noah Claypole and Charlotte came "advancing towards London by the Great North Road" and in *The Holly Tree Inn* we are told of the coach "rattling for Highgate Archway over the hardest ground I have ever heard the ring of iron shoes on."

"At the Archway toll over at Highgate" Bucket first picked up the trail of Lady Dedlock.

The old Great North Road to Highgate runs to the left of the Archway Tavern, ascending Highgate Hill ; Bill Sikes "went through Islington" when endeavouring to escape after the murder of Nancy ; and "strode up the hill at Highgate on which stands the stone in honour of Whittington." The stone referred to is to be seen on the left, incorporated in a lamp post. When Swiveller was taunted by Quilp, he threatened to run away ; "towards Highgate I suppose" he said to himself. "Perhaps the bells might strike up 'Turn again Swiveller.' "   Joe Willet came this way when he ran away from home and Dolly ; "He went out by Islington and so on to Highgate, and sat on many stones, and gates, but there were no voices in the bells to bid him turn " says Dickens.

Bill Sikes continuing his flight, turned down to Highgate Hill, unsteady of purpose, and uncertain where to go ; struck off to the right again, almost as soon as he began to descend it ; and taking the footpath across the fields, skirted Caen Wood, and so came out on Hampstead Heath. Traversing the hollow by the Vale of Health, he mounted the opposite bank, and crossing the road which joins the villages of Hampstead and Highgate, made along the remaining portion of the Heath to the fields at North End, in one of which he laid himself down under a hedge, and slept. . . .

Where could he go, that was near and not too public, to get some meat and drink? Hendon. That was a good place, not far off, and out of most people's way. Thither he directed his steps. . . . But when he got there, all the people he met . . . seemed to view him with suspicion. Back he turned again, without the courage to purchase bit or drop, and once more he lingered on the Heath, uncertain where to go.

He wandered over miles and miles of ground, and still came back to the old place. . . .

At Highgate, where Mr. Pickwick carried out "unwearied researches" Dickens lodged for a time in 1832, at "Mrs. Goodman's next door to the Red Lion" which was in North Road itself; and it was doubtless at this period that Dickens obtained most of the local colour of the road and the district as far as Barnet which he used so successfully in *Oliver Twist* and *Barnaby Rudge*. Steerforth, Dr. Strong, and David and Dora all lived at Highgate, and in the cemetery there lie the father of Dickens, and his little daughter Dora Annie.

Hampstead Lane on the left leads past Caen Wood (mentioned above) into Spaniard's Lane and Hampstead. Caen Wood—or Ken Wood—now preserved as an open space—was Lord Mansfield's country house which the Gordon Rioters endeavoured to destroy, as described in *Barnaby Rudge*.

The Spaniard's Inn is introduced into *The Pickwick Papers* when Mrs. Bardell, Mrs. Raddle and other friends spent an afternoon there. Here she was traced by Mr. Jackson, clerk to Dodson & Fogg and conveyed thence to the Fleet Prison for the costs in the action which Mr. Pickwick had so steadfastly refused to pay.

On the left may be seen the Hampstead Ponds—the speculations on the source of which formed one of the papers communicated to the Club by Mr. Pickwick, "the man who had traced to their source the mighty ponds of Hampstead."

Hampstead Heath opens out just beyond the Spaniards. Walter Gay "knew of no better fields than those near Hampstead" for reflecting on the unknown life before him when he was ordered by the house of Dombey to sail for the Barbadoes.

A walk to Hampstead and Highgate—after a dip in the Roman Bath in the Strand, was often indulged in by David Copperfield.

Jack Straw's Castle was a very popular rendezvous with Dickens. Forster quotes the following typical letter from

Dickens proposing a walk and dinner at this hostelry: "You don't feel disposed, do you, to muffle yourself up, and start off with me for a good brisk walk over Hampstead-heath? I know a good 'ous there where we can have a red-hot chop for dinner, and a glass of good wine." This, Forster adds, "led to our first experience of Jack Straw's Castle, memorable for many happy meetings in coming years."

During the writing of *The Pickwick Papers*, after the death of his sister-in-law Mary, Dickens went for a few months to live at Hampstead; in later years—whilst writing *Bleak House* he spent a summer at Wylde's Farm, near North End.

At Finchley, Barnaby Rudge and his father, after escaping from Newgate "found in a pasture . . . a poor shed with walls of mud, and roof of grass and brambles, built for some cow herd but now deserted. Here they lay down for the rest of the night."

Abel Cottage, the home of Mr. Garland, where Kit and Barbara were employed, was at Finchley.

> To be sure, it was a beautiful little cottage with a thatched roof, and little spires at the gable ends, and pieces of stained glass in some of the windows, almost as large as pocket books.

In 1843, at Cobley's Farm, Finchley, Dickens took lodgings whilst writing a part of *Martin Chuzzlewit*.

III

In the story of *Oliver Twist* as now published, Dickens does not give any clue as to the identity of the town where Oliver Twist was born and brought up; and except for the introduction of the town of Barnet, and the information afforded by Chapter VIII of the story, that the milestone at which Oliver gazed on the morning he ran away, after he had covered more than five miles, told him it was seventy miles to London, we might have added another important incident to the Dickensian history of Rochester.

Oliver Twist was first published as a serial story in *Bentley's Miscellany* which Dickens was editing, and in the opening chapter of the story we are told that the town in question was Mudfog, a name by which Dickens often spoke of Rochester and Chatham.

According to Kitton, the town from which Oliver walked to London was either Peterborough or Grantham, probably the former. It is to be regretted that we have no evidence upon which we can locate the actual original of the seat of Bumbledom. As in the case of Eatanswill with its corruption and dissension, Dickens drew a composite picture, and it would have been extremely injudicious had he fixed upon any particular town by name, for the purpose of the exposures he had in mind.

However in the present instance we have to deal with Barnet as it appeared to Oliver Twist on the seventh morning of his freedom.

Early on the seventh morning after he had left his native place, Oliver limped slowly into the little town of Barnet. The window-shutters were closed; the street was empty; not a soul had awakened to the business of the day.   The sun was rising in all its splended beauty; but the light only served to show the boy his own lonesomeness and desolation, as he sat, with bleeding feet and covered with dust, upon a door-step. . . .

He had been crouching on the step for some time; wondering at the great number of public-houses (every other house in Barnet was a tavern, large or small), gazing listlessly at the coaches as they passed through, and thinking how strange it seemed that they could do, with ease, in a few hours, what it had taken him a whole week of courage and determination beyond his years to accomplish; when he was roused by observing that a boy, who had passed him carelessly some minutes before, had returned, and was now surveying him most earnestly from the opposite side of the way.

The boy was, of course, the Artful Dodger, who accompanied Oliver to London and introduced him to Fagin. What the Artful was doing so far from his usual beat we are not told.   The story continues:

Assisting Oliver to rise, the young gentleman took him to an adjacent chandler's shop, where he purchased a sufficiency of ready-dressed ham and a half-quartern loaf. . . . Taking the bread under his arm, the young gentleman turned into a small public-house, and led the way to a taproom in the rear of the premises.   Here a pot of beer was brought in by direction of the mysterious youth; and Oliver, falling to at his new friend's bidding, made a long and hearty meal, during the progress of which, the strange boy eyed him from time to time with great attention.

We cannot agree with those writers who state the "small public-house" to be the important coaching inn The Red Lion; "every other house in Barnet was a tavern large or small" says Dickens, so we have a very wide range of choice.

The Red Lion Inn on the London side of Barnet was well known to Dickens. Forster recalls the day in March 1838, three days after the birth of his eldest daughter Mamie, to whom Forster became Godfather, when Dickens proposed a rendezvous at the Red Lion at Barnet.

"I can do nothing this morning. What time will you ride? The sooner the better for a good long spell" wrote Dickens, and Forster tells us that they "rode out fifteen miles on the great north road, and, after dining at The Red Lion in Barnet on our way home, distinguished the already memorable day by bringing in both hacks dead lame."

The Inn is still standing, and its prominent sign is a noticeable Barnet landmark.

IV

The journey of Esther Summerson, Ada Clare and Richard Carstone to Bleak House near St. Albans takes us along this same road, which Dickens describes in the following picturesque language:

We went our way through the sunshine and the fresh air, wondering more and more at the extent of the streets, the brilliancy of the shops, the great traffic, and the crowds of people. . . . By-and-bye we began to leave the wonderful city, and to proceed through suburbs which, of themselves, would have made a pretty large town, in my eyes; and at last we got into a real country road again, with windmills, rickyards, milestones, farmers' waggons, scents of old hay, swinging signs and horse troughs; trees, fields, and hedgerows. It was delightful to see the green landscape before us, and the immense metropolis behind; and when a waggon with a train of beautiful horses furnished with red trappings and clear-sounding bells, came by us with its music, I believe we could all three have sung to the bells, so cheerful were the influences around.

"The whole road has been reminding me of my namesake Whittington" said Richard, "and that waggon is the finishing touch."

The waggon was one of Mr. Jarndyce's and the waggoner had a delightful letter of welcome to each of the party from

Bleak House is thus described by Esther:

It was one of those delightfully irregular houses where you go up and down steps out of one room into another, and where you come upon more rooms when you think you have seen all there are, and where there is a bountiful provision of little halls and passages, and where you find still older cottage-rooms in unexpected places, with lattice windows and green growth pressing through them. Mine, which we entered first, was of this kind, with an up-and-down roof, that had more corners in it than I ever counted afterwards, and a chimney (there was a wood-fire on the hearth) paved all around with pure white tiles, in every one of which a bright miniature of the fire was blazing. Out of this room, you went down two steps, into a charming little sitting-room, looking down upon a flower-garden, which room was henceforth to belong to Ada and me.

The interior, it has been pointed out, bears a striking resemblance to Elm Cottage at Petersham where Dickens lived for a short time in 1839.

The prospect from her bedroom window as viewed on the first morning after her arrival is as follows:

The day shone bright upon a cheerful landscape, prominent in which the Old Abbey Church, with its massive tower, threw a softer train of shadow on the view than seemed compatible with its rugged character. But so from rough outsides (I hope I have learnt), serene and gentle influences often proceed.

The garden was found to be "quite a delightful place; in front the pretty avenue and drive by which we had approached . . . at the back the flower garden . . . beyond the flower garden was a kitchen garden and then a paddock, and then a snug little rick yard, and then a dear little farm yard." This is somewhat reminiscent of Gad's Hill Place!

Esther continues:

As to the house itself with its three peaks in the roof; its various shaped windows, some so large, some so small, all so pretty; its trellis work against the south front for the roses and honeysuckle, and its homely, comfortable welcoming look.

There must have been some house in Dickens's mind when he wrote this and there was no such house in St. Albans with which he was familiar. We venture therefore to offer the suggestion that Bleak House was Gad's Hill Place transplanted from the south to the north.

V

When Lady Dedlock disappeared from the Dedlock town house, Inspector Bucket was charged by Sir Leicester to find her; and in order to successfully accomplish his mission, he enlisted the service and sympathy of Esther Summerson, who had only lately discovered that Lady Dedlock was her mother.

They started from London late one night, and after visiting several London police offices, and crossing and recrossing the River they "came at length from the pavement on to dark smooth roads, and began to leave the houses behind" them.

After a while, I recognised the familiar way to Saint Albans. At Barnet, fresh horses were ready for us, and we changed and went on. It was very cold indeed; and the open country was white with snow, though none was falling then.

"An old acquaintance of yours, this road, Miss Summerson" said Mr. Bucket, cheerfully.

Mr. Bucket was continually making enquiries the whole way, and consequently

With all these stoppages, it was between five and six o'clock and we were yet a few miles short of Saint Albans, when he came out of one of these houses and handed me in a cup of tea.

"She's on ahead" announced Bucket. "Passed through here on foot this evening, about eight or nine. . . .

"I heard of her first at the archway toll, over at Highgate, but couldn't make quite sure. Traced her all along, on and off. Picked her up at one place, and dropped her at another; but she's before us now, safe . . ."

"We were soon in Saint Albans, and alighted a little before day. . . . Leaving the carriage at the posting-house and ordering fresh horses to be ready, my companion gave me his arm, and we went towards home."

From Bleak House they went to the brickmakers', which Mr. Bucket was sure had been visited by Lady Dedlock. Jenny was absent; but her husband, and Liz and her husband

were there, and Jenny's husband gave out that Jenny had
"gone up to Lunnon" and the lady in exactly the opposite
direction "Nor'ard, by the high road. Ask on the road if
you doubt me, and see if it warn't so."

Actually Lady Dedlock, in Jenny's dress, had returned
to London; but Bucket was deceived, and forward he went
in search, through the thick blinding snow, thinking she
was making for Chesney Wold. At what was probably
intended to be the George at Grantham (see page 199).
Bucket came to the conclusion he was on a wild goose chase
and surprised Esther very much by ordering the carriage back
to London.

The journey back to London, is vividly described:

> It was three o'clock in the morning when the houses
> outside London did at last begin to exclude the country,
> and to close us in with streets.   We had made our way
> along roads in a far worse condition than when we had
> traversed them by daylight, both the fall and the thaw
> having lasted ever since; but the energy of my companion
> never slackened. . . . Never wavering, he never even
> stopped to make an inquiry until we were within a few
> miles of London . . . and thus we came, at between
> three and four o'clock in the morning, into Islington. . . .
> We stopped in a high-street, where there was a coach-
> stand. My companion paid our two drivers, who were as
> completely covered with splashes as if they had been drag-
> ged along the roads like the carriage itself; and giving them
> some brief direction where to take it, lifted me out of it
> and into a hackney coach he had chosen from the rest.

And so Esther at length reached the burial ground where
her mother whom she did not at first recognise, being
disguised in Jenny's dress, was discovered "cold and
dead."

The flight of Lady Dedlock through roads of such terrible
condition is looked upon as a marvellous performance—and
it finds a parallel with that of Miss Flite who walked from
London to St. Albans; says Mr. Jarndyce in Chapter XXXV,
to Esther:

> Little Miss Flite, hearing a rumour that you were ill,
> made nothing of walking down here—twenty miles, poor
> soul, in a pair of dancing shoes—to inquire. It was
> Heaven's mercy we were at home, or she would have
> walked back again.

There is a reference to St. Albans in *The Uncommercial Traveller*, in a paper entitled "Tramps," when Dickens talks of a request of one of this variety to be directed to Brighton.

A matter of some difficulty at the moment, seeing that the request comes suddenly upon you in the depths of Hertfordshire.   The more you endeavour to indicate where Brighton is . . . the less the devoted father can be made to comprehend . . . whereby, being reduced to extremity, you recommend the faithful parent to begin by going to St. Albans, and present him with half-a-crown.   It does him good, no doubt, but scarcely helps him forward, since you find him lying drunk that same evening in the wheelwright's sawpit under the shed where the felled trees are opposite the sign of the Three Jolly Hedgers.

In *David Copperfield* we are told on one occasion that Steerforth had gone away with one of his Oxford friends to see another who lived near St. Albans, and in *Pickwick* in the illustration of the story of Gabriel Grub, the Abbey depicted bears a decided resemblance to St. Albans Abbey, although the old clergyman who told the tale refers to the Abbey as being in Kent.

Rothamsted, five miles from St. Albans, has an interesting connection with Dickens.   Here Sir John Bennet Lawes the famous scientist established a working men's club to enable the agricultural labourer to enjoy his beer and his pipe apart from the public house.   This naturally interested Dickens and he visited Mr. Lawes, as he then was, and saw over the club.   The outcome of the visit was the article "The poor man and his beer" in *All the Year Round* in 1859.

VI

It is thought that Dunstable was probably the town Dickens had in mind when finding a refuge for Barnaby and his mother as described in Chapter XLV of *Barnaby Rudge*.   He says:

In a small English country town, the inhabitants of which supported themselves by the labour of their hands in plaiting and preparing straw for those who made bonnets and other articles of dress and ornaments from that material . . . dwelt Barnaby and his mother.   Their hut— for it was little more, stood on the outskirt of the town at a short distance from the high road.

Here it was of course that the blind man Stagg tracked them out and obtained money from Mrs. Rudge.

Towcester, 26½ miles distant from Dunstable, is our next place of interest, and we realise that we are now on that part of the road traversed in the last recorded journey of the Pickwickians.

From Bristol Mr. Pickwick had hired a carriage for the purpose of again visiting Mr. Winkle Senior in Birmingham—and an account of the joyous progress of the party, with Bob Sawyer and Sam Weller singing "duets in the dickey" is given on page 93.   Their arrival in Birmingham is referred to later on in the present chapter.

They returned to London in the rain, but were unable to complete the journey in the day.   "At the end of each stage it rained harder than it had done at the beginning."

"I say," remonstrated Bob Sawyer, looking in at the coach window, as they pulled up before the door of the Saracen's Head, Towcester, "this won't do, you know."

"Bless me!" said Mr. Pickwick, just awaking from a nap, "I'm afraid you're wet."

Bob Sawyer was indeed so wet that "his whole apparel shone so . . . that it might have been mistaken for a full set of prepared oilskin."

"I think it's quite impossible to go on to-night," interposed Ben.

"Out of the question, sir," remarked Sam Weller, coming to assist in the conference: "it's a cruelty to animals, sir, to ask 'em to do it.   There's beds here, sir," said Sam addressing his master, "everything clean and comfortable.   Wery good little dinner, sir, they can get ready in half an hour—pair of fowls, sir, and a weal cutlet; French beans, 'taturs, tart, and tidiness.   You'd better stop vere you are, sir, if I might recommend.   Take adwice, sir, as the doctor said."

The host of the Saracen's Head opportunely appeared at this moment, to confirm Mr. Weller's statement relative to the accommodations of the establishment, and to back his entreaties with a variety of dismal conjectures regarding the state of the roads, the doubt of fresh horses being to be had at the next stage, the dead certainty of its raining all night, the equally mortal certainty of its clearing up in the morning, and other topics of inducement familiar to innkeepers.

The Saracen's Head at Towcester had been known since 1831 as the Pomfret Arms, but with this exception, it is the same inn as it was when the Pickwickians welcomed it as a haven.

The candles were brought, the fire was stirred up, and a fresh log of wood thrown on. In ten minutes' time, a waiter was laying the cloth for dinner, the curtains were drawn, the fire was blazing brightly, and everything looked (as everything always does, in all decent English inns) as if the travellers had been expected, and their comforts prepared, for days beforehand.

Here they encountered Mr. Pott of the Eatanswill Gazette, who was on his way to a Political Ball at Birmingham.

"Now, some demon of discord, flying over the Saracen's Head" Dickens informs us, beheld the rival Slurk "established comfortably by the kitchen fire," and prompted Bob Sawyer—who was cold, the fire in their room having gone out, to remark, "It wouldn't be a bad notion to have a cigar by the kitchen fire." So forth they went, when Pott and Slurk encountered one another, with the result that the services of Mr. Weller had to be demanded in order to restore peace, and a pitched battle was the result, in which the carpet bag, fire shovel and meal bag played important parts.

Between Coventry and Towcester (see page 152) Sam Weller had beguiled the party with his dissertation on Postboys and Donkeys: "Never . . . see a dead post-boy, did you? . . . No nor never vill; and there's another thing that no man never see, and that's a dead donkey."

Expatiating upon this learned and remarkable theory, and citing many curious statistical and other facts in its support, Sam Weller beguiled the time until they reached Dunchurch, where a dry postboy and fresh horses were procured; the next stage was Daventry, and the next Towcester; and at the end of each stage it rained harder than it had done at the beginning.

Daventry, of which only a bare mention is made in the above, was the town where the coach bearing Dickens and Phiz left the main road, the Birmingham road, and reached Leamington direct, a saving of eleven miles from the route we are taking.

The next town on the road is Dunchurch, also briefly mentioned in *The Pickwick Papers*, and from there the road to Rugby branches off to the right, and in 2½ miles we reach the town immortalised by Dickens in one of his *Christmas Stories*, as Mugby Junction.

VII

The origin of Mugby Junction is told by Dolby, Dickens's manager for the reading tours, in the following words :

"On this journey a slight accident to the train led to a circumstance which gave Mr. Dickens an opportunity, for which he had long been looking, to write with the object of improving the commissariat at railway stations, which, it may be within the the experience of my readers, was at that time conducted in a most unsatisfactory manner.   On the arrival of the train at Rugby, it was discovered that the carriage in which we were travelling was on fire.   Futile efforts were made to extinguish the flames, and it was at last found necessary to transfer the passengers to another carriage, and, with this view, to detach the burning one from the train, and replace it by another.   Mr. Dickens, not being aware of this, had entered the refreshment room with Mr. Wills to get some coffee. While I was busy superintending the transfer of the light baggage, Mr. Dickens came along the platform in a state of great excitement, and requested me to accompany him to the refreshment-room.   Then, standing in the doorway, and pointing with his finger, he described the picture he particularly wished to impress on my mind.   'You see, Dolby— stove to right hand—torn cocoanut matting on floor—counter across room—coffee-urn—tea-urn—plates of rusks—piles of sawdust, sandwiches and shrunken-up oranges—bottles— tumblers—and glasses on counter—and, *behind* counter, *note particularly* OUR MISSIS. . . .'

"When the train was fairly off again, Mr. Dickens proceeded to explain.   Entering the refreshment-room, he and Mr. Wills had each asked for a cup of coffee, which was supplied to them.   While Wills was feeling in his pocket for some small change wherewith to pay, Mr. Dickens reached across the counter for the sugar and milk, when both articles were suddenly snatched away from him and placed beneath the counter, while his ears were greeted with the remark, made in shrill and shrewish tones, 'You sha'n't have any milk and sugar 'till you two fellows have paid for your coffee.

"This speech was delivered by the woman whom he had pointed out to me as 'our Missis,' and it gave infinite amusement to a page in buttons, who, with that demoniacal spirit which seems to seize some boys at the idea of somebody else 'catching it,' was so overjoyed that he burst out into an uncontrollable fit of laughter.   The discomfited travellers left their coffee on the counter, after an apology for making so free with the sugar-basin.   But it was an evil day for that 'buttons,' for he figured as 'The Boy at Mugby' in the next Christmas number of *All the Year Round*."

Up in a corner of the Down Refreshment Room at Mugby Junction, in the height of twenty-seven cross draughts (I've often counted 'em while they brush the First-Class hair twenty-seven ways), behind the bottles, among the glasses, bounded on the nor'west by the beer, stood pretty far to the right of a metallic object that's at times the tea-urn and at times the soup-tureen, according to the nature of the last twang imparted to its contents which are the same groundwork, fended off from the traveller by a barrier of stale sponge-cakes erected atop of the counter, and lastly exposed sideways to the glare of Our Missis's eye—you ask a Boy so sitiwated, next time you stop in a hurry at Mugby, for anything to drink; you take particular notice that he'll try to seem not to hear you, that he'll appear in a absent manner to survey the Line through a transparent medium composed of your head and body, and that he won't serve you as long as you can possibly bear it.   That's me.

Mugby Junction, "the maddest place in England" according to Barbox Brothers, is described as

A windy place . . . a place replete with shadowy shapes . . . in the black hours of the four-and-twenty. Mysterious goods trains, covered with palls and gliding on like vast weird funerals, conveying themselves guiltily away from the presence of the few lighted lamps, as if their freight had come to a secret and unlawful end.   Half-miles of coal pursuing in a Detective manner, following when they lead, stopping when they stop, backing when they back.   Red-hot embers showering out upon the ground, down this dark avenue, and down the other, as if torturing fires were being raked clear.

"Oh yes, there's a town, sir!   Anyways, there's town enough to put up in," volunteered Lamps and accordingly in "the deadest and buriedest time" of night, Lamps trundled "on a truck through a silent street" the two large black portmanteaus bearing "the legend 'Barbox Brothers' in large white letters on two black surfaces."

And when the owner of the legend had shivered on the pavement half an hour, what time the porter's knocks at the Inn door knocked up the whole town first, and the Inn last, he groped his way into the close air of a shut-up house, and so groped between the sheets of a shut-up bed that seemed to have been expressly refrigerated for him when last made.

This inn at which Barbox Brothers subsequently announced "that he was going to stay on for the present" so as to improve his acquaintance with the Junction, has not been located. Indeed it is probable that Dickens never visited more of Rugby than is compassed by the railway station, so it is vain to seek for the cottages up "a gentle hill of some extent," where at a low window, although the upper, of a cottage that had "but a story of one room above the ground" Phœbe could be seen with "a very bright face, lying on one cheek on the window-sill." It is likewise idle to seek for the house which Barbox Brothers ultimately took to live in to be convenient for the friends he had made at the Junction.

It was the convenient place to live in, for being joined at will to all sorts of agreeable places and persons. So he became settled there, and, his house standing in an elevated situation, it is noteworthy of him in conclusion as Polly herself might (not irreverently) have put it:

There was an Old Barbox who lived on a hill,
And if he ain't gone, he lives there still.

VIII

When Dickens and Phiz went to Leamington, their coach branched off from the Birmingham Road, at Daventry, making direct for Leamington, seventeen miles distant, instead of through Coventry and Kenilworth; a saving of eleven miles.

We cannot agree with some of the writers who have gone before in accepting Coventry as the town where Little Nell showed the figures in Mrs. Jarley's Wax Work, in spite of the fact that one of its two remaining gateways is locally known as Little Nell's Gateway; in this we are pleased that the Librarian of the City of Coventry concurs. Writing in the "Coventry Herald" for December 15th, 1922, he emphatically states, after examination of all the points and claims, that, much as he would like it to be otherwise, Dickens was not thinking of Coventry when writing the story.

Coventry however must not be overlooked in the England of Dickens, as it was here in December 1857 that Dickens gave one of his unpaid readings in aid of the local Mechanics' Institute, prior to embarking on a series of readings for his own personal benefit. The reading was given in the Corn Exchange, now the Empire Theatre.

An interesting outcome of the reading was a presentation made to him on December 4th of the following year, at a public Dinner held at the Castle Hotel, which used to be in Broadgate, of a gold watch as a mark of gratitude for his reading of *A Christmas Carol*. It was a gold repeater of special construction which Dickens, in his speech acknowledging the gift, declared "that it should be thenceforward the inseparable companion of his workings and wanderings, and reckon off the future labours of his days until he should have done with the measurement of time."

In his will, he left this watch as a special item, to his friend and biographer John Forster.

It was at Coventry, $18\frac{1}{4}$ miles from Birmingham that the Pickwickians made their first stop to change horses, on their remarkably wet ride to London. (See pages 148-9).

When they stopped to change at Coventry, the steam ascended from the horses in such clouds as wholly to obscure the hostler, whose voice was however heard to declare from the mist, that he expected the first Gold Medal from the Humane Society on their next distribution of rewards, for taking the postboy's hat off.

The name of the hotel is not mentioned, but it may possibly have been the Castle above referred to.

IX

Kenilworth was visited by Dickens and Phiz from Leamington, where they had stayed the night, as he wrote to his wife:

We started in a post chaise next morning for Kenilworth, with which we were both enraptured, and where I really think we must have lodgings next summer, please God that we are in good health and all goes well. You cannot conceive how delightful it is. To read among the ruins in fine weather would be a perfect luxury.

In his diary we find the following entry at this time:

Away to Kenilworth—delightful—beautiful beyond expression. Mem: what a summer resort—three months lie about the ruins—books—thinking—seriously turn this over next year.

But next year saw him spending his summer holidays at Broadstairs, and so far as we know Kenilworth was forgotton until *Dombey and Son* was written some eight years later, when Mr. Dombey whilst visiting Leamington commissioned Major Bagstock to take a note to Mrs. Skewton begging her "and her amiable and accomplished daughter" to accompany them for a ride to Kenilworth. Even then the charms of Kenilworth are dismissed in a few words:

A stroll among the haunted ruins of Kenilworth and more rides to more points of view; most of which, Mrs. Skewton reminded Mr. Dombey, Edith had already sketched, as he had seen in looking over her drawings; brought the day's expedition to a close.

X

When Dickens arrived at Leamington with Phiz on the 29th October, 1838, he put up at Copp's Royal Hotel (demolished a few years after his visit), where he afterwards lodged Mr. Dombey, and here, as he wrote to his wife:

We found a roaring fire, and elegant dinner, a snug room and capital beds all ready for us at Leamington, after a very agreeable but very cold ride.

Mr. Dombey and the Major went to Leamington by train as far as Birmingham, the London to Birmingham railway having been opened in 1838 and Chapter XX of *Dombey and Son* contains an account of a journey by rail; but interesting as it is, one can see that Dickens's heart was not in this mode of travelling; the road of iron had no romance for him.

Away with a shriek and a roar, and a rattle, through the fields, through the woods, through the corn, through the hay, through the chalk, through the clay, through the rock, among objects close at hand, and almost in the grasp, ever flying from the traveller, and a deceitful distance ever moving slowly with him; like as in the track of the remorseless monster, Death.

At Birmingham "Post horses were harnessed and the carriage ready" to take them to their destination, and when evening came on it found them trotting through the green and leafy road near Leamington . . . to the Royal Hotel, where rooms and dinner had been ordered.

The next morning in the vicinity of the Pump Room, Mrs. Granger and her daughter Edith were encountered, with the result that all readers of the book know full well.

On the next day but one Mr. Dombey and the Major encountered the Honourable Mrs. Skewton and her daughter in the Pump Room, on the day after that they met them again very near the place where they had met them first.

Subsequently a visit was paid to Mrs. Skewton's lodgings which were "fashionable enough and dear enough, but rather limited in point of space and conveniences; so that the Honourable Mrs. Skewton being in bed had her feet in the window and her head in the fire-place."

The maid was "quartered in a closet within the drawing room, so extremely small, that, to avoid developing the whole of its accommodation, she was obliged to writhe in and out of the door like a beautiful serpent.

Dickens gave two readings in Leamington on November 2nd, 1858, and wrote, "Little Leamington is represented as the dullest and worst of audiences, I found it very good indeed, even in the morning."

His second—and last—visit to the town was on January 1st, 1862, when he again read in the same hall, the Music Hall, Bath Street.

XI

Of Warwick, Dickens wrote to his wife on November 1st, 1838:

We went on to Warwick Castle, which is an ancient building, newly restored and possessing no very great attraction beyond a fine view and some beautiful pictures.

Eight years later it proved a great attraction to Mr. Dombey who took Mrs. Skewton and her daughter Edith for a ride there from Leamington.

"The Castle is charming" said Mrs. Skewton, "associations of the Middle Ages—and all that—which is so truly exquisite."

Edith confessed to have been to Warwick several times, but that did not deter her mother from expressing her desire that they should accompany Mr. Dombey:

cleared up, through miles of cinder paths, and blazing furnaces, and roaring steam engines, and such a mass of dirt,
gloom, and misery, as I never before witnessed."

It is very probable however that Dickens had visited
Birmingham at least prior to, or during, the writing of *The
Pickwick Papers*, for towards the end of the travels of Mr.
Pickwick and his friends, they made a journey to Birmingham
for the express purpose of visiting Mr. Winkle Senior in
respect to his son's love affair with Arabella Allen.

The boisterous ride of the party from Bristol to Birmingham
and thence to London is dealt with elsewhere (see pages 93
and 148) but of their coming into Birmingham we read:

> It was quite dark when Mr. Pickwick roused himself
> sufficiently to look out of the window. The straggling
> cottages by the roadside, the dingy hue of every object
> visible, the murky atmosphere, the paths of cinders and
> brick-dust, the deep red glow of furnace fires in the dis-
> tance, the volumes of dense smoke issuing heavily forth
> from high toppling chimneys, blackening and obscuring
> everything around; the glare of distant lights, the pond-
> erous waggons which toiled along the road, laden with
> flashing rods of iron, or piled with heavy goods—all
> betoken their rapid approach to the great working town
> of Birmingham.

They "rattled through the narrow thoroughfares leading
to the heart of the turmoil" and drove briskly "through the
open streets, and past the handsome and well-lighted shops
which intervene between the outskirts of the town and the
Old Royal Hotel."

The Old Royal Hotel, considerably altered externally,
still exists in Temple Row.

On their arrival at the Royal Hotel they were shown into a
comfortable apartment, and Mr. Pickwick at once propounded a question to the waiter concerning the whereabout
of Mr. Winkle's residence :

"Close by, sir," said the waiter, "not about five hundred
yards, sir. Mr. Winkle is a wharfinger, sir, at the canal, sir.
Private residence is not—oh dear no, sir, *not* five hundred
yards, sir."

The district of the Old Wharf is doubtless that referred to,
and the house almost adjacent to the Old Wharf at the corner
of Easy Row and Edmund Street which, together with parts
of the Old Wharf itself was demolished some years ago, used
to be called Mr. Winkle's house.

Dickens describes the house as follows:

About a quarter of a mile off, in a quiet, substantial-looking street, stood an old red-brick house with three steps before the door, and a brass plate upon it, bearing in fat Roman capitals, the words, "Mr. Winkle." The steps were very white, and the bricks were very red, and the house was very clean; and here stood Mr. Pickwick Mr. Benjamin Allen, and Mr. Bob Sawyer, as the clock struck ten.

The party was viewed somewhat askance by the servant maid, but ultimately ushered into:
"A floor-clothed back parlour, half office and half dressing-room, in which the principal useful and ornamental articles of furniture, were a desk, a wash-hand stand, a shaving glass . . . a high stove, four chairs, a table, and an old eight day clock."

According to photographs the demolished house at the corner of Easy Row had six steps before the door, whereas Mr. Winkle's had only three, and another claimant has now come forward who occupies the premises at No. 11, which has the necessary three steps and therefore claims to be the original.

In April 1840, Dickens with his wife were again in the Midlands and Forster joined them and recounts an amusing incident:

The day of the first publication of *Master Humphrey* (Saturday, April 4th), had by this time come, and according to the rule observed in his two other great ventures, he left town with Mrs. Dickens on Friday the 3rd. With Maclise we had been together at Richmond the previous night; and I joined him at Birmingham the day following, with news of the sale of the whole sixty thousand copies to which the first working had been limited, and of orders already in hand for ten thousand more! The excitement of the success somewhat lengthened our holiday; and, after visiting Shakespeare's house at Stratford, and Johnson's at Lichfield, we found our resources so straitened in returning, that, employing as our messenger of need his younger brother Alfred, who had joined us from Tamworth where he was a student-engineer, we had to pawn our gold watches at Birmingham.

That they also visited the Black Country between Birmingham and Wolverhampton is evident from a letter of Dickens "to nearly six thousand people" and the design they had generously helped.

The presentation was made at a breakfast held at the Hen and Chickens Hotel in New Street on the Saturday following his last reading.

Dickens's next visit to Birmingham was as a paid reader in 1858, when on October 18th, he appeared at the Music Hall in Broad Street, now converted into the Prince of Wales Theatre. He appeared here for three nights, giving three selections each night occupying a little over two hours.

On October 26th 1859, he gave a one night reading also at the same place, and he was again reading at the Music Hall on the 30th and 31st December, 1861.

In 1866, on May 10th, he appeared as a reader at the Town Hall, when a curious blunder was made, as he wrote to Miss Hogarth at the time.

We had a tremendous hall at Birmingham last night, £230 odd, 2100 people; and I made a most ridiculous mistake. Had Nickleby on my list to finish with, instead of Trial. Read Nickleby with great go, and the people remained. Went back again at 10 o'clock, and explained the accident; but said if they liked I would give them the Trial. They did like;—and I had another half hour of it in that enormous place.

On February 13th 1867, he was again at the Town Hall and his Farewell readings were given at the same place on the 1st and 2nd April, 1869.

This was not his last visit to Birmingham, for on September 27th 1869, he delivered his inaugural address at the Town Hall as President of the Institute for which he had given his first public reading. Then in the following year, on the 6th January, he distributed the prizes to the successful students at the Institute.

XIV

Dickens first became acquainted with Wolverhampton during the late autumn of 1838 when accompanied by Hablot K. Browne (Phiz) he visited it in the tour to which we have already referred. They had been to Leamington, Warwick, Kenilworth and Stratford-on-Avon and finding it impracticable to get from Stratford to Shrewsbury by way of Bridgnorth, as there were no coaches, Dickens wrote to his wife from the Lion Hotel, Shrewsbury on November 1st, 1838:

We were compelled to come here by way of Birmingham and Wolverhampton, starting at eight o'clock through a cold, wet fog, and travelling, when the day had cleared up, through miles of cinder paths and blazing furnaces and roaring steam engines, and such a mass of dirt, gloom, and misery, as I have never before witnessed.

In Dickens's Diary for 1838, now in the Victoria and Albert Museum, and not published in any complete form, there is this reference under date October 31st:

> Journey to Shrewsbury—Birmingham—Factory Road—White Lion.

Kitton, in " The Dickens Country," on the authority of this Diary, says that Dickens spent the night at the White Lion, in Factory Road, Wolverhampton. This is not correct, as the Diary clearly shows that the day of October 31st was spent in travelling from Stratford-on-Avon to Birmingham (where 4s. was spent in mulled wine!) and thence to Shrewsbury, where, as confirmed by the letter written to his wife on November 1st, the night was spent. There is no Factory Road in Wolverhampton—nor was there one in 1838. The note " Factory Road " is surely a description of the road between Birmingham and Wolverhampton; and the meaning of " White Lion," if it is not a note of the inn at Shrewsbury where he stayed (actually the Lion) may possibly refer to the White Lion Inn at Wolverhampton where a meal may have been taken.

This hostelry stood next door to the present Town Hall, which itself was built on the site of an old inn, the Red Lion, which ceased to exist as an inn at about the very time Dickens visited the town.

The journey was continued via Tong to Shrewsbury, and Tong, as we all know, has been immortalised as the last resting-place of Little Nell.

In April, 1840, on the publication of the first part of *Master Humphrey's Clock*, Dickens and his wife, in accordance with a rule he had observed with his two previous publications, went for a holiday into the Midlands, being joined at Birmingham by his friend and biographer, John Forster, and together they visited Stratford and Lichfield.

It is highly probable, too, that Wolverhampton was again visited in this excursion, and Tong, too, perhaps, for later on, when writing the account of the flight of Little Nell in the October following, he wrote to Forster: " You will

brought him to level ground.   Rich also is the Swan in
wholesome well-cooked dinner, and in tender chine of
beef, so brave in size that the mining of all the powerful
Ironmasters is but a sufficient outlet for its gravy.   Rich
in things wholesome and sound and unpretending is the
Swan, except that we would recommend the good bird not
to dip its beak into its sherry.   Under the change from
snow and wind to hot soup, drawn red curtains, fire and
candle, we observe our demonstrations at first to be very
like the engine's at the little station; but they subside, and
we dine vigorously—another tribute to a winter walk!

The bill of the Swan is to be commended as not out of
proportion to its plumage; and now, our walking shoes
being dried and baked, we must get them on somehow—
for the rosy driver with his carriage and pair who is to
take us among the fires on the blasted heath by Bilston
announces from under a few shawls, and the collars of
three or four coats, that we must be going.   Away we go,
obedient to the summons, and, having taken leave of the
lady in the Swan's bar opposite the door, who is almost
rustled out of her glass case and blown upstairs whenever
the door opens, we are presently in outer darkness grinding
the snow.

The article concludes with an account of a night ride by
carriage through the blazing furnace country between Wolverhampton and Bilston, from which place Dickens took train
back into Birmingham.

Of his first Reading in Wolverhampton, on August 11th,
1858, Dickens wrote to his daughter:

A wonderful audience last night at Wolverhampton.
If such a thing can be, they were even quicker and more
intelligent than the audience I had in Edinburgh.   They
were so wonderfully good and were so much on the alert
this morning at nine o'clock for another reading, that we
are going back there at about our Bradford time.   I never
saw such people and the local agent would take no money
and charge no expenses of his own.

This latter fact was later on communicated to John
Forster in a letter in which Dickens wrote:

Did I tell you that the agents for our tickets who are
also book-sellers, say very generally that the readings
decidedly increase the sale of the books they are taken
from?   We were first told this by a Mr. Parke, a wealthy

old gentleman in a very large way at Wolverhampton who did all the business for love, and would not take a farthing. Since then, we have constantly come upon it.

This Mr. Parke had his place of business in High Street, and lived at The Deanery, where it is said Dickens visited him on the occasion of a subsequent visit.

Dickens stayed at the Swan on the night of this reading, and from it wrote a letter to Wilkie Collins, saying: "This is a stupid letter, but I write it before dressing to read, and you know what a brute I am at such times." Curiously enough the letter is addressed as from the Swan at Worcester; he was at Worcester the night before, and no doubt that was how the error occurred; there is no Swan Hotel in Worcester.

It was during the first visit that " in consequence of the illustrious author honouring the town with his presence " *Oliver Twist* was played at the theatre, with John L. Toole in the part of the Artful Dodger.

The theatre was situated at the bottom of the yard of the Swan; its site is now partly covered by the cinema.

When he paid the promised second visit to the town, on the 3rd November of the same year, he came on there from Leamington, and wrote to Miss Hogarth:

The evening being fine, and blue being to be seen in the sky beyond the smoke, we expect to have a full hall. . . . We came through a part of the Black Country that you know and it looked at its blackest. All the furnaces seemed in full blast, and all the coal-pits to be working. It is market day here, and the ironmasters are standing out in the street (where they always hold high change) making such an iron hum and buzz, that they confuse me horribly. In addition there is a bellman announcing something—not the readings, I beg to say—and there is an excavation being made in the centre of the open place, for a statue, or a pump, or a lamp-post, or something or other, round which all the Wolverhampton boys are yelling and struggling.

This letter was addressed from " Wolverhampton third November 1858," and it is probable that he again stayed at the Swan.

His third reading at Wolverhampton was on January 23rd, 1867, after a very bitter experience at Chester, where the reading was given in a terrible " snowstorm and a fall of ice. . . . It was the worst weather I ever knew " Dickens wrote

The only mention of Shrewsbury in the novels, has reference to its famous school, and is to be found in *A Tale of Two Cities*, where Stryver thus refers to his old schoolfellow:

> " The old Sydney Carton of Shrewsbury School . . . up one minute and down the next; now in spirits, and now in despondency. . . . Before Shrewsbury and at Shrewsbury and ever since Shrewsbury . . . you have fallen into your rank and I have fallen into mine."

XVI

It is thirty miles to Llangollen from Shrewsbury, and it was here that Dickens and Phiz stayed at the Hand Hotel the night of November 1st, 1838. The Diary described the journey thus:

> Post to Llangollen—pass 2 aqueducts—beautiful road between the mountains—old Abbey at top of mountains. Denis Brien or Rock Castle. Hand Hotel, Mrs. Phillips. Good.

The aqueduct of Pont-y-Lycylltan is seen on the left just before reaching Llangollen and close by is the Valle Crucis Abbey to which Dickens refers.

The next stage of the journey was to Capel Curig, and then the next day the party reached Chester, where apparently the whole of Sunday was spent; but the diary is quite lacking in details, being simply a record of the cost of " Posting to Bangor £1/1/–. Bill at Capel Curig £1/10/–. Posting to Chester £1/11/6."

XVII

Chester finds no place in the topography of Dickens's novels; but he read here at the Music Hall, in Northgate Street, now a cinema, on August 13th, 1858, and again on January 30th, 1862, and no doubt the picturesque and historical old town was previously well known to him; according to a letter to his wife, quoted on page 168, he paid a visit to it during the tour he took with Phiz in the late autumn of 1838, but we do not possess any details.

Dickens was again reading in Chester on January 22nd, 1867, when he " read in a snowstorm and a fall of ice." A letter written at the time says, " I think it was the worst weather I ever saw. Nevertheless the people were enthusiastic."

On the afternoon of the day of the reading he wrote to his daughter:

I have seldom seen a place look more hopelessly frozen up than this place does. The hall is like a methodist chapel in low spirits and with a cold in its head. . . . This seems to be a very nice hotel, but it is an extremely cold one. . . . The sitting room has two large windows in it, down to the ground, and facing due east. The adjoining bedroom (mine) has also two large windows in it, down to the ground, and facing due east. The very large doors are opposite the large windows, and I feel as if I were something to eat in a pantry.

We are enlightened as to the name of this hotel by George Dolby, Dickens's Business Manager for the Reading Tours. In his book, " Charles Dickens as I Knew Him," Dolby says:

Arrived at Chester, we went to the Queen's Hotel, and here I left Mr. Dickens in what had the appearance of a most comfortable sitting room, with a blazing fire. . . . I had been absent about two hours, and on my return found him sitting on the hearthrug in front of the fire with my Turkish fez on his head, to protect him from a strong draught between the door and a double French window. . . . I asked him how he felt, " Like something good to eat being kept cool in a larder. What do you think I look like?" he asked. " Like an old chief " I replied, " but without his pipe." The idea of his looking like a chief seemed to please him and from that time I always addressed him by that name, which was generally adopted by his associates, and proclaimed as his title in the office of *All the Year Round*.

Chester was again visited—in a private capacity only—in April, 1868, whilst on the reading tour, when he spent a week-end there after reading at Leeds, and prior to a series in the Lancashire towns. Dolby tells us how the sojourn at " Chester, with its old walls and picturesque streets promised a pleasant change," and was indeed very beneficial to the delicate state of Dickens's health, but he had a very bad night there, and this led him to decide to rest on the decision of his medical adviser, which, received a little later at Preston, cancelled the remainder of the readings of the tour.

Dolby gives us an account of the drive taken by Dickens and himself from Chester, to the picturesque town of Mold, during which discussion arose as to the future of the readings and, Dolby tells us, he " had an instinctive feeling that the travelling career was at an end, if not the reading career also."

And so they left the Camden Town district behind them and proceeded in the direction of Hampstead.

> At length these streets becoming more straggling yet, dwindled and dwindled away, until there were only small garden patches bordering the road. . . . Then, came the public-house; . . . with tea-gardens and a bowling green, spurning its old neighbour with the horse-trough where the waggons stopped; then, fields; and then, some houses, one by one, of goodly size with lawns, . . . then, came a turnpike; then fields again with trees and haystacks; then, a hill; and on the top of that the traveller might stop, and—looking back at old Saint Paul's looming through the smoke, . . . might feel at last that he was clear of London.

By the way they had come it must have been quite six miles to the top of the Heath, where they refreshed themselves by the water hard by.

The journey was resumed along by roads through Cricklewood to Ealing, a very rural district in those days; and and then by the main road through Southall and Hayes to Uxbridge, as Dickens so excellently describes.

> They were now in the open country; the houses were very few and . . . often miles apart. Occasionally they came upon a cluster of poor cottages, some with a chair or low board put across the open door to keep the scrambling children from the road, others shut up close while all the family were working in the fields. . . . The farm-yard passed, then came the little inn; the humbler beer-shop; and the village tradesman's. . . . The church then peeped out modestly from a clump of trees; then there were a few more cottages; then the cage, and pound, and not unfrequently, on a bank by the wayside, a deep old dusty well. Then came the trim-hedged fields on either hand, and the open road again. They walked all day, and slept that night at a small cottage where beds were let to travellers.

This was at Uxbridge and the two travellers had completed twenty miles of their journey.

III

Dickens's description of the second day's journey was but brief. It is probable they continued mostly along the turnpike road that leads to Banbury, passing through Chalfont St. Peters, Amersham and Wendover, a total distance of twenty and a half miles from Uxbridge.

Next morning they were afoot again, and though jaded at first and very tired, recovered before long and proceeded briskly forward. . . . It was nearly five o'clock in the afternoon, when, drawing near another cluster of labourers' huts, the child looked wistfully in each, doubtful at which to ask for permission to rest awhile, and buy a draught of milk. . . . At length she stopped at one where the family were seated round a table—chiefly because there was an old man sitting in a cushioned chair beside the hearth, and she thought he was a grandfather and would feel for hers.

This was no doubt near Wendover, five miles from Aylesbury, which distance fits in with a later observation. The place must have been a fairly large one with a church, since the old cottager refers to his dead soldier son in these words:

He always said he'd be buried near the sun-dial he used to climb upon when he was a baby, did my poor boy, and his words come true—you can see the place with your own eyes; we've kept the turf up, ever since.

It was " a matter of a good five mile " to the next town or village, and the grandfather urged that they should get there that night. " Further on, further on, darling, further away if we walk till midnight." Thus showing that his readiness to do a " good five mile " after five o'clock at night, with a long day's journey already to his credit, proves that twenty or twenty-five miles a day was not an impossible distance for the elder of the two wanderers.

They had gone for a mile or so, when they got a lift in a cart to the next town, and were put down at a " path . . . leading through the churchyard."

It was Aylesbury they had reached. The present church has been twice restored since that day, once in 1848 and again in 1869.

The old man and the child quitted the gravel path, and strayed among the tombs. . . . As they passed behind the church they heard voices near at hand, and presently came on those who had spoken.

Surprise has often been expressed that Codlin and Short should have been allowed to make such use as they did of a

We should consider it likely that " Grinder's Lot " had decided to stay the night at Westbury, 4½ miles from Buckingham. Codlin, however, would not go more than a mile and a half to an inn he knew; he declared he would " put up at the Jolly Sandboys and nowhere else," and so the two parties went their different ways and our wanderers arrived at the Jolly Sandboys.

The Jolly Sandboys was a small road-side inn of pretty ancient date, with a sign, representing three Sandboys increasing their jollity with as many jugs of ale and bags of gold, creaking and swinging on its post on the opposite side of the road.

Unfortunately the identity of the Jolly Sandboys is lost— even supposing that Dickens had any particular inn on the road, in view. But we can recall the curious company assembled at supper, and those who joined them later.

v

On the fourth day, the party covered 16 miles to Banbury.

Meanwhile, they were drawing near the town where the races were to begin next day; . . . On every piece of waste or common ground, some small gambler drove his noisy trade and bellowed to the idle passers-by to stop and try their chance. It was dark before they reached the town itself, and long indeed the few last miles had been. Here all was tumult and confusion; the streets were filled with throngs of people. . . . They at length passed through the town and made for the racecourse, which was upon an open heath, situated on an eminence, a full mile distant from its furthest bounds. . . . After a scanty supper, . . . she and the old man lay down to rest in a corner of a tent and slept despite the busy preparations that were going on around them all night long.

Soon after sunrise, the next day, Nelly was up plucking the wild flowers in the fields to make into nosegays. " I'm going to try to sell some, these three days of the races," she explained.

Codlin aroused the suspicions of Little Nell, by the overtures he made accompanied with the assurances, "Codlin's your friend "; and fearing the Punch and Judy Men would take steps to have them delivered up to their friends, Nell resolved to get away from them at the earliest opportunity but both kept her well in sight for the greater part of the day; at length, however, an opportunity presented itself:

> They made a path through booths and carriages and throngs of people, . . . and creeping under the brow of the hill at a quick pace, made for the open fields . . . and at length reached the public road.   Taking their way along it for a short distance, they came to a lane, . . . A broken finger-post announced that this led to a village three miles off; and thither they resolved to bend their steps.

Warmington, five miles from Banbury, on the main Warwick road, was the village they were now approaching.

> The miles appeared so long that they sometimes thought they must have missed their road.   But at last, to their great joy, it led downward in a steep descent, with over-hanging banks over which the footpaths led; and the clustered houses of the village peeped out from the woody hollow below.   It was a very small place.   The men and boys were playing at cricket on the green. . . . There was but one old man in the little garden before his cottage, and him they were timid of approaching, for he was the schoolmaster, and had "School" written up over his window in black letters on a white board.

Nell enquired of him to be directed to a shelter for the night, but he was so struck with her youth, that he offered them the hospitality of his own cottage.

The kind schoolmaster befriended the travellers for two nights, Nell endearing herself to all the little village.   It was the morning of the seventh day of their travels that they said farewell to the schoolmaster and "turned away, walking slowly and often looking back, until they could see him no more.   At length they had left the village far behind, and even lost sight of the smoke among the trees.   They trudged onward now, at a quicker pace, resolving to keep the main road, and go wherever it might lead them."

VI

From Warmington it is 14 miles to Warwick and the road is, as Dickens describes it, a long, uninteresting one, with but few villages on the way.

But main roads stretch a long, long way.   With the exception of two or three inconsiderable clusters of cottages which they passed, without stopping, and one lonely

Through the straight streets, and narrow crooked outskirts, their trembling feet passed quickly. Up the steep hill too, crowned by the old grey castle, they toiled with rapid steps, and had not once looked behind. But as they drew nearer the ruined walls, the moon rose in all her gentle glory, and, from their venerable age, garlanded with ivy, moss, and waving grass, the child looked back upon the sleeping town, deep in the valley's shade, and on the far off river with its winding track of light, and on the distant hills.

Dickens must have had Kenilworth in his mind when writing the above description; it is five miles from Warwick, but hardly in the line of route.

They continued to walk the night through, and it was not until the sun began to shine in the sky that "they laid them down to sleep, upon a bank, hard by some water."

They were awakened by the sound of voices, proceeding from some men in "a long heavy boat which had come close to the bank."

This was on the banks of the Warwick and Birmingham Canal; the men offered them a lift, which was accepted, and Nell and her grandfather were soon "on board, and gliding smoothly down the canal." Canal travel has been ousted by the railway and the motor, and it is of interest to note that this is the only description of travelling by canal that Dickens has given us.

At a kind of wharf late in the afternoon they stopped for a time. Here Nell made a few small purchases and the men after spending some time drinking in the public house, proceeded on their journey, not without bringing on board a quantity of beer and spirits, which resulted in a very uproarious night, during which Nell was reluctantly compelled to sing songs to the three bargemen.

In the afternoon of the next day they arrived at the end of the canal journey, in the very heart of Birmingham.

They had for some time been gradually approaching the place for which they were bound. The water had become thicker and dirtier; . . . the paths of coal-ash and huts of staring brick, marked the vicinity of some great manufacturing town; while scattered streets and houses and smoke from distant furnaces, indicated that they were already in the outskirts. Now, the clustered roofs, and piles of buildings trembling with the working of engines and dimly resounding with their shrieks and throbbings

KENILWORTH CASTLE

TONG CHURCH

[*Photos by T. W. Tyrrell*

the tall chimneys vomiting forth a black vapour, which hung in a dense ill-favoured cloud above the housetops and filled the air with gloom; the clank of hammers beating upon iron, the roar of busy streets and noisy crowds; . . . announced the termination of their journey. The boat floated into the wharf to which it belonged. . . . The child and her grandfather . . . passed through a dirty lane into a crowded street and stood amid its din and tumult.

The wharf at which they stopped is usually pointed out as the Old Wharf, the one connected with Mr. Winkle Senior in *Pickwick* and the terminus of the canal from Coventry. The canal from Warwick however passed Bordesley Wharf from which "through a dirty lane" Nell and her grandfather would soon find themselves in "a crowded street" such as High Street or New Street. Mr. G. W. Davis in "The Dickensian" for October 1909 states that several iron furnaces were in those days to be met with in the Stafford Street and Dale End districts and it was no doubt one of these which afforded the travellers shelter for the night, as Dickens goes on to describe.

They did not progress very far that day, but kept to the streets near to the wharf, for we read: "Evening came on. They were still wandering up and down."

Penniless and desolate they "retraced their steps . . ." and went back to the wharf hoping to find "the boat in which they had come, and to be allowed to sleep on board that night. But here again they were disappointed, for the gate was closed, and some fierce dogs, barking at their approach, obliged them to retreat."

But they found "a deep old doorway—very dark, but quite dry and warm too" and here they met the poor furnace watcher who offered them a rest for the night before the furnace fire, in "the poorest and most wretched quarter of the town."

In this strange place and on the heap of ashes Nell "slept as peacefully, as if the room had been a palace chamber, and the bed, a bed of down."

The next morning the man enquired whither they were going.

She told him that they sought some distant country place, remote from towns or even other villages, and with a faultering tongue inquired what road they would do best to take.

"I know little of the country, he said, shaking his head, for such as I pass all our lives before our furnace doors, to the tinkling of the horses' bells, the occasional smacking of the carter's whip, the smooth rolling of the great broad wheels, the rattle of the harness, the cheery good-nights of passing travellers jogging past on little short-stepped horses—all made pleasantly indistinct by the thick awning, which seemed made for lazy listening under, till one fell asleep! . . . The waking from a sound nap as the mail came dashing past like a highway comet, with gleaming lamps and rattling hoofs, and visions of a guard behind, standing up to keep his feet warm, and of a gentleman in a fur cap opening his eyes and looking wild and stupefied— the stopping at the turnpike where the man was gone to bed, and knocking at the door until he answered with a smothered shout from under the bedclothes in the little room above. . . . The cold sharp interval between night and morning— the distant streak of light widening and spreading, and turning from grey to white, and from white to yellow, and from yellow to burnng red. . . . The coming to a town—people busy in the market; light carts and chaises round the tavern yard; tradesmen standing at their doors; men running horses up and down the street for sale; . . . the night coach changing horses—the passengers cheerless, cold, ugly, and discontented, with three month's growth of hair in one night—the coachman fresh as from a bandbox and exquisitely beautiful by contrast;—so much bustle, so many things in motion, such a variety of incidents—when was there a journey with so many delights as that journey in the waggon!

From Wolverhampton to Tong is only 9½ miles, but Dickens enlarged his canvas and pictured the journey as covering several of the towns he had visited on his earlier journey in this direction. Thus Shifnal, four miles beyond Tong, is described, also Shrewsbury; for Dickens makes the journey last three days. Some maps purporting to show the route of Little Nell, actually represent the journey as being to Shrewsbury and back to Tong, but of course that is a quite unreasonable supposition. However, if we become acquainted with these Shropshire towns, we will see how accurate were Dickens's descriptions.

At the end of the first day

They came to a large town, where the waggon stopped and where they spent a night. They passed a large church; and in the streets were a number of old houses, built of a kind of earth or plaster, crossed and re-crossed in a great many directions with black beams, which gave them a remarkable and very ancient look. The doors, too, were arched and low, some with oaken portals and quaint benches, where the former inhabitants had sat on summer evenings. The windows were latticed in little diamond panes, that seemed to wink and blink upon the passengers as if they were dim of sight. They had long since got clear of the smoke and furnaces, except in one or two solitary instances, where a factory planted among fields withered the space about it, like a burning mountain. When they had passed through this town, they entered again upon the country, and began to draw near their place of destination.

"It was not so near, however but that they spent another night upon the road" we read, not of necessity, but because the schoolmaster wanted to arrive in trim order!; and on "a fine, clear, autumn morning" they arrived at their destination. "'See—here's the church' cried the delighted schoolmaster.'"

They admired everything—the old grey porch, the mullioned windows, the venerable grave-stones dotting the green church-yard, the ancient tower, the very weathercock; the brown thatched roofs of cottage, barn and homestead, peeping from among the trees; the stream that rippled by the distant watermill; the blue Welsh mountains far away. It was for such a spot the child had wearied in the dense, dark, miserable haunts of labour. . . . It was a very aged, ghostly place; the church had been built many hundreds of years ago, and had once had a convent or monastery attached; for arches in ruins, remains of oriel windows, and fragments of blackened walls, were yet standing; while other portions of the old building, which had crumbled away and fallen down, were mingled with the church-yard earth and over-grown with grass, as if they too claimed a burying-place and sought to mix their ashes with the dust of men. Hard by these gravestones of dead years, and forming a part of the ruin which some pains had been taken to render habitable in modern times, were two small dwellings with sunken windows and oaken doors, fast hastening to decay, empty and desolate.

In one of these houses the schoolmaster was to dwell, the other was to be for Nell and her grandfather; for Nell was to have charge of the church keys and to open and close the church for services and show it to visitors.

The weather was intensely and bitterly cold; a great deal of snow fell from time to time; and the wind was intolerably keen. Mr. Squeers got down at almost every stage—to stretch his legs as he said—and as he always came back from such excursions with a very red nose, and composed himself to sleep directly, there is reason to suppose that he derived great benefit from the process.

This was reflected in a Christmas story, *The Holly Tree Inn*, when the jilted writer of the story says:

I had resolved to make a visit to a certain spot (which I need not name) on the farther borders of Yorkshire. It was endeared to me by my having first seen Angela at a farmhouse in that place, and my melancholy was gratified by the idea of taking a wintery leave of it before my expatriation.

His destination was the same as ours, Greta Bridge, and the coach ride so graphically described in the story doubtless expressed Dickens's own experiences.

The lonely day wore on, and I dozed it out, as a lonely traveller does. I was warm and valiant after eating and drinking,—particularly after dinner; cold and depressed at all other times. . . . While we changed horses the guard and coachman went stumping up and down the road, printing off their shoes in the snow, and poured so much liquid consolation into themselves without being any the worse for it, that I began to confound them, as it darkened again, with two great white casks standing on end. . . . All night long we went on in this manner. Thus we came round the clock, upon the Great North Road, to the performance of Auld Lang Syne by day again. And it snowed and snowed, and still it snowed, and never left off snowing.

II

The journey of Nicholas Nickleby into Yorkshire started from the Saracen's Head at Snow Hill, close to where now stands a modern building bearing that name and recording that fact in its history by means of a plaque on either side of the doorway, which is surmounted by a bust of Dickens.

The Coach, we read, was soon "rattling over the stones of Smithfield" and in due course got to Islington, where at the Peacock it stopped, thus enabling Nicholas to find a safer seat for the little boys in his charge who had been in danger of being jerked off the coach owing to the jolting.

Off she goes! And off she did go,—if coaches be feminine—amidst a loud flourish from the guard's horn, and the calm approval of all the judges of coaches and coach-horses congregated at the Peacock, but more especially of the helpers, who stood, with the cloths over their arms, watching the coach till it disappeared, and then lounged admiringly stablewards, bestowing various gruff encomiums on the beauty of the turn-out.

Until Eaton Socon was reached, 55 miles from London, there is no mention of the towns of Barnet, Hatfield, Stevenage, and Biggleswade, or any other place on the way.

Dickens must have been very familiar with Hatfield, although we do not know the reason for his visits there; the only record is in the Diary to which we have already referred, where on Monday, October 29th, 1838, we find the entry: "Hatfield—expenses on Saturday £1 12s." From this it would appear that Phiz was also his companion on this occasion.

Hatfield figures prominently in one portion of *Oliver Twist*.

Bill Sikes "shaped his course for Hatfield" in his flight from London after the murder of Nancy, and "turned down the hill by the church of the quiet village and plodding along the little street, crept into a small public-house, whose scanty light had guided them to the spot. There was a fire in the tap-room, and some country-labourers were drinking before it. They made room for the stranger, but he sat down in the furthest corner, and ate and drank alone."

The present main road leaves the old part of the little town, on the right, and the above description shows that Dickens knew Hatfield well.

The quaint old Eight Bells, is said to have been the "small public house" where the "antic fellow, half pedlar, half mountebank" sold the "stoof" that was the

"Infallible and invaluable composition for removing . . . wine-stains, fruit-stains, beer-stains, water-stains, paint-stains, pitch-stains, mud-stains, blood-stains! . . .
Here is a stain upon the hat of a gentleman in company, that I'll take clean out, before he can order me a pint of ale."

"Hah!" cried Sikes starting up. "Give that back."

Lord Lytton wrote a play—"Not so Bad as we Seem"—and Dickens threw himself whole heartedly into the double task of acting and stage management.

On November 3rd, 1850, we find Dickens writing to Lytton:

> I am full of confidence and resolve to do the utmost that is in me—and I well know they all will—to make the nights at Knebworth, *triumphant*. Once in a thing like this—once in everything, to my way of thinking—it must be carried out like a mighty enterprise, heart and soul. Pray regard me as wholly at the disposal of the theatricals until they shall be gloriously achieved.

The result, as Forster says, was brilliant.

On his return, Dickens wrote to Mrs. Watson, at whose house at Rockingham he had recently been playing in amateur theatricals. (See page 291.)

"Everything has gone off in a whirl of triumph and fired the whole length and breadth of the county of Hertfordshire."

The scheme progressed, and performances were given in various towns headed by the famous one at Devonshire House, at which Queen Victoria and the Prince Consort were present. A piece of land at Stevenage near by was given by Lord Lytton, and in 1865, the houses were ready, and on July 29th, the members of the Guild went to Stevenage to inspect these houses, and afterwards accepted the hospitality of Lytton at Knebworth, when Dickens proposed the health of the host in the course of which he explained:

> The Ladies and Gentlemen whom we shall invite to occupy the houses we have built, will never be placed under any social disadvantage. They will be invited to occupy them as artists and receiving them as a mark of the high respect in which they are held by their fellow workers.

Unfortunately the scheme was a failure because, in spite of the promoter's most sanguine hopes, the support, indispensable to its success, was not given to it by the very persons it was founded to support. The houses were empty for nearly twenty years, and then converted into ordinary residences.

The idea underlying the establishment of the Guild was part of Dickens's great aversion to any form of patronage of Literature which was with him the whole of his life.

To quote Forster: "It survived the failure of the Guild whereby it was hoped to establish a system of self-help, under which men engaged in literary pursuits might be as proud to receive as to give. Though there was no project of his life into which he flung himself with greater eagerness than the Guild, it was not taken up by the class it was meant to benefit, and every renewed exertion more largely added to the failure. A passage from a letter to Bulwer Lytton at its outset will be some measure of the height from which the writer fell, when all hope for what he had so set his heart upon ceased. 'I do devoutly believe that this plan, carried by the support which I trust will be given to it, will change the status of the literary man in England, and make a revolution in his position which no government, no power on earth but his own, could ever effect. I have implicit confidence in the scheme— so splendidly begun—if we carry it out with a steadfast energy. I have a strong conviction that we hold in our hands the peace and honour of men of letters for centuries to come, and that you are destined to be their best and most enduring benefactor. . . . Oh, what a procession of new years may walk out of all this for the class we belong to, after we are dust.'"

The houses founded as a result of the work of the Guild are still standing, and we pass them on the right on entering Stevenage, nearly opposite a public-house bearing the very appropriate title of Our Mutual Friend.

Dickens was a frequent visitor to Lytton at Knebworth, and in 1861 spent a week there with his daughter and Miss Hogarth, conferring with Lytton about his "Strange Story" that was to appear in *All the Year Round*. On this occasion Forster informs us that he "there met Mr. Arthur Helps, with whom and Lord Orford he visited the so-called "Hermit" near Stevenage, whom he described as Mr. Mopes in *Tom Tiddler's Ground*. With his great brother-artist he thoroughly enjoyed himself, as he invariably did; and reported *him* as "in better health and spirits than I have seen him in, in all these years—a little weird occasionally regarding magic and spirits, but always fair and frank under opposition. He was brilliantly talkative, anecdotical, and droll; looked young and well; laughed heartily; and enjoyed with great zest some games we played. In his artist-character and talk he was full of interest and matter, saying the subtlest and finest things—but that he never fails in. I enjoyed myself immensely, as we all did."

IV

The original Tom Tiddler's Ground was at Redcoats Green about five miles from Stevenage.

and sinking away among the ruined grass and the nettles, were the last perishing fragments of certain ricks; which had gradually mildewed and collapsed, until they looked like mounds of rotten honeycomb or dirty sponge.

v

All this while we have not forgotten the passengers on the coach, making for Dotheboys Hall: but they have not yet reached Eaton Socon, 23 miles away and Nicholas is still in conversation with the "good tempered man" and Squeers is at his regular leg stretching game.

So the day wore on. At Eton Slocomb there was a good coach dinner, of which the box, the four front outsides, the one inside, Nicholas, the good-tempered man, and Mr. Squeers, partook; while the five little boys were put to thaw by the fire, and regaled with sandwiches.

The correct name of this town is Eaton Socon: Dickens certainly gave it a more humorous title!

The inn that offered the "good coach dinner" for the adults and the thawing fire and sandwiches for the little boys was probably the Cock where the coaches stopped. It is no longer an inn.

A stage or two further on, the lamps were lighted, and a great to-do occasioned by the taking up, at a roadside inn, of a very fastidious lady with an infinite variety of cloaks and small parcels, who loudly lamented, for the behoof of the outsides, the non-arrival of her own carriage which was to have taken her on, and make the guard solemnly promise to stop every green chariot he saw coming; which, as it was a dark night and he was sitting with his face the other way, that officer undertook, with many fervent asseverations, to do.

This probably happened somewhere in the neighbourhood of Norman Cross or at Kate's Cabin Inn three miles further on. It had its counterpart in an actual happening to Dickens as he described in the letter to his wife :

We had a very droll male companion until seven o'clock in the evening, and a most delicious lady's-maid for twenty miles, who implored us to keep a sharp look-out at the coach windows, as she expected the carriage was coming to meet her and she was afraid of missing it. We had many delightful vauntings of the same kind; but i the end it is scarcely necessary to say that the coach did not come, but a very dirty girl did.

From this inn it is 10 miles to Stamford. "The night and the snow came on together, and dismal enough they were. There was no sound to be heard but the howling of the wind; for the noise of the wheels, and the tread of the horses' feet were rendered inaudible by the thick coating of snow which covered the ground, and was fast increasing every moment. The streets of Stamford were deserted as they passed through the town; and its old churches rose, frowning and dark, from the whitened ground."

Twenty miles further on, two of the front outside passengers wisely availing themselves of their arrival at one of the best inns in England, turned in, for the night, at the George at Grantham.

It was of the George Inn, at Grantham, that Dickens wrote to his wife from Greta Bridge on February 1st, 1838.

We reached Grantham between nine and ten on Thursday night, and found everything prepared for our reception in the very best inn I have ever put up at. It is odd enough that an old lady, who had been outside all day and came in towards dinner-time, turned out to be the mistress of a Yorkshire school returning from the holiday stay in London. She was a very queer old lady, and showed us a long letter she was carrying to one of the boys from his father, containing a severe lecture (enforced and aided by many texts of Scripture) on his refusing to eat boiled meat. She was very communicative, drank a great deal of brandy-and-water, and towards evening became insensible, in which state we left her.

It was probably as far as Grantham that Inspector Bucket and Esther got in their chase of Lady Dedlock from London and through St. Albans as described so graphically in Chapter LVII of *Bleak House*.

To avoid suspicion Lady Dedlock had changed dresses with the wife of one of the brickmakers at St. Albans and had doubled back to London, Jenny the decoy walking for a few miles in the northerly direction. This deceived Bucket, who thought Lady Dedlock was making for Chesney Wold and all that day Esther and he went travelling over the worst roads imaginable, in a snow-storm such as Dickens himself had experienced. In the evening they rested at an inn for

Now the identity of this Inn has puzzled many an inquirer, for since the railway came and left the little village of Greta Bridge stranded, the need for inns has greatly lessened, and several of the old inns have almost been lost in obscurity; one that was known to have existed on the left hand side of the road entering the village from London, just before reaching the Bridge, used to be called the George, and it has generally been assumed that this was the inn where the coach stopped. There was another inn at the time, about half a mile away known as the New Inn, and it was Kitton, we believe, who first put forward the very reasonable explanation that Dickens had joined the two names together when referring to the Inn in *Nicholas Nickleby*. At a later date Mr. T. P. Cooper who has long identified himself with Dickensian research in Yorkshire, endorsed this opinion in his interesting volume " With Dickens in Yorkshire," to which the writer wishes to record a debt of gratitude; but in April 1924, Mr. Cooper contributed an article to "The Dickensian" in which he was able to show conclusively from information that had since come into his possession that the George and New Inn was one inn in fact, and exists to-day in Thorpe Grange, now a pretty house about half a mile before reaching the village. The extensive stabling at the rear stands as proof of its former usage.

We are pleased Mr. Cooper has at length solved this question, for the lonely situation of Thorpe Grange fits in much better with Dickens's own description in the letter to his wife, quoted below, than does the present house by the Bridge, the old George Inn.

As we came north the snow grew deeper. About eight o'clock it began to fall heavily, and, as we crossed the wild heaths hereabout, there was no vestige of a track. The mail kept on well, however, and at eleven we reached a bare place with a house, standing alone in the midst of a dreary moor, which the guard informed us was Greta Bridge. I was in a perfect agony of apprehension, for it was fearfully cold, and there was no outward signs of anybody being up in the house. But to our great joy we discovered a comfortable room, with drawn curtains and a most blazing fire. In half an hour they gave us a smoking supper and a bottle of mulled port (in which we drank your health) and then we retired to a couple of capital bedrooms, in each of which there were a rousing fire halfway up the chimney. We have had for breakfast, toast, cakes, a Yorkshire pie, a piece of beef about the size and much

DOTHEBOYS' HALL, BOWES

[*Photo by T. W. Tyrrell*

THE GEORGE AND NEW INN, GRETA BRIDGE

the shape of my portmanteau, tea, coffee, ham and eggs; and are now going to look about us.

The George and New Inn, at Greta Bridge is also pointed out as the probable original of the Holly Tree Inn described as being on "the farther borders of Yorkshire . . . on a Yorkshire moor . . ." A similar rambling house, apparently, judging by Dickens's description of the large rooms, and long corridor; his own bedroom being "some quarter of a mile away" from the sitting-room. Its being on the road to Gretna Green fits in well with the charming story told by Boots, of Mr. and Mrs. Harry Walmers Junior.

In Dickens's day the inn was kept by George Martin, who had formerly been landlord of the minor inn the Morritt Arms, the only inn now in Greta Bridge.

Dickens playfully turned the name of Martin into Swallow, when Mrs. Squeers, arranging to follow the fugitive Smike says to Mr. Squeers: "You take the chaise and go one road: and I borrow Swallow's chaise and go the other."

"Mr. Squeers being safely landed" at the George, and having performed "the leg stretching process at the bar" "a rusty pony chaise and a cart" took the party to Dotheboys Hall, "about three miles from here . . . but you needn't call it a Hall down here" volunteered Squeers.

Dotheboys Hall was "a long cold looking house, one story high, with a few straggling outbuildings behind, and a barn and stable adjoining."

In the advertisement as drawn up by Mr. Squeers this is how it is described:

"Education—At Mr. Wackford Squeers's Academy, Dotheboys Hall, at the delightful village of Dotheboys, near Greta Bridge in Yorkshire. Youth are boarded, clothed, booked furnished with pocket-money, provided with all necessaries, instructed in all languages, living and dead, mathematics, orthography, geometry, astronomy, trigonometry, the use of the globes, algebra, single stick (if required), writing, arithmetic, fortification, and every other branch of classical literature. Terms twenty guineas per annum. No extras, no vacations, and diet unparalleled. Mr. Squeers is in town, and attends daily, from one till four, at the Saracen's Head, Snow Hill. N.B. An able assistant wanted. Annual salary £5. A Master of Arts would be preferred."

"The delightful village of Dotheboys" has its prototype in Bowes, and the "Hall" is to be seen at the far end of the her lattle boy to yon o' our schoolmeasters, while there's a house to hoold 'im a' Lunnun, or a gotther to lie asleep in."

Kitton in " The Dickens Country " says that this person, the obvious original of John Browdie—was John S—of Broadiswood, a farmer: the name Browdie being taken from Broadiswood.   But Mr. T. P. Cooper in his " With Dickens in Yorkshire," thinks, and with good reason, that Mr. Smithson would have been more likely to have given Dickens a letter of introduction to his own agent in Barnard Castle. This was Richard Barnes, and Mr. Cooper's theory is upheld by reference to a letter Dickens wrote to Mrs. S. C. Hall on December 29th, 1838, in which he says:

I went down in an assumed name, taking a plausible letter to an old Yorkshire attorney in town, telling him how a friend had been left a widow and wanted to place her boys at a Yorkshire school, in hopes of thawing the frozen compassion of her relations.   The man of business gave me an introduction to one or two schools, but at night he came down to the inn where I was stopping, and after much hesitation and confusion—he was a large-headed, flat-nosed, red-faced, old fellow—said with a degree of feeling one would not have given him credit for, that the matters had been upon his mind all day—that they were sad places for mothers to send their orphan boys to—that he hoped I would not give him up as my adviser—but that she had better do anything with them—let them hold horses, run errands—fling them in any way upon the mercy of the World—rather than trust them there.   This was an attorney, a well-fed man of business, and a rough Yorkshireman.

Not far from the Academy that was kept by Shaw, is the village church, and in the church yard Shaw and his son lie buried.   The churchyard also contains a stone to the memory of George Ashton Taylor, aged 19 "who died suddenly at Mr. William Shaw's Academy 1822."

This was the grave visited by Dickens, as he tells us in the letter above mentioned, of which this is a further extract :

The country for miles round was covered, when I was there, with deep snow.   There is an old church near the school, and the first grave-stone I stumbled on that dreary winter afternoon was placed above the grave of a boy, eighteen long years old, who had died—suddenly the inscription said; I suppose his heart broke—the camel falls down "suddenly" when they heap the last load upon his back—died at that wretched place. I think his ghost put Smike into my head, upon the spot.

The strength of this mute appeal to Dickens's sense of justice was very great, for the letter states further:

Depend upon it that the rascalities of those Yorkshire schoolmasters cannot easily be exaggerated, and that I have kept down the strong truth and thrown as much comicality over it as I could, rather than disgust and weary the reader with its fouler aspects. The identical scoundrel you speak of I saw—curiously enough. His name is Shaw; the action was tried (I believe) eight or ten years since, and if I am not much mistaken another action was brought against him by the parents of a miserable child, a cancer in whose head he opened with an inky penknife, and so caused his death.

The interview with the prototype of John Browdie already referred to, took place at the King's Head Inn, Market Place, Barnard Castle, to which house Newman Noggs had recommended Nicholas in a letter which he handed him in parting at the Saracen's Head.

If you should go near Barnard Castle, there is good ale at the King's Head. Say you know me, and I am sure they will not charge you for it. You may say Mr. Noggs there, for I was a gentleman then. I was indeed.

The end of the letter from Dickens to his wife from Greta Bridge is as follows:

We start in a post-chaise for Barnard Castle, which is only four miles off, and there I deliver the letter given me by Mitton's friend. All the schools are round about that place, and a dozen old abbeys besides, which we shall visit by some means or other to-morrow. We shall reach York on Saturday I hope, and (God willing) I trust I shall be at home on Wednesday morning.

The King's Head at Barnard Castle has more the appearance of a private house than an inn, and although it has been extended, the older portion does not differ very much from what it was when Dickens stayed there.

Thomas Humphrey, a clock maker, had premises almost opposite to the King's Head, and it is said that Dickens took from him the idea of the title for his periodical started in 1840,

The queerest place, with the strangest people in it, leading the oddest lives of dancing, newspaper reading and tables d'hote.

Some of the audience he described in a characteristic letter to Miss Hogarth:

There was one gentleman at the Little Dombey yesterday who exhibited—or rather concealed—the profoundest grief. After crying a good deal without hiding it, he covered his face with both his hands and laid it down on the back of the seat before him, and really shook with emotion. He was not in mourning, but I supposed him to have lost some child in old time. . . . There was a remarkably good fellow too, of thirty or so, who found something so very ludicrous in Toots that he *could not* compose himself at all, but laughed until he sat wiping his eyes with his handkerchief; and whenever he felt Toots coming again, be began to laugh and wipe his eyes afresh; and when Toots came once more, he gave a kind of cry, as if it were too much for him. It was uncommonly droll, and made me laugh heartily.

Harrogate and Scarborough are both mentioned in *Dombey and Son* by Edith when at Leamington, as spas visited by her and Mrs. Skewton.

From Harrogate Dickens had to fulfil an engagement at Scarborough on the Monday; and Sunday trains did not then run from York.

The piety of York obliging us to leave that place for this (Scarborough) at six this morning, and there being no night train from Harrogate, we had to engage a special engine. We got to bed at one, and were up again before five; which, after yesterday's fatigues, leaves a me little worn out at this present.

And even then they had to walk three miles to the station, as the letter explains:

After the reading last night we walked over the moor to the railway, three miles, leaving our men to follow with the luggage in a light cart. They passed us just short of the railway, and John was making the night hideous and terrifying the sleeping country, by playing the horn in prodigiously horrible and unmusical blasts.

Of the journey from Harrogate to Scarborough he wrote in a later letter:

I seem to have been doing nothing all my life but riding in railway carriages and reading. The railway of the morning brought us through Castle Howard, and under the woods of Easthorpe, and then just below Malton Abbey, where I went to poor Smithson's funeral. It was a most lovely morning, and, tired as I was, I couldn't sleep for looking out of window.

The Smithson referred to was the one mentioned on page 205, who helped Dickens to make his investigations complete in regard to the Yorkshire schools. He lived at Easthorpe Hall, Malton, and was a frequent visitor at Dickens's house.

It was he who is also mentioned in the preface to *Barnaby Rudge*, as the Yorkshire friend who "discovered an older and more gifted raven at a village public house, which he prevailed upon the landlord to part with for a consideration" and sent up to Dickens as some consolation for the loss of a raven he had previously possessed, and so became the prototype of Grip.

Dickens and his wife visited Easthorpe Hall for a few weeks in July, 1843, while writing *Martin Chuzzlewit*. An account of the visit was given in a letter to Professor Felton:

What do you think of Mrs. Gamp. . . . Ah heaven! Such green woods as I was rambling along, down in Yorkshire when I was getting that done last July. For days and weeks we never saw the sky but through green boughs: and all day long I cantered over such soft moss and turf that the horse's feet scarcely made a sound upon it. We have some friends in that part of the country, who are the jolliest of the jolly, keeping a big old country house, with an ale cellar something larger than a reasonable church, and everything, like Goldsmith's bear dances "in a concatenation accordingly."

We performed some madnesses there in the way of forfeits, picnics, rustic games, inspection of ancient monasteries at midnight, when the moon was shining that would have gone to your heart, and as Mr. Weller says "come out on the other side."

In less than a year on April 5th, 1844, Dickens was again at Malton, to stand beside his friend's grave. He was only 39 years of age.

On this occasion, Dickens prolonged his journey and availed himself of an invitation of Lord Normanby, to whom he subsequently dedicated *Dombey and Son*, to visit him at Mulgrave Castle, near Whitby.

had a palpitation of the heart, if any of our people stumbled up or down a stair. I am sure I never acted better, but the anxiety of my mind was so intense, and the relief at last so great, that I am half dead to-day, and have not yet been able to eat or drink anything or to stir out of my room. I shall never forget it. As to the short time we had for getting the theatre up; as to the upsetting, by a runaway pair of horses, of one of the vans at the Newcastle railway station with all the scenery in it, every atom of which was turned over; as to the fatigue of our carpenters, who have now been up four nights, and who were lying dead asleep in the entrances last night; I say nothing, after the other gigantic night-mare, except that Sloman's splendid knowledge of his business, and the good temper and cheerfulness of all the workmen are capital. I mean to give them a supper at Liverpool, and address them in a neat and appropriate speech. We dine at two to-day (it is now one) and go to Sheffield at four, arriving there at about ten. I had been as fresh as a daisy; walked from Nottingham to Derby, and from Newcastle here; but seem to have had my nerves crumpled up last night, and have an excruciating head ache. That's all at present. I shall never be able to bear the smell of new deal and fresh mortar again as long as I live.

His next visit to Sunderland was on his reading tour when he read *A Christmas Carol* at the Theatre Royal on September 23rd, 1858.

I read at Sunderland in a beautiful new theatre and (I thought to myself) quite wonderfully. Such an audience I never beheld for rapidity and enthusiasm. The room in which we acted (converted into a theatre afterwards) was burnt to the ground a year or two ago. We found the hotel so bad in our time, really good.

I walked from Durham to Sunderland and from Sunderland to Newcastle.

On the previous visit, it will be remembered, he had walked from Newcastle to Sunderland (13 miles).

There is a brief mention of Durham in *Little Dorrit*, and Dickens visited the city on his way to Sunderland and Newcastle in 1858 and read in the Town Hall on September 22nd. As a matter of interest it will be seen from the letters quoted above that Dickens walked from Durham to Sunderland (4 miles) and from the latter place to Newcastle (13 miles).

X

Dickens was at Newcastle-on-Tyne in 1852 with his company of players for the benefit of the funds of the Guild of Literature and Art. The performance took place on August 27th, at the Assembly Rooms in Westgate Road, still used for social events.

Into the room at Newcastle (where Lord Carlisle was by-the-bye) they squeezed six hundred people, at twelve and sixpence, into a space reasonably capable of holding three hundred.

In 1858 three readings were given in the Town Hall, on September 24th and 25th. To Forster—whose birthplace was at Newcastle-on-Tyne, he wrote "I hope I told you how splendidly Newcastle came out." On this occasion he stayed at the Station Hotel, and was joined by his two daughters who accompanied him to Berwick and on to Scotland for his readings there. (See page 217).

His next visit was in 1861 when he read at the Music Hall, Nelson Street, on November 21st, 22nd and 23rd. The warehouse below the Gaiety Picture Hall represents the Hall as it was in those days. An account of this visit is given in a letter to Forster:

At Newcastle, against the very heavy expenses, I made more than a hundred guineas profit. A finer audience there is not in England, and I suppose them to be a specially earnest people; for, while they can laugh till they shake the roof, they have a very unusual sympathy with what is pathetic or passionate. An extraordinary thing occurred on the second night. The room was tremendously crowded and my gas-apparatus fell down. There was a terrible wave among the people for an instant, and God knows what destruction of life a rush to the stairs would have caused. Fortunately a lady in the front of the stalls ran out towards me, exactly in a place where I knew that the whole hall could see her. So I addressed her, laughing, and half-asked and half-ordered her to sit down again; and, in a moment, it was all over. But the men in attendance had such a fearful sense of what might have happened (besides the real danger of Fire) that they positively shook the boards I stood on, with their trembling, when they came up to put things right. I am proud to record that the gas-man's sentiment, as delivered afterwards, was:

and nick-nacks" all described in detail, and its pictures and books, was undoubtedly Dickens's very own.

The book gives a description of the ascent of Carrock and what befell the idlers, an actual experience, as the following extract from a letter to Forster shows :

We came straight to it yesterday. Nobody goes up. Guides have forgotten it. Master of a little inn, excellent north-countryman, volunteered. Went up, in a tremendous rain. C. D. beat Mr. Porter (name of landlord) in half a mile. Mr. P. done up in no time. Three nevertheless went on. Mr. P. again leading; C. D. and C. (Mr. Wilkie Collins) following. Rain terrific, black mists, darkness of night. Mr. P. agitated. C. D. confident. C. (a long way down in perspective) submissive. All wet through. No poles. Not so much as a walking-stick in the party. Reach the summit at about one in the day. Dead darkness as of night. Mr. P. (excellent fellow to the last) uneasy. C. D. produces compass from pocket. Mr. P. reassured. Farm-house where dog-cart was left, N.N.W. Mr. P. complimentary. Descent commenced. C. D. with compass triumphant, until compass, with the heat and wet of C. D.'s pocket, breaks. Mr. P. (who never had a compass), inconsolable, confesses he has not been on Carrick Fell for twenty years, and he don't know the way down. Darker and darker. Nobody discernible two yards off, by the other two. Mr. P. makes suggestions, but no way. It becomes clear to C. D. and to C. that Mr. P. is going round and round the mountain, and never coming down. Mr. P. sits on angular granite, and says he is "just fairly doon." C. D. revives Mr. P. with laughter, the only restorative in the company. Mr. P. again complimentary. Descent tried once more. Mr. P. worse and worse. Council of war. Proposals from C. D. to go "slap down." Seconded by C. Mr. P. objects, on account of precipice called The Black Arches, and terror of the countryside. More wandering. Mr. P. terror-stricken, but game. Watercourse, thundering and roaring, reached. C. D. suggests that it must run to the river, and had best be followed, subject to all gymnastic hazards. Mr. P. opposes, but gives in. Watercourse followed accordingly. Leaps, splashes, and tumbles, for two hours. C. lost. C. D. whoops. Cries for assistance from behind. C. D. returns. C. with horribly sprained ankle, lying in rivulet.

Allonby, Cumberland
Wednesdy Night, Ninth September
1857

My Dear George

I walked over to Maryport
to-day, to see what letters there were, and
to ask the Postmaster to send any more
he might have, over here. I found none
from you; but hardly supposed I should,
so soon.

Think of Collins's usual
luck with me!!! We went up a Cumberland
mountain yesterday — a huge black
hill, 1500 feet high. We took for
a Guide, a capital Innkeeper hard
by. It rained in torrents — as it only
does rain in a hill country — the whole
time. At the top, there were black
mists and the darkness of night. It
then came out that the Innkeeper
had not been up for 20 years — and
he lost his head and himself
altogether, and we couldn't get down
again! What wonders the Inimitable
performed with his compass until it

We got down at last in the wildest place, preposterously out of the course; and, propping up C. against stones, sent Mr. P. to the other side of Cumberland for dog-cart, so got back to his inn, and changed. Shoe or stocking on the bad foot out of the question. Foot bundled up in a flannel waistcoat. C. D. carrying C. melo-dramatically (Wardour to the life) everywhere; into and out of carriages; up and down stairs; to bed; every step. And so to Wigton, got doctor, and here we are! A pretty business, we flatter ourselves!

To his sister-in-law he wrote a more concise account in a letter from Allonby dated Wednesday, September 9th, 1857:

Think of Collins's usual luck with me. We went up a Cumberland mountain yesterday—a huge black hill, fifteen hundred feet high. We took for a guide a capital inn-keeper hard by. It rained in torrents—as it only does rain in a hill country—the whole time. At the top, there were black mists and the darkness of night. It then came out that the inn-keeper had not been up for twenty years, and he lost his head and himself altogether; and we couldn't get down again! What wonders the Inimitable performed with his compass until it broke with the heat and wet of his pocket no matter; it did break, and then we wandered about, until it was clear to the Inimitable that the night must be passed there, and the enterprising travellers probably die of cold. We took our own way about coming down, struck, and declared that the guide might wander where he would, but we would follow a watercourse we lighted upon, and which must come at last to the river. This necessitated amazing gymnastics; in the course of which performances, Collins fell into the said watercourse with his ankle sprained, and the great ligament of the foot swollen I don't know how big.

How I enacted Wardour over again in carrying him down, and what a business it was to get him down; I may say in Gibb's words: "Vi lascio a giudicare!" but he was got down somehow and we got off the mountain somehow; and now I carry him to bed, and into and out of carriages, exactly like Wardour in private life. I don't believe he will stand for a month to come. He has had a doctor, and can wear neither shoe nor stocking, and has his foot wrapped up in a flannel waistcoat, and has a breakfast saucer of liniment, and a horrible dabbling of lotion incessantly in progress. We laugh at it all, but I do idleness," during a long day, and, it is stated "There are reasons . . . for not publically indicating the exact direction in which that journey lay, or the place in which it ended."

Canon Rawnsley thinks that Ireby was the village referred to.

It was at a little town, still in Cumberland, that they halted for the night—a very little town with the purple and brown moor close upon its one street: a curious little ancient market-cross set up in the midst of it: and the town itself looking much as if it were a collection of great stones piled on end by the Druids long ago, which a few recluse people had since hollowed out for habitations.

Here Dr. Speddie (actually Dr. Speake) attended to Idle, which led to the telling of the story about Arthur Holliday and the Doncaster Races.

The next day they managed to get to Allonby which Mr. Goodchild had discovered—from the county map—was "the most delicious piece of sea-coast to be found . . . on the coast of Cumberland." It was "approached by a coach road, from a railway station called Aspatria" shortened by the Cumberland people into "Spatter." And they came to "the most delightful place ever seen" to the Ship Hotel presided over by "the most comfortable of landladies . . . and the most attentive of landlords."

The account goes on to give a good description of this primitive place, of no street, with plenty of fishermen who never fished, but "got their living entirely by looking at the ocean" and a number of children "who were always upside down on the public buildings (two small bridges over the brook) . . . The houses people lodged in were nowhere in particular, and were in capital accordance with the beach."

In a letter to Forster we are given a further description of Allonby:

A small, untidy, outlandish place; rough stone houses in half mourning, a few coarse yellow-stone lodging-houses with black roofs (bills in all the windows), five bathing machines, five girls in straw hats, five men in straw hats (wishing they had not come); very much what Broadstairs would have been if it had been born Irish, and had not inherited a cliff.

d to Miss Hogarth he wrote at the same time:

This is a little place with fifty houses, five bathing-machines, five girls in straw hats, five men in straw hats, and no other company. The little houses are all in half-mourning—yellow stone on white stone, and black; and it reminds me of what Broadstairs might have been if it had not inherited a cliff, and had been an Irishman. But this is a capital little homely inn, looking out upon the sea; and we are really very comfortably lodged. I can just stand upright in my bedroom. Otherwise, it is a good deal like one of Ballard's top-rooms. We have a very obliging and comfortable landlady; and it is a clean nice place in a rough wild country. We came here haphazard, but could not have done better.

The Ship Hotel, which still exists, was further described in the letter to Forster:

But this is a capital little homely inn, looking out upon the sea; with the coast of Scotland, mountainous and romantic, over against the windows; and though I can just stand upright in my bedroom, we are really well lodged. It is a clean nice place in a rough wild country, and we have a very obliging and comfortable landlady.

In a later letter to Miss Hogarth, on September 12th, we find that, curiously enough, the landlady had made Dickens's acquaintance some twenty years before:

The landlady of the little inn at Allonby lived at Greta Bridge, in Yorkshire, when I went down there before "Nickleby" and was smuggled into the room to see me, when I was secretly found out. She is an immensely fat woman now. "But I could tuck my arm round her waist then, Mr. Dickens," the landlord said when she told me the story as I was going to bed the night before last. "And can't you do it now" I said, "you insensible dog? Look at me! Here's a picture!" Accordingly I got round as much of her as I could; and this gallant action was the most successful I have ever performed, on the whole. I think it was the dullest little place I ever entered; and what with the monotony of an idle sea, and what with the monotony of another sea in the room (occasioned by Collins's perpetually holding his ankle over a pail of salt water, and laving it with a milk jug), I struck yesterday, and came away.

They remained at Allonby for two days—and much enjoyed the fine sunsets, "when the low flat beach, with its pools of

ments, very good attendants; altogether a remarkable place,"
adding that he saw there "long groves of blighted men-and-
women trees: interminable avenues of hopeless faces."

The reception they had at Carlisle and Lancaster was referred
to by Dickens in an interesting letter to Miss Hogarth:

> Accustomed as you are to the homage which men delight
> to render to the Inimitable, you would be scarcely prepared
> for the proportions it assumes in this northern country.
> Station-masters assist him to alight from carriages, deputa-
> tions await him in hotel entries, innkeepers bow down
> before him and put him into regal rooms, the town goes
> down to the platform to see him off, and Collins's ankle
> goes into the newspapers!!!

> It is a great deal better than it was, and he can get into
> new hotels and up the stairs with two thick sticks, like an
> admiral in a farce. His spirits have improved in a corres-
> ponding degree, and he contemplates cheerfully the keeping
> house at Doncaster. I thought (as I told you) he would
> never have gone there, but he seems quite up to the mark
> now. Of course he can never walk out, or see anything of
> any place. We have done our first paper for H.W., and
> sent it up to the printer's.

Lancaster and the King's Arms are both mentioned in
Doctor Marigold's Prescriptions, written in 1865:

> We were down at Lancaster, and I had done two nights
> more than fair average business (though I cannot in honour
> recommend them as a quick audience) in the open square
> there, near the end of the street where Mr. Sly's King's
> Arms and Royal Hotel stands. Mim's travelling giant,
> otherwise Pickleson, happened at the self-same time to be
> trying it on in the town. The genteel lay was adopted
> with him. No hint of a van. Green baize alcove leading
> up to Pickleson in a Auction Room.

And it was between Lancaster and Carlisle that Dr. Marigold again discovered the "strange young man" following the
van. He turned out to be deaf and dumb, like the Sophy
whom he subsequently married.

v

From Lancaster the Idle apprentices went to Doncaster
by way of Leeds, of which, unfortunately, Dickens did not
appear to have a very good opinion.

Dickens's first recorded visit to Leeds was in 1847, when he presided at a soiree of the Leeds Mechanics' Institution on December 1st in the Music Hall, Albion Street. Among the other speakers was George Stephenson. This was the third such institute that Dickens had addressed on the subject of the excellent educational work they were doing, and in his concluding remarks he expressed the hope "that institutions such as this will be the means of refining and improving that social edifice which has been so often mentioned to-night, until . . . it shall end in sweet accord and harmony amongst all classes of its builders," and he closed with this expression of his earnest desires:

"Ladies and Gentlemen, most respectfully and heartily I bid you good-night and good-bye, and trust the next time we meet it will be in even greater numbers, and in a larger room, and that we often shall meet again to recall this evening, then of the past, and remember it as one of a series of increasing triumphs of your excellent institution."

The Institution is still flourishing and is known as the Leeds Institute of Science, Art and Literature, and occupies a handsome building in Cookridge Street.

Dickens, however, does not appear to have met the Leeds people again for more than ten years, when he appeared before them as a reader from his own works on September 15th, 1858.

In the meantime, however, the Lazy Tour took him there in September, 1857.

Leeds has changed wondrously since Idle and Goodchild arrived at the station with "a little rotten platform (converted into artificial touchwood by smoke and ashes) " by way of the "branchless woods of vague black chimneys . . . of the manufacturing bosom of Yorkshire." The great manufacturing towns "looked in the cinderous wet, as though they had one and all been on fire and were just put out."

Of the "enterprising and important centre of Leeds," Dickens remarked that "it may be observed with delicacy that you must either like it very much or not at all." And he emphasised his dislike of Leeds in a letter to Miss Hogarth from Lancaster on September 12th, 1857, when, proposing to go to Doncaster on the following day (Sunday) he wrote that he found the trains so inconvenient that he feared he would have to sleep the night at Leeds, "which I partcularly detest as an odious place."

arrangement, and exquisite neatness. We breakfast at half-past eight, and fall to work for H.W. afterwards. Then I go out, and—hem! look for subjects.

Collins, we are told, "once established in the hotel, with his leg on one cushion and his back against another, formally declined taking the slightest interest in any circumstance whatever connected with the races." He was, as Goodchild said of him, "absolutely and literally . . . the only individual in Doncaster who stands by the brink of the full-flowing race stream, and is not swept away by it in common with all the rest of the species."

The attraction of the races was not the sole topic of the town's interest, for the letter informs us that a civic reception of the two authors was proposed, and declined.

The mayor called this morning to do the honours of the town, whom it pleased the Inimitable to receive with great courtesy and affability. He propounded invitation to public *dejeuner*, which it did *not* please the Inimitable to receive, and which he graciously rejected.

The story of Arthur Holliday, told by the Cumberland Doctor, Mr. Speddie, concerns an adventure in Doncaster in "the middle of a race week" and has for its theme the difficulty in securing a bed at that time "at the principal hotel" and what happened when a bed was ultimately secured at an inn on the outskirts called the Two Robins: a weird story, probably the only portion of the journal of the tour that was written solely by Collins.

They stayed the week through: as he explained in his letter dated Tuesday, September 15th:

The races begin to-day and last till Friday, which is the Cup Day. I am not going to the course this morning, but have engaged a carriage (open, and pair) for to-morrow and Friday . . . That's all the news. Everything I can describe by hook or by crook, I describe for H. W. So there is nothing of that sort left for letters.

In spite of that, however, he did write at least one descriptive letter to Forster, who thus introduces it: "The impressions received from the race-week were not favourable. It was noise and turmoil all day long, and a gathering of vagabonds from all parts of the racing earth. Every bad face that had ever caught wickedness from an innocent horse had its representative in the streets; and as Dickens, like Gulliver looking down upon his fellow-men after coming from the horse country, looked down into Doncaster High Street from his inn-window, he seemed to see everywhere a then notorious personage who had just poisoned his betting-companion."

Everywhere I see the late Mr. Palmer with his betting-book in his hand. Mr. Palmer sits next me at the theatre; Mr. Palmer goes before me down the street; Mr. Palmer follows me into the chemist's shop where I go to buy rose water after breakfast, and says to the chemist "Give us soom sal volatile or soom damned thing o' that soort, in wather —my head's bad!" And I look at the back of his bad head repeated in long, long lines on the race course, and in the betting stand and outside the betting rooms in the town, and I vow to God that I can see nothing in it but cruelty, covetousness, calculation, insensibility, and low wickedness.

"Even a half-appealing kind of luck was not absent from my friend's experiences at the racecourse" adds Forster, " when, what he called a 'wonderful, paralysing, coincidence' befell him. He bought the card; facetiously wrote down three names for the winners of the three chief races (never in his life having heard or thought of any of the horses, except that the winner of the Derby, who proved to be nowhere, had been mentioned to him); 'and, if you can believe it without your hair standing on end, those three races were won, one after another, by those three horses!!!' That was the St. Leger day, of which he also thought it noticeable, that, though the losses were enormous, nobody had won, for there was nothing but grinding of teeth and blaspheming of ill-luck. Nor had matters mended on the Cup day, after which celebra-tion 'a groaning phantom' lay in the doorway of his bedroom and howled all night. The landlord came up in the morning to apologise, 'and said it was a gentleman who had lost £1,500 or £2,000; and he had drunk a deal afterwards; and then they put him to bed, and then he—took the terrors, and got up, and yelled till morning!"

VII

The lazy tour of the idle apprentices ended at Doncaster, but we idle Dickensians have a little more concern with one or two other Yorkshire towns; and this being a real idle tour, we will give a glance at them before we end it.

One of the earliest readings by Dickens in aid of the funds of Working Men's Institutes, was given in Bradford.

of my going down to Sheffield on Friday (December 21st) to read there—in the bitter winter—with journey back to Paris, before me" he wrote. After the reading Dickens was presented with a case of cutlery, a pair of silver fish carvers and a pair of razors, all the product of local works.

Writing of this reading Dickens said:

> Enormous success at Sheffield . . . they were most enthusiastically demonstrative, and they took the line "and to Tiny Tim who did NOT die" with a most prodigious shout and roll of thunder.

Three years later, on September 17th, 1858, Dickens gave a paid reading at the Music Hall. During this visit he stayed at the King's Head in Change Alley, since rebuilt, and from which he wrote:

> The run upon the tickets here is so immense that Arthur is obliged to get bills out, signifying that no more can be sold. It will be by no means easy to get into the place the numbers who have already paid. It is the hall we acted in, crammed to the roof and the passages.

So many were unable to obtain admission to this reading that Dickens had to pay a return visit on October 29th.

The next visit was more than ten years later, this time under the auspices of the Sheffield Athenæum. The reading was again at the Music Hall, and the date March 31st, 1869. This building was later converted into a High School for girls, and is now the Central Lending Library and Reading Room.

IX

Dickens's first visit to Hull was on September 14th, 1858, when he read *A Christmas Carol* at the Music Hall in Jarratt Street, now known as the Assembly Rooms. Forster remarked of his great reception on that occasion. "At Hull the vast concourse had to be addressed by Mr. Smith (Dickens's manager) on the gallery stairs, and additional readings had to be given day and night, for the people out of town and for the people in town."

Of this Dickens has left a record in a letter to his daughter, Mamie, dated September 15th, 1858:

> The Hull people (not generally considered excitable, even on their own showing) were so enthusiastic, that we were obliged to promise to go back there for two readings. I have positively resolved not to lengthen out the time of my tour, so we are now arranging to drop some

small places, and substitute Hull again and York again.
. . . Arthur (Smith) told you, I suppose, that he had his
shirt front and waistcoat torn off last night? He was perfectly enraptured in consequence. Our men got so knocked
about that he gave them five shillings apiece on the
spot. John passed several minutes upside-down against
a wall, with his head amongst the people's boots. He
came out of the difficulty in an exceedingly tousled
condition, and with his face much flushed. For all this,
and their being packed, as you may conceive they
would be packed, they settled down the instant I went in,
and never wavered in the closest attention for an instant.
It was a very high room and required a great effort.

The last reading in Hull was on Wednesday, March 10th,
1869, also at the Music Hall. A further reading was fixed for
the following Friday, but was cancelled owing to the funeral
of Emerson Tennent, which Dickens attended, and to which
we have already referred on page 209.

Dickens paid only one visit to Huddersfield on his reading
tours, and that was on Wednesday, September 8th, 1858,
when he read *A Christmas Carol* in the Gymnasium Hall in
Ramsden Street.

X

We have now to refer to a few towns in the Midlands
possessing a Dickens' interest, which did not come within
the scope of our seventh chapter.

It was probably of Stafford, described as "one of the
chiefest towns of Staffordshire . . . by no means a lively
town" that Dickens wrote in "A Plated Article" in *Household
Words*, afterwards published in *Reprinted Pieces*. Here we
find a reference to "two old churchyards near to the High
Street" and "the stiff square where the Town Hall stands
like a brick and mortar private on parade."

The Dodo Inn at which he stayed is said to be a picture of
The Swan:

I have paced the streets, and stared at the houses, and
am come back to the blank bow window of the Dodo . . .
If the Dodo were only a gregarious bird—if he had only
some confused idea of making a comfortable next—I could
hope to get through the hours between this and bed-time,
without being consumed by devouring melancholy. But,
the Dodo's habits are all wrong. It provides me with a
trackless desert of sitting-room, with a chair for every
day in the year, a table for every month, and a waste of

CHAPTER ELEVEN

THE HARD TIMES COUNTRY

I

THE country of that "triumph of fact," Coketown, was necessarily centred in Lancashire, although we do not for one minute believe that Manchester stood for the principal place in *Hard Times*, in spite of some ardent Dickensians in that city wishing to claim it as such.

Coketown is another of the composite pictures to vie with Eatanswill and Muggleton, and it is a somewhat useless task to attempt to identify any one particular place as the original. Dickens's description of it was typical of the great Lancashire manufacturing towns:

It was a town of red brick, or of brick that would have been red if the smoke and ashes had allowed it; but as matters stood it was a town of unnatural red and black like the painted face of a savage. It was a town of machinery and tall chimneys, out of which interminable serpents of smoke trailed themselves for ever and ever, and never got uncoiled. It had a black canal in it, and a river that ran purple with ill-smelling dye, and vast piles of building full of windows where there was a rattling and trembling all day long, and where the piston of the steam-engine worked monotonously up and down, like the head of an elephant in a state of melancholy madness. It contained several large streets all very like one another, and many small streets still more like one another, inhabited by people equally like one another, who all went in and out at the same hours, with the same sound upon the same pavements, to do the same work, and to whom every day was the same as yesterday and to-morrow, and every year the counter-part of last and next.

We shall look in vain for Mr. Gradgrind's house, Stone Lodge, which we are told was "situated on a moor within a mile or two of a great town, called Coketown in the present faithful guide-book," and for the house of Mr. Bounderby, which was situated on a hill, and was

> A Red house with black outside shutters, green inside blinds a black street door up two white steps with "Bounderby" upon a brazen plate and a round brazen door handle underneath it, like a brazen full stop.

Nor has Mr. Bounderby's bank been located. It was "a size larger than Mr. Bounderby's house" but nevertheless strictly according to pattern . . . a red house with black outside shutters, green inside blinds, a black street door up two white steps, a brazen door plate and a brazen door handle full stop."

Neither have we discovered Pod's End and the Pegasus's Arms, where Mr. Sleary delivered his philosophy, "People mutht be amuthed, Thquire thomehow; they can't be alwayth a working, nor yet they can't be alwayth a learning. Make the betht of uth, not the wurtht."

II

Manchester is proud of Dickens's long connection with the city.

His first visit appears to have been in the autumn of 1838, when on holiday with Phiz, as we have described in Chapter Seven. Forster had joined them at Liverpool and in the Diary, under date Tuesday, November 6th, there is this record, "3 fares to Manchester 3 times." We have unfortunately failed to find a reason for the three friends journeying to Manchester three times in the day—or possibly two days.

There is no doubt that it was during this time that Dickens met the brothers Grant, who stood for the famous Cheeryble Brothers in *Nicholas Nickleby*. It was to Harrison Ainsworth that Dickens owed the introduction, for this is what Forster has to say on the subject in the Life: "A friend now especially welcome, was the novelist Mr. Ainsworth . . . with whom we visited, . . . friends of art and letters in his native Manchester, from among whom Dickens brought away his Brothers Cheeryble."

It was at the house of Ainsworth's friend Gilbert Winter, who lived at the Stocks, Cheetham Hill Road (demolished in 1884), that Dickens met the two brothers Daniel and William. Their place of business was in Cannon Street, which before its demolition in 1907 was known as Cheeryble

On August the 21st and 22nd of the same year Dickens
played in "The Frozen Deep" at the same Hall in aid of the
Douglas Jerrold Memorial Fund.

Dickens's brother Alfred died in Manchester in July 1860,
and Dickens made a hurried visit there, as he explained in a
letter to Forster :

> I was telegraphed for to Manchester on Friday night.
> Arrived there at a quarter-past ten, but he had been dead
> three hours, poor fellow!   He is to be buried at Highgate
> on Wednesday. I brought the poor young widow back
> with me yesterday.

Alfred Dickens had been previously living in York, where
he was often visited by his famous brother (see page 209)

III

Dickens had so often been before the Manchester public
in support of worthy objects, that it is not to be wondered
at that when he plunged into the regular series of readings for
his own benefit, the reception he received from Manchester
should be absolutely overwhelming. This was in September
1858, of which occasion Forster says: "The reception
that awaited him at Manchester had very special warmth in it
occasioned by an adverse tone taken in the comment of one of
the Manchester daily papers on the letter which by a breach
of confidence had been then recently printed. 'My vio-
lated letter' Dickens always called it."

> When I came to Manchester on Saturday I found seven
> hundred stalls taken! When I went into the room at
> night 2500 people had paid, and more were being turned
> away from every door. The welcome they gave me was
> astounding in its affectionate recognition of the late
> trouble, and fairly for once unmanned me. I never saw
> such a sight or heard such a sound. When they had
> thoroughly done it, they settled down to enjoy themselves
> and certainly did enjoy themselves most heartily to the last
> minute.

On Saturdays October the 16th and 23rd, 1858, the readings were repeated with equal success.

On December 3rd, in the same year, Dickens was again
in Manchester, presiding at the annual meeting of the
Institutional Association of Lancashire and Cheshire at the
Free Trade Hall, and presented prizes to candidates from over
one hundred Mechanics' Institutes affiliated to the Association

MR.

CHARLES DICKENS

WILL READ AT THE

FESTIVAL CONCERT ROOM,

YORK,

ON

MONDAY EVENING,

OCTOBER 25th, at 8 o'Clock,

THE POOR TRAVELLER,

BOOTS AT THE HOLLY TREE INN,

AND

MRS. GAMP.

PLACES FOR THE READINGS

Stalls, (numbered and reserved)	-	Four Shillings.
Gallery, -	-	Two Shillings.
Back Seats,	-	One Shilling.

Tickets to be had of Mr. HENRY BANKS, Music Warehouse, Stonegate, York,

Where a Plan of the Reserved Seats may be seen.

☞ On only one occasion, within Mr. DICKENS's experience, some ladies and gentlemen in the Stalls caused great inconvenience and confusion (no doubt, unintentionally), by leaving their places during the last quarter of an hour of the Reading, when the general attention could least bear to be disturbed. This elicited a strong disposition in other parts of the Hall towards an angry but not unreasonable protest.

In case any portion of the company should be under the necessity of leaving before the close of the Reading in the apprehension of losing railway trains, they are respectfully intreated, as an act of consideration and courtesy towards the remainder, to avail themselves of the opportunity afforded by the interval between the parts when Mr. DICKENS retires for five minutes.

THE READING WILL LAST TWO HOURS.

"NASSAU STEAM PRESS," 60, St. Martin's Lane.

POSTER ANNOUNCING A READING BY DICKENS AT YORK

246

It was nearly three years before Dickens again appeared publicly in the city. This was on Saturday, December 14th, 1861, when he read at Free Trade Hall. He described his reception as "magnificent," adding:

> When I went in (there was a very fine hall) they applauded in the most tremendous manner and the extent to which they were taken aback and taken by storm by *Copperfield* was really a fine thing to see.

In the January following two readings were given on the 25th. There was an interval of over four years before Dickens again read in Manchester. This was on April 12th, 1866, when he had, as he himself said "such a prodigious demonstration . . . that I was obliged (contrary to my principles in such cases) to go back." Forster informs us: "The success everywhere went far beyond even the former successes. A single night at Manchester, when eight hundred stalls were let, two thousand five hundred and sixty-five people admitted, and the receipts amounted to more than three hundred pounds, was followed in nearly the same proportion by all the greater towns."

"The reception at Manchester last night" he wrote to Miss Hogarth, of this occasion, "was quite a magnificent sight; the whole of the immense audience standing up and cheering."

The return visit was on April 26th.

In 1867 there were two readings in the February: the fisrt on the 2nd of the month, and the second on the 16th, of which occasion he wrote to his daughter from Glasgow:

> Manchester last night was a splendid spectacle. They cheered to that extent after it was over that I was obliged to huddle on my clothes (for I was undressing to prepare for the journey) and go back again. After so heavy a week, it *was* rather stiff to start on this long journey at a quarter to two in the morning; but I got more sleep than I ever got in a railway carriage before. . . . I have, as I had in the last series of readings, a curious feeling of soreness all round the body—which I suppose to arise from the great exertion of voice.

In 1868 Dickens gave two special Saturday evening readings at the Free Trade Hall, on April 12th and 26th. During his autumn reading tour of that year, the Saturday readings at Manchester were quite a feature, October 10th, 17th, 24th and 31st, being reserved for them at the Free Trade Hall.

to speculate on her feet having a good or an ill tempered look,—on her knees,—on her waist,—until finally her face came into view, and settled the question. From this it will be seen that I was timid, and that the cellar steps were steep, and that the doorway was very low.

The story centres around Hoghton Towers, to which he is taken in a cart.

I found that we were mounting a steep hill, where the road was a rutty by-road through a field. And so, by fragments of an ancient terrace, and by some rugged out-buildings that had once been fortified, and passing under a ruined gateway we came to the old farm-house in the thick stone wall outside the old quadrangle of Hoghton Towers; which I looked at like a stupid savage, seeing no speciality in, seeing no antiquity in; assuming all farm-houses to resemble it.

The impression obtained on that short visit was a very vivid one, as the following description shows: the reference to James I is the story attaching to the Towers, that here that Monarch knighted the loin of beef ("Sirloin")!

What do I know now of Hoghton Towers? Very little; for I have been gratefully unwilling to disturb my first impressions. A house, centuries old, on high ground a mile or so removed from the road between Preston and Blackburn, where the first James of England, in his hurry to make money by making baronets, perhaps made some of those remunerative dignitaries. A house, centuries old, deserted and falling to pieces, its woods and gardens long since grass land or ploughed up, the Rivers Ribble and Darwen glancing below it, and a vague haze of smoke, against which not even the supernatural prescience of the first Stuart could foresee a counter-blast, hinting at steam-power, powerful in two distances.

What did I know then of Hoghton Towers? When I first peeped in at the gate of the lifeless quadrangle, and started from the mouldering statue becoming visible to me like its guardian ghost; when I stole round by the back of the farm-house, and got in among the ancient rooms, many of them with their floors and ceilings falling, the beams and rafters hanging dangerously down, the plaster dropping as I trod, the oaken panels stripped away, the windows half walled up, half broken; when I discovered a gallery commanding the old kitchen, and looked down between balustrades upon a massive old table and benches, fearing to see I know not what dead-alive creatures come in and seat themselves, and look up with I know not what dreadful eyes, or lack of eyes, at me; when all over the house I was awed by gaps and chinks where the sky stared sorrowfully at me, where the birds passed, and the ivy rustled, and the stains of winter weather blotched the rotten floors, when down at the bottom of dark pits of staircase, into which the stairs had sunk, green leaves trembled, butterflies fluttered, and bees hummed in and out through the broken doorways; when encircling the whole ruin were sweet scents, and sights of fresh green growth, and ever-renewing life, that I had never dreamed of,—I say, when I passed into such clouded perception of these things as my dark soul could compass, what did I know then of Hoghton Towers?

As an example of how environment had so strong an influence on Dickens, it must be added that after the story had been published he wrote to Wills, "it is very curious that I did not in the least see how to begin his state of mind until I walked into Hoghton Towers one bright April day."

It was at Preston in April 1869 that the reading tour came to an abrupt conclusion. Dickens had had a very bad attack at Chester the week before and from there had written to his Doctor, Mr. Carr Beard. The readings that week had been gone through with difficulty, but a week-end at Blackpool had revived Dickens's spirits and health very considerably.

"I telegraphed to the Imperial Hotel for apartments" says Dolby, "which, on our arrival there, we found most comfortable and the fresh breeze blowing from the sea was most invigorating and beneficial to Mr. Dickens, who revived in a wonderful manner."

Dolby was hoping that the rest would enable Dickens to get comfortably through the two remaining readings of the week, Preston and Warrington, but such was not to be, for at Preston the rest of the reading tour was cancelled on doctors' advice, and Dickens returned to Gad's Hill.

From the Imperial Hotel at Blackpool Dickens wrote the following letter to Miss Hogarth in regard to his health:

I have come to this Sea Beach Hotel (charming) for a day's rest. I am much better than I was on Sunday; but shall want careful looking to, to get through the readings. My weakness and deadness are all on the left side; and if

April 26th, 1867, when he saw Hoghton Tower for the first
time.   On this occasion he read in the Town Hall Assembly
Room.

The nest visit was almost two years later, Wednesday,
April 19th, 1869, when he read at the Exchange Assembly
Room, now a cinema.   It was announced as "The last Mr.
Dickens will ever give in Blackburn."   It was almost his last
provincial reading, and he was apparantly in a bad state of
health, to judge from a letter written to Mrs. Watson, from
Blackburn the day after the reading :

> I don't wonder at the papers being confused regarding
> my whereabouts, when I am confused myself.   I am in a
> different place every day . . . I shall be gone from here
> before noon to-morrow: I shall be gone from there (I
> forget where "there" is) before noon next day.   Nothing
> would uphold me through such work but the prospect of
> soon working it out.

.   .   .   .   .

Bolton has a melancholy interest, in the fact that the last
provincial reading took place at the Temperance Hall there
on Tuesday, April 20th, 1869.   The day following Dickens
went to Blackpool to get refreshed by the sea air.   A reading
at Southport was actually contemplated on that day, but was
cancelled so as to allow the remaining two readings of the
week, at Preston and Warrington, to be carried out.   The
reading at Preston on the Thursday was abandoned at the
last hour as we have already shown.

.   .   .   .   .

Warrington, where the reading on Friday, April 23rd, 1869
was cancelled after the breakdown the day previously, was
visited on May 2nd, 1867 for a reading at the Public Hall,
on the site of which the Royal Court Theatre now stands.
This reading ended the 1867 tour.

VI

There was no town in England, outside London itself,
that was more often visited by Dickens, and a favourite with
him too, than Liverpool.

In the *Life of Dickens*, Forster tells us, under date of
1838, how he joined Dickens in Liverpool during the latter's
visit to North Wales with Phiz, on the occasion of which we
have had something to say in Chapter Seven.   This was

probably the novelist's first visit to Liverpool. "Between the completion of *Oliver* and its publication, Dickens went to see something of North Wales; and joining him at Liverpool, I returned with him," writes Forster, to whom Dickens had written from Llangollen on November 3rd, 1838: "Go straight to Liverpool by the first Birmingham train on Monday morning, and at the Adelphi Hotel in that town you will find me."

It was from Liverpool that Dickens and his wife set sail in the *Britannia* for the United States on January 4th, 1842. On this occasion he again stayed at the Adelphi Hotel, to which he was faithful on all his subsequent visits. In *American Notes* he tells us:

I have not inquired among my medical acquaintance, whether Turtle, and cold Punch, with Hock, Champagne, and Claret, and all the slight et cetera usually included in an unlimited order for a good dinner—especially when it is left to the liberal construction of my faultless friend, Mr. Radley, of the Adelphi Hotel—are peculiarly calculated to suffer a sea-change; or whether a plain muttonchop, and a glass or two of sherry, would be less likely of conversion into foreign and disconcerting material. My own opinion is, that whether one is discreet or indiscreet in these particulars, on the eve of a sea-voyage, is a matter of little consequence; and that, to use a common phrase, "it comes to very much the same thing in the end." Be this as it may, I know that the dinner of that day was undeniably perfect; that it comprehended all these items, and a great many more; and that we all did ample justice to it. And I know, too, that, bating a certain tacit avoidance of any allusion to to-morrow; such as may be supposed to prevail between delicate-minded turnkeys, and a sensitive prisoner who is to be hanged next morning; we got on very well, and, all things considered, were merry enough.

A new Adelphi Hotel now rears its stately head on the site of the hotel kept by James Radley to which Dickens was so very partial. Dolby, in " Charles Dickens as I Knew Him " has something interesting to say respecting Dickens's fondness for this hotel. He is referring to a reading at the neighbouring city of Manchester :

"After the reading on the 12th, we returned the same night to Liverpool, as amongst the hotels in the large towns in England none was such a favourite with Mr. Dickens as the Adelphi at Liverpool—then kept by the late Mr. James went to look at it with him. It is an enormous place, and the tickets have been selling at two and even three guineas apiece. The lecture-room, in which the celebration is held, will accommodate over thirteen hundred people. It was being fitted with gas after the manner of the ring at Astley's. I should think it an easy place to speak in, being a semi-circle with seats rising one above another to the ceiling, and will have eight hundred ladies to-night, in full dress. I am rather shaky just now, but shall pull up, I have no doubt. At dinner-time to-morrow you will receive, I hope, a facetious document hastily penned after I return to-night, telling you how it all went off.

The promised "facetious document" was duly enclosed and read as follows:

OUT OF THE COMMON—PLEASE

Dickens *against* The World

Charles Dickens, of No. 1, Devonshire Terrace, York Gate, Regent's Park, in the county of Middlesex, gentleman, the successful plaintiff in the above cause, maketh oath and saith: That on the day and date hereof, to wit at seven o'clock in the evening, he, this deponent, took the chair at a large assembly of the Mechanics' Institution at Liverpool, and that having been received with tremendous and enthusiastic plaudits, he, this deponent, did immediately dash into a vigorous, brilliant, humorous, pathetic, eloquent, fervid, and impassioned speech. That the said speech was enlivened by thirteen hundred persons with frequent, vehement, uproarious, and defeaning cheers, and to the best of this deponent's knowledge and belief, he, this deponent, did speak up like a man, and did to the best of his knowledge and belief, considerably distinguish himself. That after the proceedings of the opening were over, and a vote of thanks was proposed to this deponent, he, this deponent, did again distinguish himself, and that the cheering at that time, accompanied with clapping of hands and stamping of feet, was in this deponent's case thundering and awful. And this deponent further saith, that his white-and-black or magpie waistcoat, did create a strong sensation, and that during the hours of promenading, this deponent heard from persons surrounding him such exclamations as, "What is it!

it a waistcoat? No, it's a shirt"—and the like—all of which this deponent believes to have been complimentary and gratifying; but this deponent further saith that he is now going to supper, and wishes he may have an appetite to eat it.

CHARLES DICKENS.

Sworn before me at the Adelphi
Hotel, Liverpool, on February
26th, 1844.

S. RADLEY.

The letter further tells how he met here his sister Fanny, lately married to Mr. Burnet of Manchester, and went with her to visit Captain Hewett and the s.s. *Britannia* which had taken them to America two years before.

When I came back here, I found Fanny and Hewett had picked me up just before. We all went off straight to the *Britannia*, which lay where she did when we went on board. We went into the old little cabin and the ladies' cabin, but Mrs. Bean had gone to Scotland, as the ship does not sail again before May. In the saloon we had some champagne and biscuits, and Hewett had set out upon the table a block of Boston ice, weighing fifty pounds.

On Wednesday, July 28th, 1847, he appeared in "Every Man in his Humour" with his illustrious company of amateur actors at the Theatre Royal for the benefit of the fund being raised for Leigh Hunt; and the following year, on June 5th, the company performed at the Amphitheatre for the benefit of the fund for the endowment of a perpetual curatorship at Shakespeare's house at Stratford-on-Avon. It was some four years later before he again appeared as an actor in Liverpool. This time it was in aid of the funds of the Guild of Literature and Art, on February 13th and 14th, 1852, at the Philharmonic Hall. These performances concluded the little tour. To Lytton, who had been with him at the Manchester performance a night or two before, Dickens wrote from London the day after:

At Liverpool I had a Round Robin on the stage after the play was over, a place being left for your signature, and as I am going to have it framed, I'll tell Green to send it to Lincoln's-Inn-Fields. You have no idea how good Tenniel, Topham and Collins have been in what they had to do.

There was very severe weather at that time, which affected the sale of tickets in the better parts of the hall, "it being next to impossible for people to come out at night with horses," and his letter further speaks of the delay in the Atlantic mail-boats causing great anxiety. The weather did not deter him from his accustomed walks. "We have been out for four hours in the bitter east wind, and walking on the sea shore, where there is a broad strip of great blocks of ice."

On February 15th he again wrote to his sister-in-law of his previous night's reading at Liverpool:

We had an enormous turn-away last night, and do not doubt about having a cram to-night. The day has been very fine, and I have turned it to the wholesomest account by walking on the sands at New Brighton all the morning. I am not quite right within, but believe it to be an effect of the railway shaking. There is no doubt of the fact that, after the Staplehurst experience, it tells more and more (railway shaking, that is) instead of, as one might have expected, less and less. The charming room here greatly lessens the fatigue of this fatiguing week. I read last night with no more exertion than if I had been at Gad's and yet to eleven hundred people and with astonishing effect.

Early in August, 1867, Dickens was in Liverpool seeing his manager, Dolby, off to America, to report upon the prospects of a reading tour there, which being very favourable, Dickens left Liverpool on November 9th in s.s. *Cuba* for his second visit to the United States.

On his return to England in 1868, Dickens gave further readings in the St. George's Hall on October 12th, 13th, 14th, 26th, 27th and 28th, and six months later gave his final readings in Liverpool. These were four in number, and were given on April 5th, 6th, 8th and 9th, 1869, at the Theatre Royal. On the conclusion, at the invitation of the Mayor, Dickens was entertained at a puclic banquet in the St. George's Hall on April 10th, when Lord Dufferin presided, and in the course of his reply to the toast of his health, Dickens said:

"It is no homage to Liverpool based upon a moment's untrustworthy enthusiasm, but it is the solid fact, built upon the rock of experience, that when I first made up my mind, after considerable deliberation, systematically to meet my readers in large numbers, face to face, to try to express myself to them through the breath of life, Liverpool stood foremost among the great places out of London to which I had looked with eager confidence and pleasure. And why was this? Not merely because of the reputation of its citizens for generous estimation of the arts; not merely because I had unworthily filled the chair of its great self-educational institution long ago; not merely because the place had been a home to me since the well-remembered day when its blessed roofs and steeples dipped into the Mersey behind me on the occasion of my first sailing away to see my generous friends across the Atlantic twenty-seven years ago. Not for one of those considerations, but because it had been my happiness to have a public opportunity of testing the spirit of its people. I had asked Liverpool for help towards the worthy preservation of Shakespeare's house. On another occasion I had ventured to address Liverpool in the names of Leigh Hunt and Sheridan Knowles. On still another occasion I had addressed it in the cause of brotherhood and sisterhood of letters and the kindred arts, and on each and on all the response had been unsurpassable, spontaneous, open-handed, and munificent."

Dolby tells us that after this speech "Mr. Dickens walked to the station, and the good feeling of the people of Liverpool showed itself heartily in the street; for during his progress to the station he was repeatedly stopped by persons of the working classes wanting to shake hands with him, and all of them eager to thank him for the pleasure his books had afforded them. This, however, was not a new experience to him in the large manufacturing towns."

Although Liverpool saw a great deal of Dickens and it played an important part in his life; yet there is only a bare mention of the city in several of his writings, and then mostly as the port of embarkation for the New World. Thus, even before he made the passage of the Atlantic himself he caused Mr. Vincent Crummles to set off from Liverpool to America, and at a later date made Martin Chuzzlewit to follow his example. In neither case is there more than a passing reference to Liverpool; but when Martin and Mark returned to England by the *Screw*, we have a cheerful picture of the scene on their arrival.

It was mid-day, and high water in the English port for which the *Screw* was bound, when, borne in gallantly upon the fulness of the tide, she let go her anchor in the river.

Thus it came about that the second pilgrimage of the Pickwickians was through Essex into Suffolk, for whatever may be the true identity of the town of Eatanswill, Mr. Pickwick travelled by the Norwich coach and from Eatanswill took another coach to Bury St. Edmunds.

The journey to Ipswich was made at a subsequent date from the Bull Inn, Whitechapel, when Tony Weller himself was the coachman and the best account of the road is given in that chapter of *The Pickwick Papers* dealing with the journey; but unfortunately after leaving the Whitechapel district, details are lacking of the road through which they passed.

According to "Cary's Itinerary," the Norwich coaches which started from the Bull in Whitechapel went via Sudbury, and that is one of the best reasons for supposing Sudbury, rather than Ipswich, to have stood for Eatanswill.

In later years David Copperfield was made to traverse this very same road, as the first portion of his journey to and from Yarmouth.

The composite route we propose taking is via Chigwell to Chelmsford, Sudbury, Bury St. Edmunds, Ipswich, Norwich and Yarmouth.

Although Chigwell is only a dozen miles from London, it has far escaped the ruthless hand of the builder, and presents all the rural charms of a village in the heart of the country.

The sole claim of Chigwell to Dickensian interest rests in its connection with *Barnaby Rudge*: but what a claim that is!

It is doubtful if Dickens has endeared us more to any of the Inns which he described, than he has to the Maypole at Chigwell; how alluring is his description at the very outset of the story of the "house of public entertainment called the Maypole" that, "in the year 1775 . . . stood upon the borders of Epping Forest, at a distance of about twelve miles from London," with its "emblem reared on the roadside over against the house": how attractive are the characters that we first meet round the blazing fire; old John Willet the landlord with his staring, stolid face; little Solomon Daisy "the parish clerk and bell-ringer of Chigwell: a village hard by" and the teller of "the famous Maypole story"; "short Tom Cobb the general chandler," and "long Phil Parkes, the ranger."

But first, the description of the Maypole itself:

The Maypole was an old building, with more gable ends than a lazy man would care to count on a sunny day; huge zig-zag chimneys, out of which it seemed as though even smoke could not choose but come in more than naturally fantastic shapes, imparted to it in its tortuous progress; and vast stables, gloomy, ruinous, and empty. The place was said to have been built in the days of King Henry the Eighth; and there was a legend, not only that Queen Elizabeth had slept there one night while upon a hunting excursion, to wit, in a certain oak-panelled room with a deep bay window, but that next morning, while standing on a mounting block before the door with one foot in the stirrup, the virgin monarch had then and there boxed and cuffed an unlucky page for some neglect of duty. . . .

Whether these, and many other stories of the like nature, were true or untrue, the Maypole was really an old house, a very old house, perhaps as old as it claimed to be, and perhaps older, which will sometimes happen with houses of an uncertain, as with ladies of a certain age. Its windows were old diamond-pane lattices, its floors were sunken and uneven, its ceilings blackened by the hand of time, and heavy with massive beams. Over the doorway was an ancient porch, quaintly and grotesquely carved; and here on summer evenings the more favoured customers smoked and drank—ay, and sang many a good song too, sometimes—reposing on two grim-looking high-backed settles, which, like the twin dragons of some fairy tale, guarded the entrance to the mansion.

In the chimneys of the disused rooms, swallows had built their nests for many a long year, and from earliest spring to latest autumn whole colonies of sparrows chirped and twittered in the eaves. There were more pigeons about the dreary stable yard and out-buildings than anybody but the landlord could reckon up. . . . With its overhanging stories, drowsy little panes of glass, and front bulging out and projecting over the pathway, the old house looked as if it were nodding in its sleep. Indeed, it needed no very great stretch of fancy to detect in it other resemblances to humanity. The bricks of which it was built had originally been a deep dark red, but had grown yellow and discoloured like an old man's skin; the sturdy timbers had decayed like teeth; and here and there the ivy, like a warm garment to comfort it in its age, wrapt its green leaves closely round the time-worn walls.

The whole story of *Barnaby Rudge* centres round the Maypole, and Dickens describes it fully both inside and out, with a little exaggeration at times that is the writer's license. It is somewhat remarkable therefore that Dickens should have chosen to give it a fictitious name, for there is no Maypole at Chigwell, the only inn there being the King's Head, the name it has borne for over a couple of centuries. There is, however, at Chigwell Row, which is referred to by Solomon Daisy in his story, as being a mile and a half away, a Maypole Inn whose name may possibly have suggested itself to Dickens as a more suitable one for his story.

Dickens must have been very familiar with Chigwell long before *Barnaby Rudge* was written. After its publication we find him writing to Forster on March 25th, 1841, appointing the place for a pleasant gathering:

> Chigwell, my dear fellow, is the greatest place in the world. Name your day for going. Such a delicious old Inn, opposite the Church-yard—such a lovely ride—such beautiful forest scenery—such an out of the way, rural, place—such a sexton! I say again name your day.

In quoting this letter Forster adds a note which completes the identity of the "delicious old inn opposite the church-yard" with the Maypole of *Barnaby Rudge*.

> The day was named at once, and the whitest of stones marks it, in now sorrowful memory. Dickens's promise was exceeded by our enjoyment; and his delight in the double recognition of himself and of Barnaby, by the Landlord of the nice old Inn, far exceeded any pride he would have taken in what the world thinks the highest sort of honour.

The exterior of the King's Head presents a very quaint appearance, and the solitude of its surroundings is an enhancement to its picturesqueness.

If, from the interior, we miss the kitchen with its cosy chimney corner which was so alluring to Gabriel Varden that he often went out of his way to avoid the Mapyole on his way home from the Warren, rather than break his promise to his wife by looking in, we have the pleasure of taking our refreshment in the Chester Room—the "best apartment, spacious enough in all conscience, occupying the whole depth of the house, and having at either end a great bay window, as large as many modern rooms . . . although the best room in the Inn, it had the melancholy aspect of grandeur in decay and was much too vast for comfort," and of reviewing there all the comings and goings at the Maypole described in the story.

Mr. Haredale's house, the Warren, figures largely in the story and was ultimately destroyed by the rioters—at which

THE MAYPOLE, CHIGWELL

THE ANGEL, BURY ST. EDMUNDS

[*Photos by T. W. Tyrrell*

time Nemesis overtook the elder Rudge who, in the first chapter, asked questions about the house while in disguise at the Maypole.

"What house is that which stands a mile or so from here?"

"Public-house!" said the landlord, with his usual deliberation.

"Public-house, father!" exclaimed Joe, "where's the public-house within a mile or so of the Maypole? He means the great house—the Warren—naturally and of course. The old red brick house, sir, that stands in its own grounds—"

"Aye" said the stranger.

"And that fifteen or twenty years ago stood in a park five times as broad, which with other and richer property has bit by bit changed hands and dwindled away—more's the pity!" pursued the young man.

There is no such house in the district to-day: nor have we been able to trace one in Dickens's day to answer the description: but there was a Warren House in existence in 1770, about a mile away from the church, the residence of Sir Peter Warren, M.P. for Westminster, and Dickens may have heard of it. He usually called it the Warren, but in chapter thirty-four it is referred to as Warren House. It is thus described in chapter thirteen:

It was a dreary, silent building, with echoing courtyards, desolated turret-chambers, and whole suites of rooms shut up and mouldering to ruin.

The terrace-garden, dark with the shade of overhanging trees, had an air of melancholy that was quite oppressive. Great iron gates, disused for many years, and red with rust, drooping on their hinges and overgrown with long rank grass, seemed as though they tried to sink into the ground, and hide their fallen state among the friendly weeds. The fantastic monsters on the walls, green with age and damp, and covered here and there with moss, looked grim and desolate. There was a sombre aspect even on that part of the mansion which was inhabited and kept in good repair, that struck the beholder with a sense of sadness; of something forlorn and failing, whence cheerfulness was banished. It would have been difficult to imagine a bright fire blazing in the dull and darkened rooms, or to picture any gaiety of heart or revelry that the frowning walls shut in. It seemed a place where such things had been, but could be no more—the very ghost of a house, haunting the old spot in its old outward form, and that was all.

From Chigwell, our way lies through Abridge and Ongar and we join the main Ipswich–Norwich road at Chelmsford, 29½ miles from London. We do not hear that the presentiment of Dickens was realised, so we presume he reached Chelmsford without causing mortal harm to any person, whether an "only child" or otherwise. Chelmsford possesses a modern inn with an old name, the Black Boy, a famous coaching house in its time.

It was the elder Weller who gave Mr. Pickwick the clue to the presence of Jingle at Ipswich by informing him, that, working the Ipswich coach for a friend of his, he had met both Job Trotter and Jingle "at the Black Boy at Chelmsford——the wery place they'd come to—and I took 'em up, right through to Ipswich."

Thereupon Mr. Pickwick started off in pursuit, but we do not hear that the coach made a stop at the Black Boy on the way.

From Chelmsford, the quickest way to Ipswich is through Colchester, 21¾ miles distant; this was the direct road Mr. Pickwick took in company with Mr. Magnus, but no mention is made of Colchester on the way. Nevertheless it has an interest to us, as it was at Colchester that Dickens gave a reading in the Theatre, on November 1st, 1861. He refers to the evident success of the reading in a letter written that day from the Great White Horse Hotel in Ipswich:

At mid-day we go on to Colchester, where I shall expect the young Morgans. I sent a telegram on yesterday, after receiving your note, to secure places for them. The answer returned by telegraph was: "No box-seats left but on the fourth row." If they prefer to sit on the stage (for I read in the theatre, there being no other large public room), they shall. Meantime I have told John, who went forward this morning with the other men, to let the people at the inn know that if three travellers answering that description appear before my dinner-time, they are to dine with me.

However, avoiding Colchester in the present journey, we proceed on the main Norwich Road 25½ miles to Sudbury.

Before leaving Essex for Suffolk we must not forget that the mouth of the River Thames divides that county from Kent, and there are often casual references in the novels to the Essex side of the river, notably in *David Copperfield*, and

Bleak House, in which latter book we are introduced to the fog on the Essex Marshes.

Magwitch in *Great Expectations* was "as near as possible" born in Essex, for he tells Pip:

> I've no more notion where I was born, than you have—if so much. I first became aware of myself, down in Essex, a thieving turnips for my living. Summun had run away from me—a man—a tinker—and he'd took the fire with him, and left me wery cold.

and, according to my friend, Colonel Gadd, it was on Canvey Island, at the Lobster Smack Inn, that the final scenes of the chase, and death of Magwitch, took place.

II

Suffolk was the county, other than Kent, that Dickens was fairly acquainted with, before he wrote *The Pickwick Papers*. In 1834 he wrote "A Passage in the Life of Mr. Watkins Tottle," which appeared in the " Monthly Magazine " for January and February, 1835, and in this we read:

> When I was in Suffolk . . . which is now some years ago, business led me to the town of Bury St. Edmunds. I had to stop at the principal places in my way, and, there-fore, for the sake of convenience, I travelled in a gig. I left Sudbury one dark night . . .

In the July of that year (1834) Dickens, then 22 years of age, went to Sudbury, to report the Parliamentary bye-election.

In *The Pickwick Papers*, the Pickwickians arrive at Bury St. Edmunds from Eatanswill, and this, in our opinion, is the best reason that can be advanced for declaring Sudbury as the original of that famous town, whose origin has for long been a matter of discussion in the Dickens world. Dickens knew Sudbury only in relation to the Norwich road running through Bury St. Edmunds—not in relation with Ipswich, which has still some ardent supporters who declare it to be the one and only Eatanswill. To Ipswich, it will be remembered, the Pickwickians made a special journey from London, after returning from Bury St. Edmunds.

Eatanswill—like Muggleton—is one of the few towns in *The Pickwick Papers* that Dickens disguised. The name is sufficiently suggestive. Some say he derived it from the town of Eaton Socon—which in *Nicholas Nickleby* he humorously calls Eton Slocomb (see page 198). Be that as it may, Eatanswill was on the road to Norwich, and the London side of Bury St. Edmunds.

Ipswich is on one of the main roads leading to Norwich, and it was this way that David Copperfield undoubtedly travelled to and from Yarmouth, as we shall see later on.

It was at the tavern off Cheapside—"second court on the right hand side—last house but vun on the same side the vay—" ("Mr. Weller's knowledge of London was extensive and peculiar") that old Tony Weller declared that the "chap, slim and tall, with long hair, and the gift o' the gab wery galloping . . . and a black haired chap in mulberry livery" were at Ipswich. And so Mr. Pickwick decided to follow him, adding "We may as well see Ipswich as any other place." Accordingly, from the Bull Inn, Whitechapel, in the coach driven by old Tony, Mr. Pickwick and Sam went to Ipswich, the tediousness of the journey being beguiled by the two Wellers with "conversation possessing the inestimable charm of blending amusement with instruction" and particularly dealing with oysters and pike keepers: and enlivened by Mr. Magnus and his anxiety concerning the safety of "the two bags, the leather hat box, and the brown paper parcel."

There is no account given of the road to Ipswich and we are plunged all at once into a description of the town of Ipswich and its noted hostelry :

In the main street of Ipswich, on the left-hand side of the way, a short distance after you have passed through the open space fronting the Town Hall, stands an inn known far and wide by the appellation of the Great White Horse, rendered the more conspicuous by a stone statue of some rampacious animal with flowing mane and tail, distantly resembling an insane cart-horse, which is elevated above the principal door. The Great White Horse is famous in the neighbourhood, in the same degree as a prize ox, or county paper-chronicled turnip, or unwieldy pig—for its enormous size. Never were such labyrinths of uncarpeted passages, such clusters of mouldy, ill-lighted rooms, such huge numbers of small dens for eating or sleeping in, beneath any one roof, as are collected together between the four walls of the Great White Horse at Ipswich.

It was at the door of this overgrown tavern that the London coach stopped, at the same hour every evening; and it was from this same London coach, that Mr. Pickwick, Sam Weller, and Mr. Peter Magnus dismounted, on the

THE GREAT WHITE HORSE, IPSWICH

[*Photo by Walter Dexter*

particular evening to which this chapter of our history bears reference.

Upon Mr. Pickwick's enquiring "is there any gentleman of the name of Tupman here, waiter?"

A corpulent man, with a fortnight's napkin under his arm, and coeval stockings on his legs, slowly desisted from his occupation of staring down the street, on this question being put to him by Mr. Pickwick; and, after minutely inspecting that gentleman's appearance, from the crown of his hat to the lowest button of his gaiters, replied emphatically: "No."

Thereupon Mr. Pickwick and Mr. Magnus decided to dine alone, and asked the waiter to show them a private room.

On this request being preferred, the corpulent man condescended to order the boots to bring in the gentlemen's luggage and preceding them down a long dark passage, ushered them into a large badly-furnished apartment, with a dirty grate, in which a small fire was making a wretched attempt to be cheerful, but was fast sinking beneath the dispiriting influence of the place. After the lapse of an hour, a bit of a fish and a steak was served up to the travellers and when the dinner was cleared away, Mr. Pickwick and Mr. Peter Magnus drew their chairs up to the fire, and having ordered a bottle of the worst posssible port wine, at the highest possible price, for the good of the house, drank brandy and water for their own.

It is said that Dickens had a grudge against the Inn; and it would certainly appear that he had!

Dickens was in Ipswich in 1835 to report the speeches at the Parliamentary Election of that year; and on the authority of the "Suffolk Chronicle"—for which it is said he was working, he stayed at the Great White Horse for two or three weeks, and it is surmised that the adventure, ascribed to Mr. Pickwick with "the middle-aged lady in the yellow curl papers" was an experience of young Dickens himself, and he was so incensed against the place that he wrote of it in the disparaging way to which we have referred.

But, it is pleasant to notice that the hotel is to-day proud of the fact that its name has been handed down to posterity in the pages of *Pickwick*, and nothing gives the manager so much pleasure as to direct you to the room which Mr.

T

Pickwick mistook for his own; and there you can see the identical (?) four-poster bedstead, out from the curtains of which Mr. Pickwick peeped, to behold the "Middle-aged lady, in yellow curl-papers, busily engaged in brushing what ladies call their 'back hair.'"

It is also interesting to note that on the occasions of his visits in 1859 and 1861 for the readings, Dickens stayed at the Great White Horse, as his letters testify.

It is typical of all Dickens's topography, that it has crept into the language and become a part of it, with its characters real living beings, and in a guide book to England that is not given to "writing up" any particular place, but which consists of a quantity of well-marshalled and interesting facts, we should hardly expect to find such references as these, under the headings of Ipswich and Bury respectively:

"Running E. from Cornhill is Tavern Street, with the Great White Horse Hotel (leaden sign) in which occurred Mr. Pickwick's remarkable adventure with the lady in yellow curl-papers. . . . In St. Clement's Lane, off Fore Street, Sam Weller saw Job Trotter coming out of the green garden gate.

Opposite (the Abbey) is the Angel Hotel where Sam Weller first encountered Job Trotter."

Yet these extracts are taken from "England," in Muirhead's "Blue" Guide Series, a noteworthy set now in course of publication.

The next morning we are introduced to the two Wellers taking their morning repast at the Great White Horse "in a small room in the vicinity of the stable-yard" when the elder one remarks on the "wery good power o' suction" that his son possesses, and gives that amusing dissertation on the subject of Widders.

When the two parted, the elder to his London coach, Sam, we are told, bent his steps "towards St. Clements Church" and "endeavoured to dissipate his melancholy, by strolling among its ancient precincts."

Here in St. Clement's Lane was the house with "a green gate," at the far end of a "kind of courtyard of venerable appearance—which he discovered had no other outlet than the turning by which he had entered." Sam was fortunate enough to recognise Job Trotter despite his attempt to disguise himself by "contorting his face into the most fearful and astonishing grimaces that ever were beheld."

This, of course, was the house of Mr. Nupkins, the Mayor of Ipswich, before whom Mr. Pickwick was brought for a breach of the peace concerning the middle-aged lady with the yellow curl papers: and the account of the "trial" is quite as amusing as the other and more famous Trial to be engaged in later on.

This house provided Sam with a sweetheart: for Mary was the Mayor's housemaid, and the famous valentine he penned her later, signed—in "poetry"

<blockquote>
"Your love sick
Pickwick"
</blockquote>

was addressed "Mary, Housemaid at Mr. Nupkins, Mayor's, Ipswich, Suffolk."

The main road between London and Yarmouth, through Ipswich, was often traversed by David Copperfield, and particular mention of the fact is made in chapter fifty-five on the day of the great storm which resulted in the death of Ham and Steerforth:

> When the day broke, it blew harder and harder. . . . We came to Ipswich—very late, having had to fight every inch of ground since we were ten miles out of London; and found a cluster of people in the market-place, who had risen from their beds in the night, fearful of falling chimneys. Some of these congregating about the inn-yard while we changed horses, told us of the great sheets of lead having been ripped off a high church-tower, and flung into a bye-street, which they then blocked up. Others had to tell of country people, coming in from neighbouring villages, who had seen great trees lying torn out of the earth, and whole ricks scattered about the roads and fields.

The Inn yard mentioned was doubtless that of the Great White Horse.

It was at Ipswich that Doctor Marigold courted his wife "from the footboard of the cart. She was a Suffolk young woman, and it was at Ipswich Market Place, right opposite the cornchandler's shop."

Dickens visited Ipswich three times on his reading tours. The first reading was on October 10th, 1859, in the Hall of what was then the Mechanics' Institute, now known as the Ipswich Institute, when he wrote home referring to the fine perception of the audience and a " demonstrativeness equal to the great working towns."

The reading on October 31st, 1861, was given in the Public Hall and his Farewell Reading was in the same hall on March 17th, 1869.

v

The Pickwickians never went farther east than Bury St. Edmunds and Ipswich: our tour now becomes solely associated with *David Copperfield*. There is a direct road from Ipswich to Norwich of 42 miles: and we go to Norwich first, before visiting Yarmouth to get an introduction to the Copperfield country in the same manner as Dickens himself obtained it.

In 1848 Dickens was searching for an objective for a winter jaunt with Mark Lemon, John Leech and Forster, on the same lines as the one they had taken earlier in the year in the neighbourhood of Stonehenge (see page 114). He first proposed Blackgang Chine in the Isle of Wight, but that fell through and then Dickens wrote to Forster: " It would be better to make an outburst to some old cathedral city we don't know, and what do you say to Norwich and Stanfield Hall? "

"Thither accordingly the three friends went," says Forster, "illness at the last disabling me; and of the result I heard (January 12th, 1849) that Stanfield Hall, the scene of a recent frightful tragedy, had nothing attractive unless the term might be applied to 'a murderous look that seemed to invite such a crime. We arrived,' continued Dickens, 'between the Hall and Potass farm, as the search was going on for the pistol in a manner so consummately stupid, that there was nothing on earth to prevent any of Rush's labourers from accepting five pounds from Rush Junior to find the weapon and give it to him.' "

The murder was that of the Recorder of Norwich, by Rush, who was executed at Norwich Castle.

We do not know why Dickens should have written Forster: "Norwich a disappointment, all save its place of execution, which we found fit for a gigantic scoundrel's exit. Perhaps it was overshadowed by what follows:

" But the success of the trip, for me, was to come. Yarmouth, sir, where we went afterwards, is the strangest place in the wide world: one hundred and forty-six miles of hill-less march between it and London. More when we meet. I shall certainly try my hand at it."

Thus it came about that a great part of *David Copperfield* is centred in the Yarmouth district.

On October 11th and 12th, 1859, Dickens made his first appearance in Norwich as a reader. "The Norwich people were a noble audience," he wrote, "we had a demonstration of the great working towns, and a much finer perception."

Dickens's second series of readings started with two nights at Norwich in 1861. His old friend and manager, Arthur Smith, had lately died: he had not yet engaged his later manager, George Dolby, and was evidently much out of sorts, for, after the first reading, on Monday, October 28th, he wrote from the Royal Hotel, Norwich (now no longer in existence).

I cannot say that we began well last night. We had not a good hall, and they were a very lumpish audience indeed. This did not tend to cheer the strangeness I felt in being without Arthur, and I was not at all myself. We have a large let for to-night, I think two hundred and fifty stalls, which is very large, and I hope that both they and I will go better. I could have done perfectly last night, if the audience had been bright, but they were an intent and staring audience. They laughed though very well, and the storm made them shake themselves again. But they were not magnetic, and the great big place was out of sorts somehow.

To Wilkie Collins he wrote in somewhat the same strain, and referred to St. Andrew's Hall, in which he read, a fine example of perpendicular architecture, and originally the nave of the church of the Dominicans.

The first night at Norwich was a dismal beginning— altogether unwonted and strange. We had not a good let and (the place of reading being a great cold stone paved Gothic Hall) the audience appeared to be afraid of me and of each other. I was out of sorts. Everything seemed forlorn and strange to me. Poor dear Arthur gone, and the very wind in the arches (—— them!) seemed to howl about it. . . . Next night was *Nickleby* and *The Trial*. I had had a good walk in the bright air, and time to reason myself up a bit. There was a brilliant audience. . . . The people were really quite ridiculous to to see when Squeers read the boys' letters.

To Miss Hogarth he wrote more cheerfully the next day from Bury:

"The rooks—what has become of them?" asked Miss Betsey.

"There have not been any since we have lived here," said my mother. "We thought—Mr. Copperfield thought —it was quite a large rookery; but the nests were very old ones, and the birds have deserted them a long while."

"David Copperfield all over!" cried Miss Betsey. "David Copperfield from head to foot! Calls a house a rookery when there's not a rook near it, and takes the birds on trust, because he sees the nests!"

There is no doubt that the Rectory at Blundeston is the original of the "Rookery," although little David's account of the "long passage" leading to the kitchen might have been taken from Blundeston Hall, now called The Lodge, which it is said Dickens visited at this time.

On the ground-floor is Peggotty's kitchen, opening into a back yard; with a pigeon-house on a pole, in the centre, without any pigeons in it; a great dog-kennel in a corner, without any dog; and a quantity of fowls that look terribly tall to me, walking about, in a menacing and ferocious manner.

.   .   .   .   .   .

Here is a long passage—what an enormous perspective I make of it!—leading from Peggotty's kitchen to the front door. A dark store-room opens out of it, and that is a place to be run past at night; for I don't know what may be among those tubs and jars and old tea chests, when there is nobody in there with a dimly-burning light, letting a mouldy air come out at the door, in which there is the smell of soap, pickles, pepper, candles, and coffee, all at one whiff. Then there are the two parlors; the parlor in which we sit of an evening, my mother and I and Peggotty. . . .

And now I see the outside of our house, with the latticed bed-room windows standing open to let in the sweet-smelling air, and the ragged old rooks'-nests still dangling in the elm-trees at the bottom of the front garden. Now I am in the garden at the back, beyond the yard where the empty pigeon-house and dog-kennel are—a very preserve of butterflies, as I remember it, with a high fence, and a gate and padlock.

In a later chapter we are given some of those personal

BLUNDESTONE RECTORY

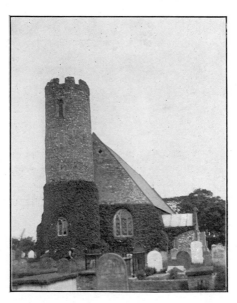

BLUNDESTONE CHURCH

[Photo by Walter Dexter

touches which go to show how much of Dickens's self was put into the story, among which is a picture of

> A summer evening, the boys at play in the church-yard, and I sitting on my bed, reading as if for life. Every barn in the neighbourhood, every stone in the church, and every foot of the churchyard, had some association of its own, in my mind, connected with these books, and stood for some locality made famous in them. I have seen Tom Pipes go climbing up the church-steeple; I have watched Strap, with the knapsack on his back, stopping to rest himself upon the wicket-gate; and I *know* that Commodore Trunnion held that club with Mr. Pickle, in the parlor of our little village alehouse.

Thus do we to-day pursue our topographical enquiries only in the way that Dickens himself did!

In chapter two there is a reference to the Church:

> There is nothing half so green that I know anywhere, as the grass of that churchyard; nothing half so shady as its trees; nothing half so quiet as its tomb-stones. The sheep are feeding there, when I kneel up, early in the morning, in my little bed in a closet within my mother's room, to look out at it; and I see the red light shining on the sun-dial, and think within myself, "Is the sun-dial glad, I wonder, that it can tell the time again?"

This is a proof that the Rookery must have been the Rectory as the churchyard is not visible from the Hall. The visitor will notice the sundial over the porch, and will recall David's recollection of the high-backed pew they occupied in the church, near a window out of which their house could be seen.

The Plough Inn at Blundeston is "our little village ale house" and from here Mr. Barkis's cart used to start for Yarmouth. It is said that when Dickens visited the place the name of the carrier was Barker!

In 1853 Dickens, in writing to Mrs. Watson, said:

> Lowestoft I know, by walking over there from Yarmouth when I went down on an exploring expedition previous to *Copperfield*. It is a fine place.

Lowestoft has an interesting connection with *David Copperfield*—the Royal Hotel there being no less than the birthplace of that immortal expression "Brooks of Sheffield" (see page 237).

It was before the second and disastrous marriage of David's mother, that her admirer, Mr. Murdstone, said to her that he was going to Lowestoft to see some friends who were there with a yacht, and merrily proposed "to take young David on the saddle before him if he would like the ride."

And so David accompanied him, and "went to a hotel by the sea, where two gentlemen were smoking cigars."

This was undoubtedly the Royal Hotel, and here his mother was referred to as "bewitching" and "pretty little widow," which occasioned Mr. Murdstone to say:

> "Take care, if you please, somebody's sharp!"
> "Who is?" asked the gentleman laughing.
> I looked up quickly, being anxious to know.
> "Only Brooks of Sheffield" said Mr. Murdstone.

and here later they drank in sherry "Confusion to Brooks of Sheffield," with much laughter.

VII

Just prior to Mrs. Copperfield's second marriage, Peggotty took David for a fortnight's holiday to her brother's house at Yarmouth. They went by Barkis's cart by "so many deviations up and down lanes and were such a long time delivering a bedstead at a public house." It is suggested that the Village Maid at Lound was the public-house in question.

Here too, when later on, Barkis again drove Peggotty and David into Yarmouth, they no doubt stopped:

> He was so polite as to stop at a public-house, expressly on our account, and entertain us with broiled mutton and beer. . . . But as we drew nearer to the end of our journey, he had more to do and less time for gallantry; and when we got on Yarmouth pavement, we were all too much shaken and jolted, I apprehend, to have any leisure for anything else.

Later in the same chapter, we read that Peggotty's Wedding Breakfast was taken in "a little inn in a bye road"—perhaps it was the same inn as the one previously referred to, as Barkis was not a man to vary his places of call.

David Copperfield often traversed the road between Blundeston and Yarmouth, and on the occasion of the burial of Mr. Barkis at Blunderstone, he tells us how he parted from the two Peggottys and "instead of going back, waited a little distance on the road to Lowestoft.   Then I turned, and walked back towards Yarmouth," stopping to dine at a "decent ale house some mile or two from the ferry."   This, says Mr. Matz in "Dickensian Inns and Taverns" was probably the Feathers at Gorleston.

To resume little David's account of his first visit to Yarmouth:

I was quite tired and very glad when we saw Yarmouth. It looked rather spongy and soppy, I thought, as I carried my eye over the great dull waste that lay across the river; and I could not help wondering, if the world were really as round as my geography-book said, how any part of it came to be so flat.   But I reflected that Yarmouth might be situated at one of the poles; which would account for it.

As we drew a little nearer, and saw the whole adjacent prospect lying a straight low line under the sky, I hinted to Peggotty that a mound or so might have improved it; and also that if the land had been a little more separated from the sea, and the town and the tide had not been quite so much mixed up, like toast and water, it would have been nicer.   But Peggotty said, with greater emphasis than usual, that we must take things as we found them, and that, for her part, she was proud to call herself a Yarmouth Bloater.

When we got into the street (which was strange enough to me), and smelt the fish, and pitch, and oakum, and tar, and saw the sailors walking about, and the carts jingling up and down over the stones, I felt that I had done so busy a place an injustice; and said as much to Peggotty, who heard my expressions of delight with great complacency, and told me it was well known (I suppose to those who had the good fortune to be born Bloaters) that Yarmouth was, upon the whole, the finest place in the universe.

The Buck Inn is suggested as the likely public house where Peggotty met her " 'Am—growed out of knowledge " and they started off for Dan'l Peggotty's house.

We turned down lanes bestrewn with bits of chips and little hillocks of sand, and went past gas-works, rope-walks, boat-builders' yards, ship-wrights' yards, ship-breakers'

yards, riggers' lofts, smiths' forges, and a great litter of
such places, until we came out upon the dull waste I had
already seen at a distance; when Ham said:

"Yon's our house, Mas'r Davy!"

I looked in all directions, as far as I could stare over the
wilderness, and away at the sea, and away at the river, but
no house could *I* make out.   There was a black barge, or
some other kind of superannuated boat, not far off, high
and dry on the ground, with an iron funnel sticking out of
it for a chimney and smoking very cosily; but nothing else
in the way of a habitation that was visible to *me*.

"That's not it?" said I.   "That ship-looking thing?"

"That's it, Mas'r Davy," returned Ham.

If it had been Aladdin's palace, roc's egg and all, I
suppose I could not have been more charmed with the
romantic idea of living in it.   There was a delightful door
cut in the side, and it was roofed in, and there were little
windows in it; but the wonderful charm of it was, that it
was a real boat which had no doubt been upon the water
hundreds of times, and which had never been intended
to be lived in, on dry land.   That was the captivation of it
to me.   If it had ever been meant to be lived in, I might
have thought it small, or inconvenient, or lonely; but
never having been designed for any such use, it became
a perfect abode.

The original of this "wonderful house" (there have been
many imitations since) was James Sharman's Black Hut
which stood near the Nelson Monument.   In those days a
sandy waste stretched from Kimberley Terrace to the Nelson
Monument, such as Dickens describes.

The inn at Yarmouth from which David travelled to
London, in disgrace, for Salem House School, where "the
coach was in the yard, shining very much all over, but
without any horses to it as yet: and it looked in that state
as if nothing was more unlikely than its ever going to
London" and where "the friendly waiter" assisted David
in eating an enormous dinner, is The Duke's Head, which
Mr. B. W. Matz points out was the principal coaching inn
in the town.   The same authority locates the inn where
David stayed with Steerforth when he first introduced him
to the Peggotty household, as the Star Hotel.

We went down by the Mail . . . and Steerforth said
as we drove through the dark streets to the inn . . . it
was a good, queer, out of the way kind of hole. . . . We

went to bed on our arrival (I observed a pair of dirty shoes
and gaiters in connection with my old friend the Dolphin
as we passed that door).

David had made the acquaintance of this inn much earlier,
on the occasion of his first holiday from school, when he saw
his mother for the last time.

When we arrived before day at the inn where the mail
stopped, which was not the inn where my friend the
waiter lived, I was shown up to a nice little bedroom, with
Dolphin painted on the door. Very cold I was, I know,
notwithstanding the hot tea they had given me before a
large fire down stairs; and very glad I was to turn into the
Dolphin's bed, pull the Dolphin's blankets round my head,
and go to sleep.

Another Yarmouth inn connected with the book is the
Willing Mind, Peggotty's "house of call" where Steerforth
used to ingratiate himself by standing treat to the fishermen.
There is no inn of such a name in the town, but the name
savours somewhat of the Village Maid at Lound, to which
we have already referred.

One other Yarmouth landmark, and that is the shop of
Omer, the undertaker, where David heard the men making his
mother's coffin:

We walked away to a shop in a narrow street, on which
was written Omer, Draper, Tailor, Haberdasher, Funeral
Furnisher, etc. It was a close and stifling little shop; full
of all sorts of clothing, made and unmade, including one
window full of beaver-hats and bonnets. We went into
a little back-parlour behind the shop, where we found
three young women at work on a quantity of black
materials. . . .

The three young women, who appeared to be very indus-
trious and comfortable, raised their heads to look at me,
and then went on with their work. Stitch, stitch, stitch.
At the same time there came from a workshop across a little
yard outside the window a regular sound of hammering that
kept a kind of tune: Rat—tat-tat. Rat—tat-tat, Rat—tat-
tat, without any variation.

This is identified with the quaint shop of a carpenter and
coffin-maker, in the quaint old street called Middlegate Street:
the number is 74.

VIII

Our next point of interest in this eastern part of England, is Peterborough, one hundred miles from Yarmouth by way of Norwich and King's Lynn.

Among the early readings that Dickens gave for the benefit of local working men's institutions, was one at Peterborough on December 18th, 1855. This was in aid of the Peterborough Mechanics' Institute, and the meeting was held in the Wentworth Rooms, attached to the Wentworth Hotel, on the site of which the Grand Hotel now stands. The Mechanics' Institute ceased to exist in the 'eighties.

The following interesting letter was written to his friend, Mrs. Watson, of Rockingham Castle—to which we refer later in this chapter—and dated September 16th, 1855:

Now I wish to tell you that I have been appointed to read at Peterboro' on Tuesday the eighteenth of December. I have told the Dean that I cannot accept his hospitality, that I am going with Mr. Wills to the inn, therefore I shall be absolutely at your disposal, and shall be more than disappointed if you don't stay with us. As the time approaches will you let me know your arrangements, and whether Mr. Wills can bespeak any rooms for you in arranging for me.

In the December Dickens was in Paris, and according to a letter which he wrote to Wilkie Collins on December 12th, he crossed over to Engand specially for the Peterborough meeting.

We cannot find any record of the hotel at which Dickens stayed, but it was probably the Wentworth.

The Watsons undoubtedly joined him on that occasion, because on December 23rd, after he had read at Sheffield (to which place he had travelled after leaving Peterborough) he wrote to Mrs. Watson, "Enormous effect at Sheffield. But really not a better audience perceptively than at Peterborough, for that could hardly be."

There is a touch of Mugby Junction (see page 150) about Dickens's experience at the refreshment room on Peterborough Station, to judge from a letter written to Miss Mary Boyle in 1856. He was returning after the reading and presentation at Sheffield (page 238) and

At two or three o'clock in the morning I stopped at Peterborough again and thought of you all. The Lady in the refreshment room was very hard upon me, harder even than those fair enslavers usually are. She gave me a cup of tea as if I were a hyena, and she my cruel keeper with a strong dislike to me. I mingled my tears with it, and had a petrified bun of enormous antiquity in miserable meekness.

Dickens paid only one other visit to Peterborough. This was when he read in the Corn Exchange on Wednesday, October 19th, 1859.

On that day he addressed the following letter from Peterborough to Frank Stone:

This is a place which—except the cathedral, with the loveliest front I ever saw—is like the back door to some other place. It is, I should hope, the deadest and most utterly inert little town in the British Dominions. The magnates have taken places, and the bookseller is of opinion that "such is the determination to do honour to Mr. Dickens, that the doors must be opened half an hour before the appointed time." You will picture to yourself Arthur's quiet indignation at this, and the manner in which he remarked to me at dinner "that he turned away twice Peterborough last night."

A very pretty room—though a Corn Exchange—and a room we should have been glad of at Cambridge, as it is large, bright and cheerful, and wonderfully well lighted.

The difficulty in getting to Bradford from here to-morrow at any time convenient to us, turned out to be so great, that we are all going in for Leeds (only three quarters of an hour from Bradford) to-night after the reading, at a quarter past eleven. We are due in Leeds a quarter before three.

The note about turning away "twice Peterborough last night" referred to the previous day's reading at Manchester.

IX

It was during the holiday in Switzerland in 1846 that Dickens first met the Hon. Richard and Mrs. Watson who became his life-long friends. At their beautiful home at Rockingham Castle he spent some most enjoyable times and in addition to dedicating his "favourite child" *David Copperfield* to the Watsons, he has left us as a legacy a descriptive picture of the mansion in *Bleak House* where it figures as "Chesney Wold in Lincolnshire."

Rockingham Castle is in Northamptonshire and is quite as conveniently reached by rail from Peterborough as by road. The latter way takes you through Oundle and along the Market Harborough road where 2½ miles beyond Corby, the Uppingham road leads past the castle grounds.

During his first visit in 1849, Dickens wrote to Forster as follows:

Rockingham Castle: Friday, thirtieth of November, 1849. Picture to yourself, my dear F., a large old castle, approached by an ancient keep, portcullis, &c., &c., filled with company, waited on by six-and-twenty servants; . . . and you will have a faint idea of the mansion in which I am at present staying. I should have written to you yesterday, but for having had a very busy day. Among the guests is a Miss B. (Mary Boyle). . . . This lady is renowned as an amateur actress, so last night we got up in the great hall some scenes from *The School for Scandal*; the scene with the lunatic on the wall, from the *Nicholas Nickleby* . . . some conjuring; and then finished off with country dances; of which we had two admirably good ones, quite new to me, though really old. Getting the words, and making the preparations, occupied (as you may believe) the whole day; and it was three o'clock before I got to bed. It was an excellent entertainment, and we were all uncommonly merry. . . . We leave here this afternoon. . . . Of all the country-houses and estates I have yet seen in England, I think this is by far the best. Everything undertaken eventuates in a most magnificent hospitality; . . . I regard it as a fortunate circumstance for the neighbouring community that this patrimony should have fallen to my spirited and enlightened host. Every one has profited by it, and the labouring people in especial are thoroughly well cared-for and looked after. To see all the household, headed by an enormously fat housekeeper, occupying the back benches last night, laughing and applauding without any restraint; and to see a blushing sleek-headed footman produce, for the watch-trick, a silver watch of the most portentous dimensions, amidst the rapturous delight of his brethren and sisterhood; was a very pleasant spectacle.

Of this first visit he wrote to his French friend de Cerjat on December 29th, 1849:

We had a most delightful time at Watsons' (for both of them we have preserved and strengthened a real affection)

ROCKINGHAM CASTLE

THE SONDES ARMS, ROCKINGHAM

[Photo by Walter Dexter

and were the gayest of the gay. There was a Miss Boyle staying in the house, who is an excellent amateur actress and she and I got up some scenes from "The School for Scandal" and from *Nickleby*, with immense success. We played in the old hall, with the audience filled up and running over with servants. The entertainments concluded with feats of legerdemain (for the performance of which I have a pretty good apparatus, collected at divers times and in divers places), and we then fell to country dances of a most frantic description, and danced all night.

Unfortunately Mr. Watson died in 1852, but Dickens's friendship with Mrs. Watson continued, and he continued a regular visitor to Rockingham.

Forster adds that Dickens "during the too brief time his excellent friend was spared to him, often repeated his visits to Rockingham, always a surpassing enjoyment; and in the winter of 1850 he accomplished there, with help of the country carpenter 'a very elegant little theatre' of which he constituted himself manager. . . . It will be one more added to the many examples I have given of his untiring energy both in work and play, if I mention the fact that this theatre was opened at Rockingham for their first representation on Wednesday the 15th of January; that after the performance there was a country dance which lasted far into the morning; and that on the next evening, after a railway journey of more than 120 miles, he dined in London with the Prime Minister, Lord John Russell."

The pieces played were "Used Up," "The Day After the Wedding" and "Animal Magnetism," for which latter he wrote a special "tag" for the occasion, the last lines of which were:

> Stay yet again. Among us all I feel
> One subtle, all-pervading influence steal,
> Stirring one wish within our heart and head;
> Bright be the path our host and hostess tread!
> Blest be their children, happy be their race,
> Long may they live, this ancient hall to grace;
> Long bear of English virtues noble fruit—
> Green-hearted Rockingham! Strike deep thy root.

It is probable that the following description from *A Christmas Tree*, published in 1850, was prompted by his visits to Rockingham:

U

On, by low-lying misty grounds, through fens and fogs, up long hills, winding dark as caverns between thick plantations, almost shutting out the sparkling stars; so, out on broad heights, until we stop at last, with sudden silence, at an avenue. The gate-bell has a deep half-awful sound in the frosty air; the gate swings open on its hinges; and, as we drive up to a great house, the glancing lights grow larger in the windows and the opposing rows of trees seem to fall solemnly back on either side, to give us place. . . . And so, the lights growing larger, and the trees falling back before us, and closing up again behind us, as if to forbid retreat, we come to the house. . . . It is an old house, full of great chimneys where wood is burnt on ancient dogs upon the hearth, and grim Portraits (some of them with grim Legends too), lower distrustfully from the oaken panels of the walls. . . . We make a generous supper with our host and hostess and their guests—it being Christmas-time, and the old house full of company—and then we go to bed. Our room is a very old room. It is hung with tapestry. . . . There are great black beams in the ceiling, and there is a great black bedstead, supported at the foot by two great black figures, who seem to have come off a couple of tombs in the Old Baronial Church in the Park, for our particular accommodation.

All authorities agree that Lady Dedlock's "place in Lincolnshire" in *Bleak House* was founded on Rockingham Castle in the neighbouring county, and we have Dickens's confession to Mrs. Watson in a letter dated August 27th, 1853, that:

In some of the descriptions of Chesney Wold, I have taken many bits, chiefly about trees and shadows, from observations made at Rockingham. I wonder whether you have ever thought so!

Our first introduction in the book to this delightful spot is during the wet wintry weather—and it was November time when Dickens first saw it.

The vases on the stone terrace in the foreground catch the rain all day; and the heavy drops fall, drip, drip, drip, drip, upon the broad flagged pavement, called, from old time, the Ghost's Walk, all night. . . . The rain is ever falling, drip, drip, drip, by day and night, upon the broad flagged terrace-pavement, the Ghost's Walk. The weather is so very bad down in Lincolnshire, that the liveliest imagination can scarcely apprehend its ever being fine again. . . .

The discontented goose, who stoops to pass under the old gateway, twenty feet high, may gabble out, if we only knew it, a waddling preference for weather when the gateway casts its shadow on the ground. . . . The horses in the stables—the long stables in a barren, red-brick courtyard, where there is a great bell in a turret, and a clock with a large face, which the pigeons who life near it, and who love to perch upon its shoulders, seem to be always consulting.

Although Rockingham Castle is on an eminence, the River Welland in the valley below often overflows, and thus was obtained the suggestion of the Lincolnshire Fens which Dickens transposed into the description.

The old gateway to which Dickens refers in the above extract is the remains of the former Norman castle, and passing through it we find ourselves facing the north front of the mansion which contains the drawing-room, so often figuring in the story. The Hall, in which the plays were given, is a magnificent specimen of Elizabethan architecture and contains some of the family portraits ("no end to the Dedlocks" as Mr. Guppy thought when he went to see them).

It is not difficult to associate with the Yew Walk the Ghost's Walk of *Bleak House*, although the stone paving is lacking.

A fuller description of the house was given later by Esther Summerson when she and her guardian visited Mr. Boythorn who was neighbour of Sir Leicester Dedlock, between whom a deadly feud existed regarding a right of way which necessitated Mr. Boythorn going two miles out of his way from the village to reach his house.

The park, as then, is open to the public, upon application to the gardener. It will be remembered that much of dramatic importance occurs in the grounds of Chesney Wold; Esther's description of the house and grounds is as follows:

It was a picturesque old house, in a fine park richly wooded. . . . O, the solemn woods over which the light and shadow travelled swiftly, as if Heavenly wings were sweeping on benignant errands through the summer air; the smooth green slopes, the glittering water, the garden where the flowers were so symmetrically arranged in clusters of the richest colours, how beautiful they looked! The house with gable and chimney, and tower, and turret, and dark doorway, and broad terrace-walk, twining among the balustrades of which, and lying heaped upon the vases, there was one great flush of roses, seemed scarcely real in its light solidity, and in the serene and peaceful hush that rested on all around it. . . . On everything, house, garden, terrace, green slopes, water, old oaks, fern, moss, woods again, and far away across the openings in the prospect, to the distance lying wide before us with a purple bloom upon it, there seemed to be such undisturbed repose. . . .

I passed before the terrace garden with its fragrant odours, and its broad walks, and its well-kept beds and smooth turf; and I saw how beautiful and grave it was, and how the old stone balustrades and parapets, and wide flights of shallow steps, were seamed by time and weather; and how the trained moss and ivy grew about them, and around the old stone pedestal of the sundial; and I heard the fountain falling. Then the way went by long lines of dark windows, diversified by turreted towers, and porches, of eccentric shapes, where old stone lions and grotesque monsters bristled outside dens of shadow, and snarled at the evening gloom over the escutcheons they held in their grip. Thence the path wound underneath a gateway, and through a court-yard where the principal entrance was (I hurried quickly on), and by the stables where none but deep voices seemed to be, whether in the murmuring of the wind through the strong mass of ivy holding to a high red wall, or in the low complaining of the weathercock, or in the barking of the dogs, or in the slow striking of a clock. So, encountering presently a sweet smell of limes, whose rustling I could hear, I turned with the turning of the path, to the south front; and there, above me, were the balustrades of the Ghost's Walk, and one lighted window that might be my mother's.

When Esther made her first acquaintance with "the most friendly of villages" she came down by coach with Mr. Jarndyce and Harold Skimpole and it was undoubtedly at Market Harborough, nine miles distant, that they alighted, to meet Mr. Boythorn " waiting with an open carriage to take us to his house which was a few miles off."

Late in the afternoon we came to the market-town where we were to alight from the coach—a dull little town, with a church-spire, and a market-place, and a market-cross, and one intensely sunny street, and a pond with an old horse cooling his legs in it, and a very few men sleepily

ROCKINGHAM CASTLE.

On WEDNESDAY Evening, January 15th, 1851.

Will be presented

USED UP!

Sir Charles Coldstream		Mr. CHARLES DICKENS.
Sir Adonis Leech		Mr. WILLIAM STOPFORD.
The Honourable Tom Saville		Mr. GOWRAN VERNON.
Wurzel	(a Farmer)	Captain CAVENDISH BOYLE.
John Ironbrace	(a Blacksmith)	Mr. STAFFORD.
Mr. Fennel	(a Lawyer)	The Hon. Captain QUIN.
James	(a Tiger)	Master BENGAL.
Mary		Miss MARY BOYLE.
Lady Clutterbuck		Mrs. CHARLES DICKENS.

To be followed by the INTERLUDE of

A DAY AFTER THE WEDDING

Colonel Freelove	Mr. CHARLES DICKENS.
Lord Rivers	Mr. GOWRAN VERNON.
James	Captain CAVENDISH BOYLE.
Lady Elizabeth Freelove	Miss MARY BOYLE.
Mrs. Davies	The Hon. Mrs. SPENCER LYTTLETON.

The Performances will conclude with Mrs. INCHBALD's Farce,

ANIMAL MAGNETISM.

The Doctor	Mr. CHARLES DICKENS.
La Fleur	Captain CAVENDISH BOYLE.
The Marquis de Lancy	Mr. STAFFORD
Jeffrey	Mr. WILLIAM STOPFORD.
Constance	Miss HOGARTH.
Lisette	Miss MARY BOYLE.

Costumiers, Messrs. NATHAN, of Tichborne Street, Haymarket.   Perruquier, Mr. WILSON, of the Strand.

ACTING AND STAGE MANAGER   -   -   -   Mr. CHARLES DICKENS.

The Theatre will be opened at a QUARTER BEFORE EIGHT, and the Performances will commence at EIGHT O'CLOCK

GOD SAVE THE QUEEN!

FACSIMILE OF A PLAY BILL OF AMATEUR THEATRICALS AT
ROCKINGHAM CASTLE

296

lying and standing about in narrow little bits of shade. After the rustling of the leaves and the waving of the corn all along the road, it looked as still, as hot, as motionless a little town as England could produce.

At length they came to "the little village and passed a small inn with the sign of the Dedlock Arms swinging over the road in front." This has its prototype in the Sondes Arms, Sondes being the family name of the Watson family who still inhabit the castle.

The "shady, ancient, solemn little church in the park" is reached by a pathway from the village street—the disputed pathway that always roused the ire of Mr. Boythorn.

We arrived at his house on a Saturday. On the Sunday morning we all set forth to walk to the little church in the park. Entering the park, almost immediately by the disputed ground, we pursued a pleasant footpath winding among the verdant turf and the beautiful trees, until it brought us to the church-porch.

In an earlier chapter we are told:

On Sundays, the little church in the park is mouldy; the oaken pulpit breaks out into a cold sweat; and there is a general smell and taste as of the ancient Dedlocks in their graves.

Mr. Boythorn "lived in a pretty house, formerly the Parsonage-house." It is described as:

A real old house, with settles in the chimney of the brick-floored kitchen, and great beams across the ceilings. On one side of it was the terrible piece of ground in dispute, where Mr. Boythorn maintained a sentry in a smock-frock, day and night, whose duty was supposed to be, in cases of aggression, immediately to ring a large bell hung up there for the purpose, to unchain a great bull-dog established in a kennel as his ally, and generally to deal destruction on the enemy. Not content with these precautions, Mr. Boythorn had himself composed and posted there, on painted boards to which his name was attached in large letters, the following solemn warnings: "Beware of the Bull-dog. He is most ferocious. Lawrence Boythorn." "The blunderbuss is loaded with slugs. Lawrence Boythorn." "Man-traps and spring-guns are set here at all times of the day and night. Lawrence Boythorn."

x

Cambridge, like its sister city Oxford, is not often referred to by Dickens.

In *Great Expectations* we are told that Mr. Pocket had "distinguished himself at Cambridge" and from *A Tale of Two Cities* we learn that Charles Darnay read with undergraduates at Cambridge as "a sort of tolerated smuggler who drove a contraband trade in European languages." There are equally minor references in "George Silverman's Explanation" and *Mrs. Lirriper*.

It was, however, not overlooked in his reading tours. Dickens's first reading was on October 17th, 1859, in the Guildhall, when he read the *Carol* and the Pickwick *Trial*. The following night he read *The Story of Little Dombey* and *Mrs. Gamp*, and the next day wrote the following letter to Frank Stone from Peterborough:

> We had a splendid rush last night. They were a far finer audience than the previous night. I think the finest I have ever read to. They took every word of the Dombey in quite an amazing manner, and after the child's death, paused a little, then set up a shout that it did one good to hear. Mrs. Gamp then set in with a roar, which lasted till I had done. I think everybody for the time forgot everything but the matter in hand. It was as fine an instance of thorough absorbtion in a fiction, as any of us are likely to see ever again.

On March 27th, 1867, he again read at Cambridge, and on this occasion wrote to Forster:

> The reception at Cambridge was something to be proud of in such a place. The colleges mustered in full force, from the biggest guns to the smallest: and went beyond even Manchester in the roars of welcome and rounds of cheers. The place was crammed, and all through the reading everything was taken with the utmost heartiness of enjoyment.

His farewell reading was two years later, on March 18th, 1869, also at the Guildhall.

INDEX TO PLACES

All places named have an association either with Dickens or his books.

The figures after the titles of books indicate the chapter in the book in which the place is mentioned.

Abbreviated references only are given to the London and Kent places.

PRINTED IN GREAT BRITAIN BY PURNELL AND SONS
PAULTON, SOMERSET, ENGLAND